VOLUME LXI

PROCEEDINGS OF
THE AMERICAN CATHOLIC
PHILOSOPHICAL
ASSOCIATION

THE METAPHYSICS
OF SUBSTANCE

Edited by

Daniel O. Dahlstrom

Issued by the National Office of
The American Catholic Philosophical Association
Washington, D.C. 20064

Table of Contents

VOLUME LXI

PROCEEDINGS OF

THE AMERICAN CATHOLIC

PHILOSOPHICAL

ASSOCIATION

THE METAPHYSICS OF SUBSTANCE

Edited by

Daniel O. Dahlstrom

Issued by the National Office of
The American Catholic Philosophical Association
Washington, D.C. 20064

Presidential Address:
Substance in Aquinas's Metaphysics

by John F. Wippel

When we turn to Thomas Aquinas's many discussions of substance, we are immediately struck by his heavy dependence upon Aristotle. This occasions little surprise, of course, in light of Thomas's considerable debt to the Stagirite for so much of his philosophical reflection. At the same time, many elements of Thomas's metaphysical thought are not to be found in the texts of Aristotle. Thus Aquinas's theory of distinction and composition of essence and act of being (*esse*) in finite beings, his metaphysics of participation, his views concerning creation, to mention but three items, these are as absent from Aristotle's metaphysics as they are central to his own.[1]

What, then, of Thomas's understanding of substance? Even as we acknowledge his considerable debt to Aristotle in developing this topic, do we find truly original elements in his analysis of substance? In addressing myself today to some facets of Thomas's teaching on substance, I shall also attempt to keep in the background the issue of his debt to Aristotle concerning the same.[2] And in my concluding remarks I shall briefly return to this.

Because the points associated with Thomas's metaphysics of substance are many and varied, in this paper I shall limit myself to the following four: (1) substance and being (*ens*); (2) substance taken as individual subject (*suppositum*) and substance taken as nature or quiddity; (3) the "definition" of substance; (4) substance and *esse* (act of being).

1. Substance and Being (Ens)

Here we should recall that throughout his career Thomas repeatedly insists that what the intellect first conceives, and that to which it reduces its other conceptions, is being (*ens*).[3] As I understand this, the priority Thomas has in mind applies to the order of resolution (analysis). This is to say that no matter what we may discover about a given entity, for instance that it is large or small, moving or stationary, living or nonliving, etc., eventual analysis will lead us to recognize that for it to be any of these things it must first and foremost enjoy being. As Thomas explains in *De veritate,* qu. 1, a. 1, that which the intellect first conceives and into which it resolves all its other conceptions is being (*ens*). Other conceptions of the intellect are gained by

2

some kind of addition to being. But nothing can be added to being from without, as if it were extrinsic to it, in the way a difference is added to a genus or an accident to a subject. This is so, continues Thomas, because every nature is being essentially, i.e., intrinsically. And Aristotle has shown in *Metaphysics* III that being itself is not a genus.[4]

In this same context Thomas goes on to note that certain things are said to "add" to being insofar as they express a mode which is not expressed by the name being itself. This can happen in two ways. It may be that the mode expressed by such a name is some special mode of being. There are differing grades or degrees of entity, and therefore different modes of being. Corresponding to these, the different genera of things are derived.[5] Here Thomas has in mind the division of being into its ten supreme genera or categories or predicaments. As he puts it, substance does not add to being any difference which might be regarded as a nature superadded from without. Rather by the name substance a certain special mode of being is expressed, i.e., being per se.[6] As is also well known, Thomas goes on in this same context to single out certain general modes of being which are as broad in extension as being itself or, as he phrases it, which follow upon every being. These result in what subsequent scholasticism often refers to as the transcendental properties of being.[7]

For our purposes, however, Thomas's reference to certain special modes of being, i.e., to the predicaments, and in particular, to substance, is all-important. First of all, this suggests that within the range of finite being Thomas does not think that we first discover accidental modes of being, or accidents, and then reason from our awareness of these to knowledge of an underlying subject or substratum which we would identify as substance. On the contrary, what we first recognize intellectually is either explicitly or implicitly grasped as being or as a being. Once we have thus discovered being, subsequent analysis should enable us to distinguish explicitly therein between that which exists in itself, or substance, and that which does not but only in something else, or accidental being.[8]

Secondly, I can hardly overemphasize the importance in Thomas's metaphysics of his view that substance and the other predicaments, when viewed ontologically, are themselves modes of *being*. He certainly acknowledges that the predicaments may be regarded as supreme and generically distinct kinds of predicates which may be affirmed of a subject. But more significant is his repeated association of these modes of predication with the modes of being which they both express and presuppose. This is implied by our text from *De veritate*, qu. 1, a. 1, and is brought out explicitly in his derivations of the predicaments both in his Commentaries on *Metaphysics* V and on *Physics* III.[9]

In sum, as Thomas sees things, it is because to exist in itself is a supreme way or mode in which being is realized that we can understand it that way, derive a kind of predicate which expresses this understanding or concept, and therefore speak of substance. And because there are other supreme ways in which being is realized as existing in something else, corresponding to our understanding or concepts of these, we derive other names or predicaments for them, i.e., for the nine classes of accidents. In the order of discovery, our reflection upon these supreme kinds of predicates (which we may regard as predicaments in the logical sense) may assist us in arriving at more explicit knowledge of the corresponding underlying modes of being (which we may regard as predicaments in the ontological sense). But in the order of reality, for Thomas there can be no doubt. Primacy is to be assigned to being. Because there are these different levels or modes of being, we understand them in different fashion and are justified in assigning different predicaments to each of them.[10]

In light of his emphasis on the primacy of being when it comes to our discovery of the predicaments, we are not surprised to find Thomas agreeing with Aristotle that substance is the prime instance of being itself. Thus in *Metaphysics* IV, ch. 2, Aristotle comes to grips with the fact that the name being is used in different ways. This seems to pose some threat to his claim in ch. 1 that there is a science, i.e., one science, that studies being as being. Aristotle counters with his theory of *pros hen* equivocation and maintains that all secondary instances of being are so named by reason of their relation to the primary instance of being, *ousia* or substance.[11]

Thomas follows Aristotle's thinking on this point, and gives it a central role in developing his own theory of analogy of being.[12] This is clearly brought out in Thomas's Commentary on *Metaphysics* IV, ch. 2; but this thinking is already present in his discussion of analogy at the very beginning of his career, as can be seen in his *De principiis naturae*. The presentation offered there of analogical predication is modelled on Aristotle's discussion in *Metaphysics* IV, ch. 2, and is also deeply indebted to Averroes' Commentary on the same text. This is so even though neither Aristotle nor the Latin translation of Averroes uses the term "analogy" in the contexts in question.[13]

To return to Thomas's Commentary on *Metaphysics* IV, there we find him writing that some things are described as beings because they enjoy being in themselves. These of course are substances. Substances alone are beings in the primary sense. All other instances of being are so named because in some way they are related to substance.[14] After reproducing Aristotle's somewhat haphazard listing of a number of other ways in which things may be named beings because of their relationship to substance, Thomas sums this up in his own fashion. These different modes of being, he writes, may be reduced to four types: (1) negations and privations; (2) generations and corruptions; (3) things that do not exist in their own right but only in something else, such as quantities, qualities, and the properties of substance; (4) that which exists in reality and enjoys what Thomas calls a firm and solid being (*esse*). This alone exists in itself and is again identified by Thomas as substance.[15] In this reduced listing of the different ways in which being may be realized, most important for our purpose are the members of classes three and four, that is to say, quantities, qualities, and the other accidents we may presume (class 3), and substances (class 4). Substance is being in the primary sense, Thomas again reminds us.[16]

In preparing to derive the ten predicaments in his Commentary on *Metaphysics* V, Thomas first mentions substance. In this case, he notes, the predicate or predicament is said to signify or be predicated of what he now calls "first substance." And he identifies "first substance" as the particular or individual substance of which everything else is predicated, as for instance, when we say "Socrates is an animal," the predicate animal is affirmed of Socrates—the first substance.[17] I mention this to show that Thomas is familiar with Aristotle's distinction between first substance and second substance in his *Categories*. Nonetheless, the more frequent and, I think, more important contrast for Thomas is not between first substance and second substance, but between the subject or suppositum (first substance) and nature or essence. But we shall return to this below.[18]

In *Lectio* 10 of his Commentary on this same Bk. V (ch. 8) of the *Metaphysics*, Thomas there finds Aristotle singling out four modes or kinds of substance. First of all there are individual substances such as simple bodies and even mixed bodies when they are composed of similar parts as in the case of stones and living things and their parts. These are said to be substances because other things are predicated of them. Thomas identifies these as the first substances mentioned by Aristotle in the *Categories*. As a second mode or kind of substance Thomas lists the intrinsic formal cause (*causa essendi*) of a first substance, i.e., its substantial form. As a third mode of substance he mentions the parts of substances which set limits to them in some way, i.e., lines, points and numbers. (These are regarded as substances by some.) Finally, as the fourth mode or kind of substance he names the quiddity of a thing which its definition signifies. Concerning this fourth mode, Thomas notes that it is according to this mode—substance taken as quiddity—that genus and species are said to be the "substance" of that of which they are predicated.[19]

Following Aristotle's lead, Thomas quickly reduces these four modes to two. He immediately eliminates the members of class three, i.e., the limiting or terminating parts of substance, as viable candidates for the title substance. Substance in the first sense, i.e., the ultimate subject or first substance, continues to be regarded as substance in the primary sense and is referred to as a *hoc aliquid* ("this particular something") which subsists in itself and is separate; for it is distinct from all else and is not communicable to others.[20] By denying that the individual substance or subject can be communicated to others, I take Thomas to mean that it is not predicated of anything else, to be sure. But even more important for Thomas is the fact that it cannot be shared in by others in the way a common nature or essence might be shared in by individual instances of the same.[21]

In order to complete his reduction of Aristotle's classes of substances to two, Thomas now combines substance taken as form (i.e., as substantial form) with substance taken as quiddity. Both substantial form and quiddity may be regarded as principles by means of which something is. But when we speak of (substantial) form, writes Thomas, we view it as a principle which is directly ordered to its appropriate matter. When we speak of quiddity, we rather have in mind the quiddity as ordered to its subject or suppositum, that is to say, to that which is signified as having the quiddity or essence.[22] In effect, therefore, he is subsuming substance taken as form under substance taken as essence or quiddity. We should not conclude from this, however, that for Thomas the quiddity of a material being is reducible to and identical with its substantial form. Substantial form is rather included within the quiddity or essence, along with prime matter, Thomas would always maintain, even though this does not in fact appear to have been Aristotle's position.[23] Thomas's reduction of this fourfold division of substance to a twofold division brings us to Part II of our paper.

2. Substance as the Individual Subject (Suppositum) and Substance as Nature or Quiddity

For Thomas's purposes this appears to be the most important division of substance. This is evident from his clearly independent writings, that is, writings in which he is not commenting on Aristotle or others. For instance, in *Summa theologiae* I, qu. 29, a. 2, he notes that substance may indicate either (1) the quiddity of a thing which its definition signifies—i.e., *ousia* or *essentia* to give the Greek and Latin equivalents; or (2) the subject or suppositum which subsists within the genus substance. As Thomas puts this in *Summa theologiae* III, qu. 17, a. 1, ad 7 (and in qu. 2, a. 6, ad 3), substance may be expressed either as essence or nature, on the one hand, or as subject (i.e., *suppositum* or *hypostasis*), on the other. Or as he had explained in his earlier *Summa contra gentiles* IV, ch. 49, substance may be understood as a subject within the genus substance, and when it is so used it is also known as *hypostasis.* Or it may be taken as signifying a thing's quiddity (*quod quid est*), i.e., its nature.[24]

It is true that in a much earlier discussion in his Commentary on I *Sentences* (dist. 25, qu. 1, a. 1, ad 7), Thomas offers a somewhat different division. There he is defending the Boethian definition of a person as an individual substance of a rational nature. He notes that the term substance is spoken of in four ways: (1) as essence (taken this way the name applies to all genera including accidents, just as does essence); (2) as an individual within the genus substance, i.e., first substance or *hypostasis*; (3) as second substance; (4) in a more general way which abstracts from first substance and second substance. In fact, remarks Thomas, it is in this fourth way that the term is used in Boethius's definition of person, a point which he also makes much later in his career (see *De potentia*, qu. 9, a. 2, ad 7; ST I, qu. 29, a. 1, ad 2). But of more immediate interest to us are the second and third usages of substance mentioned here, that is, first substance and second substance.[25] Should we not conclude from this that Thomas's more frequent contrast between subject (*suppositum*) and nature is really the same as that between first substance and second substance? Or to put this another way, should we not identify substance taken as nature or essence or quiddity with second substance?[26]

Other texts strongly suggest that any such identification would be ill advised. For instance, Thomas discusses the relationship between nature and suppositum in considerable detail in *De potentia*, qu. 9, a. 1. There he is considering the relationship between person, on the one hand, and essence, subsistence, and hypostasis, on the other. Once again he recalls that according to Aristotle substance is used in two ways. It may signify the ultimate subject which is not predicated of anything else, i.e., an individual within the genus substance. Or it may signify the form or nature of a subject. To support this distinction Thomas recalls that many individual subjects, for instance, many men, share in a given nature. Therefore we must distinguish between that which is one and that which is multiplied. The common nature is signified by the definition which indicates what the thing is. Because of this, this common nature is also known as essence or quiddity. But certain items are found in an individual substance which are not included in the common nature, i.e., individual matter and the individual accidents which determine such matter.[27]

From this Thomas concludes that essence is related to an individual substance in which it is realized as a formal part of the latter. For instance, it is in this way—as part to whole—that humanity (standing for essence) is related to Socrates (an individual subject). Therefore in matter-form composites we cannot say that an essence is completely identical with its subject. Consequently, the essence cannot be predicated of the subject. Thus we cannot say that Socrates is humanity.[28] In simple substances, however, there is no such distinction between an essence and the subject in which it is realized; for in them there is no matter to individuate a common nature. In them essence and what Thomas now calls subsistence are identical.[29]

Thomas also notes that substance taken as subject (*suppositum*) enjoys two distinctive characteristics. First, it needs no extrinsic subject to serve as its support; therefore it subsists, or exists in itself and is known as οὐσιώσις in Greek or as *subsistentia* in Latin. Second, it also serves as a foundation for accidents and is therefore said to "stand under" them. Because of this it is also known as *hypostasis* by the Greeks and as "first substance" by the Latins. Hence if hypostasis and (first) substance differ logically or conceptually, they are one and the same reality.[30]

From all of this we may conclude that in material entities substance taken as essence or nature is not completely identical with substance taken as subject. Nor are the two totally diverse. As realized in a concrete individual, they stand in a part-whole relationship to one another.[31] And the contrast between them is not to be identified with that between first substance and second substance. Second substance can be predicated directly of its subject, whereas, in material beings, a nature, when taken as a part, cannot be predicated directly of its subject or suppositum. While we can say Socrates is a man (second substance), we cannot say that Socrates is humanity (nature).

For confirmation of the points we have just made we may turn to Thomas's Commentary on *Metaphysics* VII, ch. 3. There he is explaining Aristotle's preliminary division of substance (*ousia*) into four modes: (1) quiddity, essence or nature (*quod quid erat esse*); (2) the universal, viewed as substance by the defenders of Platonic forms; (3) the primary genus for a thing, i.e., unity and being according to some; (4) the subject, that is, the particular substance of which all else is predicated. Once more Thomas identifies substance taken as subject (see class 4) with the first substance of Aristotle's *Categories*. He adds that second substances, i.e., genera and species, stand under accidents, but only by reason of first substance.[32]

But Thomas also notes that the first member of this fourfold division of substance—substance as essence, nature or quiddity—does not appear in the division in the *Categories*. Hence it is neither first substance nor second substance. This is so, explains Thomas, because quiddity taken as such does not enter into the division into the predicaments except insofar as it serves as a principle for each. In other parts, it is not a genus or species (second substance) or an individual (first substance), but only a formal principle for each. Again, therefore, we find Thomas refusing to identify substance taken as essence, nature or quiddity with second substance.[33]

3. "Definition" of Substance

As some of the texts we have analyzed indicate, and as Thomas often notes in other contexts, a substance is that which has being in itself. And as our text from *De potentia*, qu. 9, a. 1 states, substance taken as subject (1) subsists or exists in itself, and (2) stands under or supports accidents.[34] But if a substance can fulfill this second function and support accidents, this is only because it enjoys the first, that is, because it exists in itself. Given this, we might expect Thomas to define substance as a being which exists in itself or per se—as an *ens per se*—and accident as that which exists in something else. Nonetheless, as E. Gilson pointed out in an interesting study published in 1974, almost from the beginning of his career until its end, Thomas repeatedly makes the point that "being in itself (per se)" is not the definition of substance. As Gilson also noted, in saying this Thomas finds himself in agreement with Avicenna, even though we are hard pressed to find this stated by the Muslim philosopher in those exact terms.[35]

At first sight such a view is somewhat unsettling, at least as regards the definition of substance. Given Thomas's belief in Eucharistic transubstantiation, we are not surprised to find him refusing to define an accident as "that which exists in something else" but rather as "that to which it belongs to exist in something else."[36] But why does he reject "that which exists in itself" as an appropriate definition of substance?

In what appears to be his earliest explicit discussion of this (*In I Sent.*, d. 8, qu. 4, a. 2), Thomas examines an argument in support of the claim that God falls within the predicament substance. According to this argument, a substance is that which is not in a subject but which rather is a being (*ens*) in itself (per se). Since this can also be said of God, God must be included in the genus substance.[37] Against this Thomas counters that, according to Avicenna, "that which is not in a subject" is not the definition of substance. As regards the positive part of the proposed definition—being per se, being is not a genus. And the negative part of the alleged definition—not in a subject— posits nothing. Therefore, to speak of "being which is not in a subject" is not to identify any genus.[38] The implication is that if the proposed definition cannot identify any genus, it is not a satisfactory definition.

To prove that "being which is not in a subject" does not identify any genus, Thomas reasons that whatever falls within a genus must have a quiddity which does not include *esse* (the act of being) in its intelligible content. But the name being (*ens*) does not express quiddity but the act of being (in other words, the name being—*ens*—is taken not from the essence or quiddity of a thing but from its act of being). Therefore it does not follow that if something is not in a subject that it is included in the genus substance. What does follow is this: If something has a quiddity to which it belongs to exist not in a subject, only then will it be included in the genus substance. But it cannot be said that God has a quiddity to which it belongs to exist not in a subject. Therefore God does not fall within the genus substance.[39]

We may wonder why we cannot say that God has a quiddity to which it belongs to exist not in a subject. Thomas will reply that this is because God's essence is identical with his *esse*. As Thomas had already argued in the corpus of this same article, if something is to be included in a genus, its quiddity must differ from its act of being. (Here we meet one of Thomas's ways of arguing for the distinction between essence and existence [*esse*].) To repeat, if something falls within a genus, its essence and *esse* must differ. But, continues Thomas, essence and *esse* are not distinct in God. Therefore God falls within no genus.[40]

As Thomas remarks in another helpful discussion in his Commentary on IV *Sentences*, to exist in itself is not the definition of substance. Rather its definition or "quasi-definition" is this—"a thing (*res*) to which it is given or belongs to exist not in something else."[41]

For fuller discussion of this in a somewhat later text we may turn to *Summa contra gentiles* I, ch. 25, dating from 1258-1259. There again Thomas is attempting to show that God is not contained in any genus. His fourth argument runs this way. A thing falls within a genus by reason of its quiddity because a genus is predicated in quidditative fashion. But Thomas has already shown in ch. 22 that God's quiddity is identical with his *esse*. We cannot say that God is present in a genus by reason of his *esse*, continues Thomas, for then being itself (*ens*), which signifies the act of being, would be a genus. (In other words, we cannot say that God is present in a genus by reason of his essence without implying that he is present therein by reason of his act of existing; for in God the two are identical.) But to say that God is in a genus by reason of his act of existing would be to make of *esse* and therefore of being (*ens*) a genus. Neither is acceptable to Thomas.[42]

In this same context Thomas poses this objection for himself. It might be granted that the name "substance" taken strictly does not apply to God since God does not stand under any accident. Nonetheless, the reality signified by that name is present in God. Therefore God is in the genus substance. This follows because a substance is a being in itself, and so is God.[43]

To this reasoning Thomas replies once again that being in itself is not the definition of substance. He had already argued that being is not a genus. The "in itself" (per se) part of the proposed definition implies nothing but a negation, i.e., that something does not exist in something else. From this it follows that a substance is a thing to which it belongs to exist not in a subject. In this description, the name "thing" (*res*) is taken from the substance's quiddity. Therefore, he concludes, implied in the meaning of substance is that it have a quiddity to which it belongs to exist not in something else. But this cannot be said of God. We may assume that Thomas's reason for denying that this can be said of God continues to be the same: to be so defined is by implication to have an essence that is not identical with one's *esse*.[44]

Thomas sums up much of the same thinking in a still later treatment in *De potentia*, qu. 7, a. 3, ad 4.[45] He again makes the point that being is not a genus; for nothing can be added to being which does not itself participate in being. But a difference should not participate in its genus.[46]

In this same context Thomas also writes that if substance could be defined in spite of the fact that it is a most general genus, this would be its definition—a thing (*res*) to whose quiddity it belongs to exist not in something else. In addition to reasserting his preferred "definition" of substance, here Thomas also adds to his reasons for denying that substance can be properly defined at all. Substance itself is in fact a most general genus. There can be no more general genus, such as being, of which substance would be a species.[47]

In sum, therefore, according to Aquinas "being per se" is not the definition of substance. If substance could be defined, the definition should rather be "a thing to whose quiddity it belongs to exist not in something else (or to exist in itself)." Even this is not a definition of substance in the strict sense but only a quasi-definition. This quasi-definition cannot be applied to God, since it implies distinction of essence and *esse* on the part of that which is so defined. Hence, it is clear that Thomas's theory that essence and *esse* are diverse in creatures and identical in God controls much of his thinking about the appropriate way of "defining" substance.

4. Substance and Esse (Act of Being)

In this part of my paper I wish to focus upon Thomas's understanding of *esse* as act of being and the role this plays in the ontological structure of the first substance or subsisting subject (*suppositum*). In Section 2 we have seen that Thomas correlates the individual subject or suppositum with nature as whole and as formal part, at least in material entities. This implies some kind of distinction between the two, and one that is not merely conceptual or mind-dependent. Given Thomas's view that essence and *esse* differ in created entities, this suggests another possible way for him to approach the distinction between an individual subsisting subject and its nature.

When considering this relationship, Thomas might simply appeal to the distinction between the individuating characteristics present in material substances and the nature which is realized in each. This will imply that subject and nature differ in such entities. On the other hand, he might turn to his theory of distinction of essence and act of being (*esse*). Since this distinction also applies to created spiritual entities, from this approach it would follow that even in them the distinction between the subsisting subject and its essence or nature is more than merely conceptual or mind-dependent.

Most frequently Thomas adopts the first approach. This we have already seen, especially in *De potentiä*, qu. 9, a. 1.[48] In a much earlier discussion in his Commentary on III *Sentences* (d. 5, qu. 1, art. 3), he defends the theological position that in Christ there is only one person. He notes that in certain cases nature and person differ really (*secundum rem*), and in other cases only conceptually (*secundum rationem*). He identifies nature as he uses it here with quiddity. By a person he understands this particular something which subsists with its given nature, in other words, an intellectual subsisting subject or suppositum. Because simple things lack matter, they are identical with their quiddities. But the quiddity of a matter-form composite is not to be identified with that composite entity. The meaning of the quiddity (of humanity, for instance) includes only those principles which are essential to man as such, but not the individuating characteristics which are present only in individual instances of humanity. Therefore, because humanity is taken as a part, it does not include in its meaning the whole, i.e., the subsisting subject. Hence humanity (or nature) does not subsist. The individual subject subsists as that which has humanity.[49]

In sum, in this text Thomas holds that in a simple entity such as God, nature and the subsisting subject do not really differ. And though Thomas does not spell this out in so many words, the implication appears to be that nature and the subsisting subject do not differ really in created spirits either; for in such beings there is no matter and hence no individuating characteristics in addition to specific characteristics.

Thomas makes this final point very clear elsewhere, for instance, in *Summa contra gentiles* IV, ch. 55. There he remarks that "in man nature and person differ since a man is composed of matter and form; but this is not true of an angel."[50] Hence here we have an explicit rejection of (real) distinction between nature and the individual subject in created spirits, i.e., in angels. Thomas expresses the same view in other contexts, for instance, in *De potentia,* qu. 7, a. 4 (of 1265-1266), in *De spiritualibus creaturis,* art. 5, ad 9 (ca. 1267-1268) and in his Commentary on Bk. III of the *De anima* (ca. 1266-1269).[51]

But in Quodlibet II, qu. 2, a. 2 of Christmas, 1269, a different picture emerges. In this disputation Thomas had been asked to determine whether in an angel the subsisting subject and nature differ. Again he appeals to the distinction between nature, when it is taken as signifying the substance of a thing, and the subsisting subject or suppositum. Nature signifies the substance of a thing in the sense of essence or quiddity. The subsisting subject or suppositum is an individual within the genus substance, and is also known as a *hypostasis* or first substance.[52]

Because sensible substances are better known to us, Thomas first turns to them. After presenting and criticizing a view which would identify the form of the part (substantial form) with the form of the whole (the entire essence) in such beings, he offers his own solution.[53] Nature or essence is that which is signified by the definition of a thing. In material entities this includes both matter and form. Thomas appeals to Aristotle's *Metaphysics* VII where he finds the Stagirite asking whether each and every thing is identical with its quiddity (*quod quid est*). Aristotle concludes that in things which are said to be per se, a thing (*res*) and its quiddity are one and the same. This is not so in the case of things which are said to be only per accidens.[54]

In order to determine when nature and the subsisting subject or suppositum differ, Thomas now offers a working principle: if a being is such that something can "happen" to it which is not included in the definition (*ratio*) of its nature, such a thing will differ from its quiddity (*quod quid est*). In other words, in such a being the subsisting subject differs from its nature. This is so because the definition of a thing's nature applies only to that which is included in the intelligible content of its species; but an individual subject or suppositum includes not only that, but other things which may "happen" to that subject. Therefore, Thomas reminds us again, the subject or suppositum is designated as a whole, but the nature or quiddity only as a formal part.[55]

Until this point Thomas's solution is consistent with what we have seen in earlier texts. But now he returns to the case of immaterial entities. In God and God alone is there nothing accidental in addition to his essence; for God's essence and *esse* are identical. Therefore in God the subsisting subject is completely identical with the divine essence. In angels, however, this is not the case. Something does "happen" to an angel in addition to what is included in its essence or nature. First and foremost, the *esse* of an angel is added to its essence or nature. In addition, remarks Thomas, other things also happen to an angel which belong to the angelic subsisting subject, but not to its nature. By these I take it that Thomas has in mind accidents such as operative powers and operations.[56]

Unlike his earlier treatments, therefore, in this text Thomas clearly distinguishes between the subsisting subject or suppositum and its nature even in created spirits or angels. His major reason for doing so is the distinction of essence and *esse* in such beings. As he puts this in his reply to the first objection, it is because no angel can be identified with its *esse* that something does "happen" to an angel in addition to its essence, i.e., *esse* and certain accidents. And as he specifies in replying to the second objection, *esse* is not included within the definition of a subsisting subject or suppositum. But *esse* does belong (*pertinet*) to such a subject. Therefore the subject and its nature cannot be completely identical in any entity in which essence (*res*) and *esse* differ.[57]

This discussion raises some difficulties about Thomas's final position. Various attempts have been made to reconcile his presentation in Quodlibet II with his earlier treatments. Perhaps he has simply changed his mind. If not, how are the earlier discussions to be brought into harmony with Quodlibet II?[58] In my opinion, the most promising solution has been offered by O. Schweizer. At times Thomas uses the term "suppositum" or subsisting subject to signify an individual nature which is ontologically complete in itself. At other times, as in Quodlibet II, he uses this term so as to include not only the individual essence or nature but a thing's act of being (*esse*) as well. When taken in this second and broader sense as including *esse* (and other accidents, we should add), the subject will differ from its nature in all created entities, not merely in those that are material. But when this term is taken in the narrower sense so as not to include the act of being (*esse*), the subject or suppositum will not really differ from the nature of a created spirit.[59] In sum, Schweizer's solution would resolve our problem by suggesting not that Thomas has changed his position in Quodlibet II, but that there he gives a different meaning to the suppositum or subject.[60]

Another way of approaching this problem of interpretation has occurred to me, and I would like to propose it in tentative fashion as lending additional weight to Schweizer's solution. In referring to the relationship between essence and *esse* in created beings, Thomas often uses the language of Boethius. This is to say, he often describes this as a distinction or composition of "that which is" (*quod est*) and *esse*.[61] When Thomas speaks this way, we should take it that he is emphasizing not the "is" (*est*) but the "that which" (*quod*) in the expression "that which is." Because of this emphasis on the quidditative side of a concrete entity, Thomas can say that such an entity ("that which is") is other than and enters into composition with its act of being. Even in a created spirit its "that which is" when so understood will not include its act of being (*esse*).[62]

For instance, in *De spiritualibus creaturis,* art. 1, ad 8, Thomas explains that to be composed of "that which is" and that "whereby it is" (*quo est*) is not the same as to be composed of matter and form. If form may be described as "that whereby something is," matter cannot, properly speaking, be referred to as "that which is." "That which is" (*quod est*) is what subsists in the order of being. In other words, I would interject, it is the subsisting subject or suppositum. Therefore, continues Thomas, in material entities this is the matter-form composite. In immaterial substances it is the simple form itself. And that whereby such a thing exists is its participated act of being itself (*esse*). Because of this Thomas distinguishes between "that which is" and *esse* as between essence and act of being in all created substances.[63]

Mutatis mutandis, I would suggest, we may say much the same of Thomas's understanding of suppositum in his more frequent way of contrasting this with nature. Just as the expression "that which is" may be taken as signifying the concrete subject which exists, but with the emphasis on the quidditative aspect of the same, so the suppositum or subsisting subject may be taken as signifying this same subject and with this same quidditative emphasis. When the suppositum is so understood, the individual nature or essence will be related to it as formal part to concrete whole. Because in material entities the concrete whole includes individuating characteristics in addition to the essence, there is some kind of real as opposed to merely conceptual distinction between nature and suppositum in such entities. Because such individuating characteristics are not present in angels, in them Thomas identifies nature and suppositum when he understands suppositum in this fashion, that is, when he emphasizes the quidditative aspect of the same.

On the other hand, Thomas might emphasize the "is" (*est*) in the expression "that which is" when referring to a subsisting entity. When he does this, he will understand the subsisting subject as including its act of being together with its essence or nature. When so understood, therefore, the subsisting subject or suppositum will differ really rather than merely conceptually from its nature or essence even in created spirits, not merely in material entities. It is in this way that Thomas understands suppositum in Quodlibet II, qu. 2, a. 2.

This shift in usage is significant, it seems to me, for two reasons. First, it brings out more forcefully the role of *esse* within the structure of any subsisting subject or suppositum. When such a subject is viewed as a whole and in the second way just distinguished, it must include *esse* as well as essence or nature. This is not to say that a definition of the subject or suppositum will include *esse*; for definitions are limited to the quidditative side of things. But one's full understanding of a suppositum should also include reference to its act of being.

Second, this approach brings out more clearly the distinction between Thomas's solutions for two distinct issues: (1) How can there be many individuals within the same species? This is the problem of individuation. (2) How is one to correlate and distinguish between a subsisting subject (suppositum) and its essence or nature? This is the problem we have been considering. Mere appeal to the presence of individuating factors within a matter-form composite might lead one to think that Thomas's answer to the first (in terms of his theory of individuation) is also his answer to the second. His appeal to the presence of the act of being within the subject or suppositum in resolving the second issue indicates that such is not the case.

Concluding Remarks

Thomas's understanding of substance and accidents enters into many other aspects of his metaphysics which I have not even mentioned. For instance, it controls his defense of real distinction between the soul and its powers. It is crucial for his defense of unicity of substantial form in individual substances. And it evidently enters into the difficult issue concerning whether distinct existences are to be assigned to accidents as well as to substances themselves.

Rather than dwell on these issues here, we may simply ask ourselves whether Thomas's metaphysics might be described as a metaphysics of substance, or as a metaphysics of *esse*. Substance plays a considerable role in his metaphysics, as we have now seen at least to some degree. At the same time, when it comes to his understanding of substance—the primary instance of being—Thomas builds upon and goes beyond Aristotle. In Aristotle there is nothing like Thomas's theory of distinction and composition of essence and *esse* in finite substances. Moreover, for Thomas *esse* is so important within the structure of a subsisting substance or subject that he refers to it as the actuality of all acts and the perfection of all perfections in the well-known passage from *De potentia*, qu. 7, a.2, ad 9.[64]

To put this another way, for Thomas metaphysics has as its subject being as being or being in general (*ens commune*).[65] The primary referent for the term being is substance for Thomas as well as for Aristotle. But for Thomas a substance can enjoy being in actuality only by reason of its act of being (*esse*). Hence if Thomas does have a metaphysics of substance, as indeed he does, it is a metaphysics in which *esse* plays a primary role within the structure of every existing substance. This we do not find in Aristotle.

The Catholic University of America
Washington, D.C.

NOTES

1. E. Gilson's many studies have rightly emphasized the importance of the primacy of existence in Thomas's metaphysical thought, as well as the significance of his doctrine of creation. See, for instance, *Being and Some Philosophers*, 2d ed. (Toronto, 1952); *The Christian Philosophy of St. Thomas Aquinas* (New York, 1956); *Elements of Christian Philosophy* (Garden City, N.Y., 1960); *Introduction à la philosophie chrétienne* (Paris, 1960); *Le thomisme*, 6th ed. (Paris, 1965). For an earlier work which makes Thomas's theory of distinction between essence and existence most central to his metaphysics see N. Del Prado, *De veritate fundamentali philosophiae christianae* (Fribourg, 1911). For classical studies of the importance of participation in Thomas's metaphysics see C. Fabro, *La nozione metafisica di partecipazione secondo S. Tommaso*, 2d ed. (Turin, 1950); L. Geiger, *La participation dans la philosophie de S. Thomas d'Aquin*, 2d ed. (Paris, 1953).

2. Here I shall not be concerned with the historical accuracy of his interpretations of Aristotle concerning substance, especially because Professor Verbeke has addressed himself to Aristotle's position in the first paper in this session.

3. For some of these references see *De ente et essentia*, Prooemium, (Roland-Gosselin ed., p. 1/Leonine ed., Vol. 43, p. 369); *In De Trinitate*, q. 1, a. 3, obj. 3 (*Expositio super librum Boethii De Trinitate*, B. Decker, ed. [Leiden, 1959], p. 69); see p. 73 for Thomas's reply, which indicates that he accepts this part of the objection); *In I Sent.*, d. 38, q. 1, a. 4, obj. 4 and Thomas's reply (*Scriptum super libros Sententiarum*, P. Mandonnet, ed., Vol. 1 [Paris, 1929], pp. 905, 906); *De veritate*, q. 21, a. 1 (R. Spiazzi, ed., p. 376/Leonine ed. Vol. 22.3, p. 593); *In I Met.*, lect. 2 (*In duodecim libros Metaphysicorum Aristotelis*, R. M. Spiazzi, ed. [Turin-Rome, 1950], n. 46, p.

13); *Summa theologiae,* I-IIae, q. 55, a. 4, ad 1: "...dicendum quod id quod primo cadit in intellectu, est ens: unde unicuique apprehenso a nobis attribuimus quod sit ens....Sed tamen considerandum quod sicut accidentia et formae non subsistentes dicuntur entia, non quia ipsa habeant esse, sed quia eis aliquid est...." (Turin-Rome, 1950, p. 242).

4. "Illud autem quod primo intellectus concipit quasi notissimum et in quod (with Leonine) conceptiones omnes resolvit, est ens, ut Avicenna dicit in principio suae Metaphysicae" (Spiazzi ed., p. 2/Leonine ed., Vol. 22.1, p. 5). I am taking *resolvit* as the verb for the noun *resolutio* or analysis. The same seems to be implied by Thomas's remark in ST I-IIae, q. 94, a. 2: "Nam illud quod primo cadit in apprehensione, est ens, cuius intellectus includitur in omnibus quaecumque quis apprehendit" (*ed. cit.*, p. 426). Also note Thomas's remark that every nature is being *essentialiter* in the text from the *De veritate:* "...quia quaelibet natura essentialiter est ens" (*ibid.*).

5. *Ibid.* Note in particular: "Sunt enim diversi gradus entitatis, secundum quos accipiuntur diversi modi essendi, et iuxta hos modos accipiuntur diversa rerum genera."

6. *Ibid.* "...sed nomine substantiae exprimitur quidam specialis modus essendi, scilicet ens per se; et ita est in aliis generibus."

7. *Ibid.*

8. This interpretation is reinforced by the next point in my text, i.e., that Thomas views substance and the other predicaments as supreme modes of *being,* with the emphasis on being, when we consider them ontologically rather than merely logically.

9. See *In V Met.,* lect. 9, nn. 889-890, *ed. cit.,* p. 238. Note in particular: "Unde oportet, quod ens contrahatur ad diversa genera secundum diversum modum praedicandi, qui consequitur diversum modum essendi; quia 'quoties ens dicitur,' idest quot modis aliquid praedicatur, 'toties esse significatur,' idest tot modis significatur aliquid esse." Also see *In III Physic.,* lect. 5 (*In Octo Libros Physicorum Aristotelis Expositio,* M. Maggiòlo, ed. [Turin-Rome, 1954]), n. 322, p. 158: "...sciendum est quod ens dividitur in decem praedicamenta non univoce, sicut genus in species, sed secundum diversum modum essendi. Modi autem essendi proportionales sunt modis praedicandi. Praedicando enim aliquid de aliquo altero, dicimus hoc esse illud: unde et decem genera entis dicuntur decem praedicamenta." For more on this and on Thomas's derivation of the predicaments see my "Thomas Aquinas's Derivation of the Aristotelian Categories (Predicaments)," *Journal of the History of Philosophy* 25 (1987), pp. 13-34, esp. pp. 17-19, 25.

10. See the texts and contexts cited in the previous note. Also note the following remark concerning our concepts (literally: "understandings") of things: "Licet modus significandi vocum non consequatur immediate modum essendi rerum, sed mediante modo intelligendi; quia intellectus sunt similitudines rerum, voces autem intellectuum, ut dicitur in primo Perihermenias" (*In VII Met.,* lect. 1, n. 1253). For Aristotle see *De interpretatione,* c. 1 (16a 1-5); for Thomas's Commentary on this see *In libros Peri Hermeneias expositio,* lect. 2, R. M. Spiazzi, ed., 2d ed. (Turin-Rome, 1964), n. 15.

11. 1003a 33-1003b 19. Cf. the remarks concerning this by Professor G. Verbeke in this same volume, pp. 35-51.

12. For a good overall presentation of this see B. Montagnes, *La doctrine de l'analogie de l'être d'après saint Thomas d'Aquin* (Louvain-Paris, 1963), Ch. 1, Section 1, "L'unité d'ordre par référence à un premier" (pp. 24-41).

13. See *De principiis naturae,* ch. 6 (Leonine ed., Vol. 43, pp. 46-7). For Averroes see *In IV Met.,* com. 2 (Venice, 1562), Vol. 8, ff. 65rb-va. For a comparison of these two texts see Montagnes, pp. 177-80.

14. Note that Aquinas, following Averroes, specifies that the primary instance of being — substance — is related to other instances as a subject, not as an end or as an efficient cause. He continues: "Alia enim dicuntur entia vel esse, quia per se habent esse sicut substantiae, quae

principaliter et prius entia dicuntur. Alia vero quia sunt passiones sive proprietates substantiae, sicut per se accidentia uniuscuiusque substantiae...." (*In IV Met.*, lect. 1, n. 539, p. 152).

15. *Ibid.*, nn. 540-543. Note Thomas's remarks concerning the third and fourth classes: "Tertium autem dicitur quod nihil habet de non ente admixtum, habet tamen esse debile, quia non per se, sed in alio, sicut sunt qualitates, quantitates et substantiae proprietates. Quartum autem genus est quod est perfectissimum, quod scilicet habet esse in natura absque admixtione privationis, et habet esse firmum et solidum, quasi per se existens, sicut sunt substantiae."

16. See n. 543: "Et ad hoc sicut ad primum et principale omnia alia referuntur."

17. *In V Met.*, lect. 9, n. 890. "Quia igitur eorum quae praedicantur, quaedam significant quid, idest substantiam, quaedam quale, quaedam quantum, et sic de aliis; oportet quod unicuique modo praedicandi, esse significet idem; ut cum dicitur homo est animal, esse significat substantiam." See n. 891: "Sciendum enim est quod praedicatum ad subiectum tripliciter se potest habere. Uno modo cum est id quod est subiectum, ut cum dico, Socrates est animal. Nam Socrates est id quod est animal. Et hoc praedicatum dicitur significare substantiam primam, quae est substantia particularis, de qua omnia praedicantur." On this see my "Thomas Aquinas's Derivation...," p. 20, and n. 21.

18. See section 2 below. For Aristotle see *Categories,* ch. 5.

19. *In V Met.,* lect. 10, nn. 898-902. Here Thomas does not pause to explain in what sense the parts of animals, such as hands and feet, are to be regarded as substances in this first way. He is content to mention them, along with demons, because Aristotle has done so. As regards the primary mode of substance he concludes: "Haec enim omnia praedicta dicuntur substantia, quia non dicuntur de alio subiecto, sed alia dicuntur de his. Et haec est descriptio primae substantiae in praedicamentis" (n. 898). On the fourth mode see n. 902. There Thomas distinguishes the quiddity or essence of a thing from substance taken in the second way, i.e., as substantial form. They differ as humanity differs from soul. This is because the form is a part of the essence or quiddity of a thing, and the quiddity or essence includes all the thing's essential principles. Because genus and species do not signify the form alone but the whole essence of the thing, they can be described as the substance of that of which they are predicated in this fourth way.

20. See nn. 901 and 905, for the elimination of the third mode. On substance in the first sense see n. 903. Note in particular: "...quorum unus est secundum quod substantia dicitur id quod ultimo subiicitur in propositionibus, ita quod de alio non praedicetur, sicut substantia prima. Et hoc est, quod est hoc aliquid, quasi per se subsistens, et quod est separabile, quia est ab omnibus distinctum et non communicabile multis." He goes on to develop three differences between particular or individual substance (first substance) and substance taken as universal: 1) particular substance is not predicated of any inferior, as is universal substance; 2) universal substance does not subsist except by reason of the individual substance which subsists per se; 3) universal substance is realized in many, but individual substance is not.

21. See n. 903 and note 20 above.

22. See n. 904.

23. For a helpful comparison and contrast of Aristotle and Aquinas concerning this see A. Maurer, "Form and Essence in the Philosophy of St. Thomas," *Mediaeval Studies* 13 (1951), pp. 165-76.

24. For the first text see *ed. cit.*, p. 157. There Thomas supports his twofold usage of substance by citing Aristotle's *Metaphysics* V. See ch. 8 (1017b 23-26), the text in Lectio 10 of his Commentary on the same (see nn. 903-905), and our discussion of this in the preceding paragraphs of this study. For ST III, q. 17, a. 1, ad 7 see the Marietti ed. (Turin-Rome, 1948), p. 130; for q. 2, a. 6, ad 3 see p. 30. For the *Summa contra gentiles* see *Editio leonina manualis* (Rome, 1934), p. 504. Thomas's immediately following comment expresses his personal view concerning the claim of the parts of a substance to be called "substances" (see my note 19

above): "Sed neque partes alicuius substantiae sic dicuntur particulares substantiae quasi sint per se subsistentes, sed subsistunt in toto. Unde nec hypostases possunt dici: cum nulla eorum sit substantia completa."

25. Mandonnet ed., Vol. 1, p. 605.

26. Already militating against accepting this suggestion is the fact that here Thomas has singled out essence (which we might identify with nature) as the first way in which substance is used, and distinguished this from the third way—second substance.

27. Ed. P. M. Pession (Turin-Rome, 1953), p. 226. Note especially: "Quidquid ergo est in re ad naturam communem pertinens, sub significatione essentiae continetur...."

28. *Ibid.* Note especially: "Comparatur ergo essentia ad substantiam particularem ut pars formalis ipsius, ut humanitas ad Socratem. Et ideo in rebus, ex materia et forma compositis, essentia non est omnino idem quod subiectum; unde non praedicatur de subiecto...."

29. *Ibid.* Note in particular: "In substantiis vero simplicibus, nulla est differentia essentiae et subiecti, cum non sit in eis materia individualis naturam communem individuans, sed ipsa essentia in eis est subsistentia."

30. *Ibid.* Note in particular: "Patet ergo quod hypostasis et substantia differunt ratione, sed sunt idem re."

31. "Essentia vero in substantiis quidem materialibus non est idem cum eis secundum rem, neque penitus diversum, cum se habeat ut pars formalis; in substantiis vero immaterialibus est omnino idem secundum rem, sed differens ratione" (p. 226). For more on the relation between first substance and second substance see *De pot.*, q. 9, a. 2, ad 6 (p. 228).

32. *In VII Met.*, lect. 2, nn. 1270-1274. Note his remark about substance taken as the subject: "Patet autem, quod subiectum hic dicitur, quod in *Praedicamentis* nominatur substantia prima, ex hoc, quod eadem definitio datur de subiecto hic, et ibi de substantia prima" (n. 1273). As Maurer points out, as early in his career as his *De ente,* Thomas identifies essence, quiddity and *quod quid erat esse,* and attributes this identification to Aristotle. But for Aristotle the concept of what a thing is ($τò \ τί\,\overset{?}{ε}στιν$) is not completely identical with his understanding of *quod quid erat esse* ($το \ τί\,\overset{?}{ην}\,\overset{?}{ε}ιναι$). See "Form and Essence in the Philosophy of St. Thomas," p. 172.

33. *Ibid.*, n. 1275. This text should be used to interpret Thomas's remark in *In X Met.*, lect. 3, n. 1979, that second substances signify a certain nature in the genus substance.

34. See n. 30 above and the corresponding part of our text. For some texts where Thomas identifies substance as being or existing in itself (*per se*) see *De ver.*, q. 1, a. 1 (cited above in n. 6); *In IV Met.*, lect. 1, n. 539 (see notes 14 and 15 above); *In V Met.*, lect. 10, n. 903 (see note 20); *De pot.*, q. 9, a. 1, *ed. cit.*, p. 226 ("quasi per se et non in alio existens").

35. "Quasi Definitio Substantiae," in *St. Thomas Aquinas 1274-1974: Commemorative Studies,* A. Maurer, ed. (Toronto, 1974), Vol. 1, pp. 111-29. Gilson has found what appears to be the text in Avicenna which Thomas has in mind. See *Liber de philosophia prima sive scientia divina,* S. Van Riet, ed., and G. Verbeke, intr., Tract. VIII, ch. 4 (Vol. 2, pp. 403-04). Cf. Gilson, pp. 112-14. Even so, we must admit that "to be not in a subject" is equivalent to "to be in itself," if we are to regard this as the text Thomas envisions.

36. On this see Gilson, pp. 121-25; and Ch. VII, Section 3 of the book on Aquinas's metaphysics I am now completing.

37. Mandonnet ed., Vol. 1, p. 221. See arg. 2.

38. *Ibid.*, pp. 222-23. Note especially: "Ens enim non est genus. Haec autem negatio 'non in subiecto' nihil ponit; unde hoc quod dico, ens non est in subiecto, non dicit aliquod genus...."

39. *Ibid.*, p. 223.

40. *Ibid.*, p. 222. Note in particular: "Omne quod est in genere, habet quidditatem differentem ab esse, sicut homo....In Deo autem esse suum est quidditas sua....Et ideo Deus (for: Deo) non potest esse in aliquo genere." For more on Thomas's argumentation here and elsewhere that presence in a genus entails distinction of essence and *esse* see my *Metaphysical Themes in Thomas Aquinas* (Washington, D.C., 1984), pp. 134-39.

41. *In IV Sent.*, dist. 12, qu. 1, a. 1, ql. 1, ad 2 (Moos ed., Vol. 4, p. 499): "Ad secundum dicendum quod, sicut probat Avicenna in sua *Meta.*, per se existere non est definitio substantiae; quia per hoc non demonstratur quidditas eius, sed esse eius. Et sua quidditas non est suum esse....Sed definitio vel quasi definitio substantiae est res habens quidditatem, cui acquiritur esse vel debetur non in alio."

42. *Ed. cit.*, p. 26. In order to make the point that being (*ens*) is not a genus, Thomas refers to Aristotle's procedure in *Metaphysics* III, ch. 3 (998b 22). If being were a genus, a difference would have to be identified which would restrict being to its various species. But no difference participates in a genus so as to include the genus in its intelligible content. For then a genus would be twice included in the definition of the species. Hence a difference must be something which is extrinsic to the meaning of the genus. But nothing can fall outside the intelligible content of being, since being is included within the intelligible content of those things of which it is predicated. Therefore being cannot be contracted by any difference and, consequently, is not a genus. For the dating see J. A. Weisheipl, *Friar Thomas d'Aquino,* 2d ed. (Washington, D.C., 1983), pp. 359-60.

43. *Ibid.*, p. 27.

44. *Ibid.* Note especially: "Oportet igitur quod ratio substantiae intelligatur hoc modo, quod substantia sit res cui conveniat esse non in subiecto; nomen autem rei a quidditate imponitur, sicut nomen entis ab esse; et sic in ratione substantiae intelligitur quod habeat quidditatem cui conveniat esse non in alio."

45. In this question Thomas is again attempting to show that God is not included in any genus, not even that of substance. See *ed. cit.*, pp. 193-94. Weisheipl dates this in 1265-1266 (*Friar Thomas*, p. 363).

46. *Ed. cit.*, p. 194.

47. "Sed si substantia possit habere definitionem, non obstante quod est genus generalissimum, erit eius definitio: quod substantia est res cuius quidditati debetur esse non in aliquo" (*ibid.*). Again Thomas concludes that this "definition" of substance cannot be applied to God.

48. See section 2 above, pp. 6-8, and the text cited in note 31.

49. Moos ed., Vol. 3, p. 196.

50. *Ed. cit.*, pp. 515-16, ad 4: "...quia in homine aliud est natura et persona, cum sit ex materia et forma compositus; non autem in angelo, qui immaterialis est." Note that here Thomas is meeting a series of objections against the fittingness of the Incarnation, and in this particular case, by showing that it was more fitting for the nature of man to be assumed by the Word than for an angel to be assumed precisely because of the distinction in man between nature and person.

51. For the first see *Quaestiones disputatae,* Vol. 2 (Turin-Rome, 1953), p. 195; for the second, M. Calcaterra and T. S. Centi, eds., *ibid.*, p. 390: "...dicendum quod in compositis ex materia et forma, individuum addit supra naturam speciei designationem materiae et accidentia individualia. Sed in formis abstractis non addit individuum supra naturam speciei aliquid secundum rem, quia in talibus essentia eius est ipsummet individuum *subsistens*...." (ital. mine). The term *subsistens* indicates Thomas is speaking of the suppositum, not merely of an individuated instance of nature. For the third text see *In III De anima,* A. M. Pirotta, ed. (Turin-Rome, 1959), Lect. 8, n. 706/Leonine ed., Vol. 45.1, p. 209. Note that in this context Thomas speaks of there being no distinction in such beings between *res* and *quod quid est.* By this I take him to have in mind the relationship between the subject (*res*) and its nature or quiddity (*quod quid est*). For the dates of these two last-mentioned works see Weisheipl, *Friar Thomas d'Aquino,* pp. 364, 378 (as corrected). The dating of Thomas's Commentary on the *De anima* continues to be disputed. For a review see B. Bazán, "Le commentaire de S. Thomas d'Aquin sur le *Traité de l'âme.* Un événement: l'édition critique de la commission léonine," *Revue des sciences philosophiques et théologiques* 69 (1985), p. 532. For another text see ST I, qu. 3, a. 3 (*ed. cit.*, p. 16).

52. *Quaestiones quodlibetales,* ed. by R. Spiazzi (Turin, 1956), p. 25. Note especially: "Suppositum autem est singulare in genere substantiae, quod dicitur hypostasis vel substantia prima...." For the date see Weisheipl, p. 367.

53. In his Commentary on *Metaphysics* VII Thomas assigns this position to Averroes and rejects it. See *In VII Met.,* lect. 9, nn. 1467-1468. Against this he accepts the view which he assigns to Avicenna (see n. 1469), according to which the form of the whole—the quiddity of the species—differs from the form of the part as a whole differs from its part; for the quiddity of the species is composed of matter and form, though not of this form and this individual matter. He also assigns this position to Aristotle. For discussion see Maurer, "Form and Essence...," pp. 165ff., 169ff.

54. *Ed. cit.,* p. 25. For Aristotle see *Metaphysics* VII, ch. 6 (1031a 16-1031b 28). To illustrate his point, Thomas notes that a man is nothing other than what it is to be a man (*quod quid est hominis*), presumably because a man is said to be per se. A white thing is not completely identical with what it is to be white, since it is a substance which has a quality—whiteness. Hence a white thing is an illustration of something which is said to be per accidens. Cf. *In VII Met.,* lect. 5, especially nn. 1377-1379. Thomas does not conclude from this that when quiddity is taken as a part (e.g., humanity) that it is completely identical with the concrete subject (e.g., a man). For some helpful remarks concerning this in Aristotle see A. C. Lloyd, *Form and Universal in Aristotle* (Liverpool, 1981), pp. 37-38.

55. *Ibid.* "Secundum hoc ergo, cuicumque potest aliquid accidere quod non sit de ratione suae naturae, in eo differt res et quod quid est, sive suppositum et natura....suppositum autem non solum habet haec quae ad rationem speciei pertinent, sed etiam alia quae ei accidunt; et ideo suppositum signatur per totum, natura autem, sive quidditas, ut pars formalis."

56. *Ibid.* Note especially: "In angelo autem non est omnino idem: quia aliquid accidit ei praeter id quod est de ratione suae speciei: quia et ipsum esse angeli est praeter eius essentiam seu naturam; et alia quaedam ei accidunt quae omnino pertinent ad suppositum, non autem ad naturam."

57. *Ed. cit.,* pp. 25-26. Note from the end of his long reply to objection 1: "Sed quia non est suum esse, accidit ei aliquid praeter rationem speciei, scilicet ipsum esse, et alia quaedam quae attribuuntur supposito, et non naturae; propter quod suppositum in eis non est omnino idem cum natura."

58. L. De Guzman Vicente has attempted to do this, and regards the treatment in Quodlibet II as decisive. As for texts where Thomas seems to identify nature and suppositum in created spirits, De Guzman Vicente suggests that if in these texts Thomas speaks of simple substances taken generally, he really has in mind only God. See his "De notione subsistentiae apud sanctum Thomam," *Divus Thomas* (Piacenza) 71 (1968), pp. 418-19. Unfortunately, this will not resolve the difficulty. Consultation of the above passages in which Thomas identifies nature and suppositum in immaterial beings reveals that by implication in all of them and explicitly in some he has in mind created immaterial entities, not merely God. See notes 49, 50, and 51 above.

59. *Person und hypostatische Union bei Thomas von Aquin* (Freiburg, Schweiz, 1957), pp. 85-89.

60. See p. 88. Note that Schweizer also cites ST III, q. 2, a. 2 (dating from 1272-1273). There Thomas writes that something is found in certain subsisting things which does not pertain to the intelligible content of its species, i.e., accidents and individuating principles, "sicut maxime apparet in his quae sunt ex materia et forma composita" (Turin-Rome, 1948), p. 23. In this text Thomas also writes that since in God there is nothing in addition to the divine nature, in him suppositum and nature do not really differ. Might not this be taken as implying that Thomas would again distinguish between nature and suppositum in angels because of the distinction in them between essence and *esse*? See Schweizer, pp. 97-98. While this text does not exclude that interpretation, it does not assert it; it is noncommittal concerning the issue of angels.

61. For this in Boethius see his *De Hebdomadibus,* Axiom II: "Diversum est esse et id quod est...." See his *The Theological Tractates. The Consolation of Philosophy,* ed. by H. F. Stewart, E. K. Rand, and S. J. Tester (Cambridge, Mass., 1978), p. 40.

62. For some texts where Thomas makes this contrast see *De ente,* ch. 4 (Roland Gosselin ed., pp. 35-36/Leonine ed., Vol. 43, p. 377); *In I Sent.,* d. 8, q. 5, a. 1 (Mandonnet ed., Vol. 1, p 227); *In De Hebdomadibus,* lect. 2, in *Opuscula theologica,* ed. by M. Calcaterra (Turin-Rome, 1954), p. 398, n. 32; ST I, q. 75, a. 5, ad 4; SCG II, ch. 52 (where the entire chapter is devoted to proving that in created separate substances there is composition of *esse* and *quod est* (or *substantia*); Quodlibet II, q. 2, a. 1 (*ed. cit.,* p. 24).

63. *Ed. cit.,* p. 372.

64. *Ed. cit.,* p. 192.

65. See *Sancti Thomae de Aquino Expositio super librum Boethii de Trinitate,* B. Decker, ed. (Leiden, 1959), q. 5, a. 1, ad 6 (p. 171); qu. 5, art. 4 (p. 194): "...quae habet subiectum ens in quantum est ens"; and the *Prooemium* to his Commentary on the *Metaphysics* (p. 2): "...ens commune."

Thirtieth Award of Aquinas Medal

by Edward A. Synan

Like handicappers estimating the odds on a race next week, we inevitably day-dream as to how Brother Thomas Aquinas would do his work today. Can we think that the Common Doctor would take Heidegger or Marx or Wittgenstein less seriously than he was accustomed to take Averroes and Rabbi Moyses and Aristotle? Thoroughly faithful to biblical, ecclesial, and university traditions, Saint Thomas made his mark by responding skillfully to the challenges of the 13th century. We can hardly believe that this theologian, who knew himself to be a "modern" in his own time, transferred to ours would be content to count as an "ancient."

Our Thomists ought to do nothing less. Should we not aspire to forward what an earlier medalist, William A. Wallace, O.P., has called "developmental Thomism," we could be no more than pseudo-Thomists. Surely such a one would not merit the Aquinas Medal of this Association. Our medalist this year is in no sense a pseudo-Thomist and he richly deserves the award. Philosophers like to have good reasons; may these few do service for the many that have inspired the choice.

Armand A. Maurer, a priest of the Congregation of Saint Basil, like a number of us still-young Toronto staff, is by a paradox *professor emeritus* of the University of Toronto and of the Pontifical Institute of Mediaeval Studies. That University granted him the degrees B.A., M.A., and Ph.D.; the Institute awarded him the diploma L.M.S. His cosmopolitan academic *persona* owes more than a little to a post-doctoral year in Paris at l'École des hautes études, to another year at Cambridge University, and to yet another which he divided between Rome and Harvard's Cambridge.

As a mediaevalist Armand Maurer has contributed to our understanding of a whole litany of persons and puzzles. Poor Siger of Brabant and that worthy's companion-in-arms, Boethius of Dacia, the Franciscan sages John Duns the Scot, Francis of Mayron, and William of Ockham are all better focused for us, thanks to Maurer. So are the secular Masters: Henry of Harclay, who struggled against both Franciscans and Dominicans with a fine impartiality, but had the consolation of dying as Bishop of Lincoln, and that even more notable Master, so often under the scrutiny of Duns Scotus, Henry of Ghent. To them must be added the Arts Master John of Jandun, Cardinal Nicholas of Cusa, and the Dominican Dietrich of Freiberg and

Meister Eckhardt. Lest this catalogue of clerics make our numerous and distinguished lay members feel left out, Maurer has had not a little to say about the thought of the layman Pietro Pompanazzi and about that of the 19th century Orestes A. Brownson, thorn in the side of "Dagger John," Archbishop Hughes of New York. Nor would the catalogue be complete without a glancing mention of two more (clerics, to be sure, but at least not mediaevals) Jonathan Edwards and Yale's Samuel Johnson—not to be confused with Boswell's companion.

As for puzzles, our medalist has dealt with that most mysterious of Names, the Tetragrammaton, *baruch ha-Shem!* as well as with the myth of a mediaeval "double truth" theory. Most of all, however, he has clarified for beginners and specialists alike the endlessly fascinating, difficult, and precious thought of the "dumb ox" from the Kingdom of Sicily, Brother Thomas Aquinas of the Order of Preachers.

All of Maurer's publications are distinguished and some in a most unexpected way. A pair of his annotated Thomistic translations (soon to become a trio) not only meet exacting academic standards, but also make money. His volume, *Medieval Philosophy,* has merited a revision and a new printing; a kind Providence has effected its transfer from the commercial house it was enriching to the Publications Department of the Institute in order to enrich us. *Dignum et iustum est.*

His journal publications can be given a summary estimate. Excluding reviews of what others have published, Armand Maurer has more than 60 articles and papers in learned journals, in the proceedings of international conferences, and in encyclopedias of acknowledged authority. He was editor-in-chief as well as a contributor to the volumes with which the Pontifical Institute commemorated the septicentenary of Saint Thomas' passage into the clear light of vision.

This research accomplishment has flourished within and permeated a most notable teaching career. If strangers from less complex academic consortia will put their consternation on hold, the truth is that Professor Maurer has functioned, more or less simultaneously, on the teaching staffs of Saint Michael's College, the Pontifical Institute, the Graduate Department of Philosophy in the University of Toronto, and has managed the occasional detour through the Center for Thomistic Studies in Houston's University of Saint Thomas.

Maurer's "developmental Thomism" does not stop with these explicitly theological and philosophical issues. Like Brother Thomas himself, who counted Job's Leviathan a whale "according to the letter," *ad litteram,* Armand Maurer can bring in a literary anecdote about two whales with a grace that belies the unwieldy bulk of those enormous creatures; you will hear him do so in a moment. To his literary erudition must be added the fact that he knows about music and painting; he helps us to see that, in the end, their beauty is their being. No one who meets him in the staff dining room, week after week, can fail to know that Armand Maurer has his view, an instance of *doxa,* alas, not of *episteme,* on that most intractable of philosophical enigmas, the future contingent: the performance tomorrow of a horse on the track at Woodbine.

As might have been expected, all this has earned him honors. Beyond the academic triumphs noted, Armand Maurer has served as President of our Association; he has long been a Fellow of the Royal Society of Canada.

Honors enough, you say? There remains, thus far imperfectly expressed, a very real cloud of respect, gratitude, and affection arising from his former students. To him they owe first-class teaching and direction in research as well as the dissertations thus generated. A comparable cloud of good will arises from the ranks of his colleagues, near and far; in a sense we are his students also. Because a respectable number of both categories are members of this Association, it is a joy to present one whom Alexander Pope would allow us to call our "guide, philosopher, and friend" (*Essay on Man,* Epist. IV, 1. 390; *Imitations of Horace,* Epist. I, bk 1, 1. 177), Armand A. Maurer, C.S.B, for the 1987 award of the Aquinas Medal of the American Catholic Philosophical Association.

Pontifical Institute of Mediaeval Studies
  Toronto, Canada

Medalist's Address:
Reflections on Metaphysics and Experience

by Armand Maurer

Our President, Fr. Wippel, has set the tone of this year's conference by choosing as his theme the metaphysical notion of substance. His choice of a metaphysical topic is hardly surprising, for he is a distinguished member of that rare and somewhat endangered species—the metaphysician. In keeping with the direction Fr. Wippel has given to our conference, I should like to offer a few reflections on the relation of metaphysics to experience.

There is a widespread opinion among contemporary philosophers, especially those of a positivist and linguistic persuasion, that if metaphysics is a viable enterprise, it has little or nothing to do with experience. A few would banish metaphysical terms, like being and existence, from our vocabulary,[1] but most would contend that they are meaningful and deserve the special attention of the philosopher. They would deny, however, that their meaning, or for that matter the meaning of any metaphysical term, is derived from experience. Rather, they regard these terms as part of the categorial or linguistic structure inherent in our mind or language. As a consequence, metaphysics is not conceived as a science that can be enriched by everyday experience, or by experience in the natural or social sciences, history, poetry or music.

No one bears greater responsibility for metaphysics' flight from experience than Immanuel Kant. Kant had no intention of destroying metaphysics itself. Quite the contrary: he wrote his *Critique of Pure Reason* to save it from the morass into which he believed it had fallen in his day. Metaphysics traditionally claims to make judgments about the ultimate nature of reality as it is in itself, but Hume convinced Kant of the impossibility of making such pronouncements from experience, for they escape any possible empirical verification. Hence he concluded that they have their ground in human subjectivity, i.e., in the *a priori* categories of our understanding. Thus he accomplished a revolution in metaphysics whose effects are still with us. That revolution can be expressed succinctly in his own words: "Metaphysics is a completely isolated speculative science of reason, which soars far above the teachings of experience, and in which reason is indeed meant to be its own pupil."[2] Because, in his view, metaphysics is derived solely from pure *a priori* concepts, he saw no reason why it could not be completed within a short time, indeed within his own *Critique of Pure Reason,* leaving his successors the sole task of adapting it as they might, without adding anything to its content.³

Modern philosophers of language are too original and inventive to content themselves with the menial occupation of adding footnotes to Kant. They have brought about their own revolution in philosophy by making it a study of language—either ordinary language or an ideal language. The "linguistic turn," however, that has captivated so many contemporary philosophers, does not bring metaphysics any closer to experience, with the exception perhaps of the experience of language. For the Kantian study of the *a priori* categories and forms of knowledge, analytic philosophers have generally substituted the logical analysis of language. For them, language is the source of *a priori* knowledge in place of the Kantian categories of pure reason. This clearly emerges in Strawson's account of what he calls "descriptive metaphysics."⁴ He grants that the philosopher must examine closely the ordinary use of words—this he assures us is the only safe method in philosophy. But the metaphysician, he continues, must probe more deeply into language and reveal its hidden structure and interconnections. There he will find categories and concepts that remain fundamentally the same throughout history. This shifts the ground of metaphysics from pure reason to language, but metaphysics remains—as it was for Kant—a closed body of knowledge. It is not a science drawn from experience of the real world in all its many facets, and capable of indefinite enrichment through contact with the arts and sciences. Indeed, Strawson claims that once the philosopher has discovered the basic structure of language, it is unlikely that any new truths can be added.

Analytical philosophy has taken many forms, but its central teaching, according to Arthur Danto, is "that the problems of philosophy are *au fond* problems of language, however heavily disguised."⁵ How could it be otherwise when, in Danto's words, "the structures of language determine what are the structures of reality for those whose language it is, and that the deep order of the world, so sought by philosophers of the past, is but the cast shadow of the deep order of their grammar."⁶ This is so true, in Danto's view, that a change in language is able to effect a change in human reality. In this connection he applauds Nietzsche, who proclaimed that "we shall not get rid of God...until we get rid of grammar."

What must the world be like, asks Danto, "in order that language may get a purchase upon it"? He replies: "The world, as it were, flattens out in order to receive language: it falls into the shape of things, of facts, of qualities and of classes, depending upon the semantical vehicle applied. The facets of the receiving surface of the world are determined completely by the structure of semantical vehicles, so that language and world reflect one another faithfully *when* (and *only when*) we conceive of the world as external to language. This explains why since pre-socratic days, philosophers have spoken *as though the world were made out of language.*" "So nature is frozen language," Danto continues, "as language is liquid world."[7] In the same vein, Danto quotes J. H. Randall Jr.: "Nature displays certain 'passive powers' or potentialities of being shaped into linguistic form."[8]

We might well ask at this point: what is the fate of metaphysics, indeed of philosophy itself, if these views are correct? If the world or reality is simply the reflection, or possibly even the creation, of our language, we cannot hope to know reality as it is in itself. We know it only as it is shaped by the language we use, as, according to Kant, we know it only as it is conditioned by *a priori* categories and forms. In no sense of the word does knowledge represent or mirror reality itself.

The frightening consequences of this direction of philosophy are clearly drawn in Richard Rorty's recent book, *Philosophy and the Mirror of Nature.*[9] As Henry Veatch says, Rorty's underlying thesis "is that present-day Analytical Philosophy cannot end in anything other than a philosophy of radical Deconstruction," by which he means "a total conceptual or intellectual permissiveness."[10] The aim of philosophy, in Rorty's view, is no longer the search for truth, but rather "to sustain a conversation." As we cannot hope to *know*, in any of the classical senses of the word, the sufficient purpose of philosophy is "to keep the conversation going" or "to send the conversation off in new directions." If new objective truths result, they are not the point of philosophy, but only "accidental byproducts." Philosophy has the social function which Dewey called "breaking the crust of convention," thereby preventing a person from deluding himself with the notion that he knows himself, or anything else, except under optional descriptions.[11]

How did philosophy reach this sorry condition? Is it not because philosophers have so often cut themselves off from the wealth of human experience? Kant wanted human reason to feed upon itself, but this was found to be a very meager diet. The analytical philosophers turned to language as their mentor, but by itself this turned out to be a teacher of questionable competence.

But perhaps the plight of the philosopher is not as desperate as it appears. It is possible that some of the presuppositions of philosophy since the time of Locke, Hume and Kant just fail to withstand critical scrutiny. One of these assumptions—amounting almost to a dogma for modern philosophers—is that a statement is either necessarily true, and then it is *a priori,* underived from experience, or it is contingently true, and then it is *a posteriori* or derived from experience. Accordingly, necessary truths, like those of metaphysics, must be *a priori*; they cannot be *a posteriori,* i.e., known to be true on the basis of observation or experience of the real world.

This widely held belief has been recently challenged by Saul Kripke in a remarkable essay entitled "Identity and Necessity."[12] Kripke's treatment of the topic remains on the level of logical theory and the philosophy of language, but it has far-reaching implications for metaphysics. In contradiction to the sacrosanct dogma of modern philosophy that a statement cannot be both *a posteriori* and necessary, Kripke argues for the existence of a class of identity statements that are necessarily true but yet *a posteriori.* As an example he offers the statement: The Morning Star is identical with the Evening Star, or Phosphorus is identical with Hesperus. We know that the star, or better the planet, seen in the morning and called Venus is identical with the star seen in the evening and called by the same name. This is clearly a statement known to be true by experience and hence *a posteriori,* for both observation and reflection were required for the discovery of the identity of the planets. It is also a necessary statement, for the contrary cannot be true.

Kripke's essay suggests a reversion to a pre-Kantian notion well known to ancient and medieval philosophers, namely that experience reveals to us necessities in nature that are the basis of necessary propositions. Both Aristotle and Aquinas, for example, thought it necessarily true that when a thing exists it must exist. Thus, while Socrates is sitting he must sit. He cannot both be sitting and not sitting at the same time.[13] This necessity resides, so to speak, in the very being of Socrates. The identity of a thing with itself (expressed, for example, by the statement "Socrates is Socrates") is not simply a logical tautology, but a truth that can awaken the mind to the deep mystery of being. It can lead to the insight of Thomas Aquinas, that being (*esse*) is something stable and at rest in a thing.[14]

If experience reveals necessities in nature that are the basis of necessary statements concerning particulars, like the planet Venus or Socrates, why may there not be intelligible necessities in nature grounding general or universal necessary statements? These necessities would be known not through an empirical generalization or induction that always remains incomplete and therefore provisory, but through the intellectual power of insight, which Aristotle called *nous* and Aquinas *intellectus*: a power that enables us to read, so to speak, within nature itself.[15] The power has been widely dismissed or neglected since Kant, and yet it is difficult to deny its existence. How else could we arrive at general truths about nature which, try as we might, we cannot deny? After a lecture in which Gilson forcefully defended this power, a questioner challenged him to give an example of a universal necessary truth. The questioner probably thought Gilson would offer the principle of contradiction, for which the questioner had a ready reply. Gilson's example was unexpected and undeniable: Even the rich have need of friends. The questioner stood in silence for a moment, then quietly sat down. And indeed, do we not know from experience that the need for friendship is, so to speak, written right in human nature? Long ago Aristotle and Cicero saw the necessary connection between human nature and friendship, and nothing has happened to human nature since then to question the connection.[16]

We do not have to go to antiquity or the Middle Ages to find metaphysicians who used a concrete and experiential approach to their subject. Modern philosophy provides eminent examples of such metaphysicians. Jacques Maritain cites three: Bergson, Heidegger and Gabriel Marcel. Bergson approached being through the biological and psychological experience of duration. Toward the end of his career he turned to the experience of the mystics as he studied, so to speak experimentally, the problem of the nature and existence of God. Heidegger led his reader to an insight into being by the psychological—even the metaphysical—experience of anguish (*Angst*). In the deep feeling of anguish we experience our existence "as something saved from nothingness, snatched from nonentity." Marcel's way to being concentrates on certain moral virtues such as fidelity. The experience of fidelity, by which we dominate the flux of our life and give it unity and consistency, offers the metaphysician a glimpse of the steadfastness of our own being.[17]

To this list of modern metaphysicians who have used an experiential approach to being, Maritain might have added his own name. We all know how successfully he used poetic and mystical experience in his pursuit of being. On occasion he had recourse to biology in his philosophizing. I recall his Toronto lectures on the natural law, which began with a description of the mysterious dance of the bees.

Another name that immediately comes to mind in this connection is Etienne Gilson. His preferred method in philosophy was historical. Trained in historical methodology at the Sorbonne, he never forgot the lessons he learned in the power of historical analysis. He found reflection on the history of philosophy an indispensable aid in recognizing true philosophical principles and discovering their meaning in the light of their necessary consequences.[18] This is the empirical method he used so fruitfully in *The Unity of Philosophical Experience* and *Being and Some Philosophers*. Gilson knew well that a philosophical reflection on the data of history is not the most direct or best method in philosophy. Metaphysics, he assures us, has its own. proper method, which is the intellectual intuition of first principles and the direct insight into their truth. The experience of philosophy in history, he concedes, can only be a secondary and auxiliary method in metaphysics. It cannot replace metaphysical research properly so called. All it can do is to assist it. With his usual precision, Gilson says that the historical method in philosophy "does not make us see, but it leads us to the point from where we see."[19]

Maritain writes in the same vein that experience in the sciences can only bring the philosopher to the threshold of metaphysics. It can prepare him for the intuition of being, but it cannot give him that intuition. The experiences of metaphysicians like Bergson, Heidegger and Marcel stop short of metaphysics proper. We reach this goal, Maritain continues, "by letting the veils — too heavy with matter and too opaque — of the concrete psychological or ethical fact fall away to discover in their purity the strictly metaphysical values which such experiences concealed. There is then but one word by which we can express our discovery, namely being."[20]

Thomas Aquinas would heartily applaud these appeals to experience in metaphysics. As you know, all our knowledge, in his view, originates in and from sensory experience. This is true even of metaphysical knowledge.[21] Moreover, he considered all the arts and sciences relevant to the progress of metaphysics. Without prejudicing the formal independence of metaphysics as a wisdom, he believed that the sciences and arts provide it with data that in some cases are essential to it and in others simply useful. Thus metaphysics borrows from the philosophy of nature the notions of form, nature and motion, though it views these realities in a new light — the light of being. Some arts and sciences do not offer metaphysics data essential to it, but they contribute to its fullness of perfection (its *bene esse*).[22] One of the examples given by Thomas Aquinas is music. This may come as a surprise, for it is not at once clear how music can benefit the metaphysician — except perhaps to put him in a good mood! But on reflection we can see how the study of music can enrich the metaphysician's notion of being. The existence of music is fluid and successive, and indeed spiritual, for a musical composition, taken as a whole, must be constructed by the mind in memory.[23] It has being, therefore, only by analogy with the subsistent being that is "something stable and at rest in a thing."

The Thomist, then, is not faced with a choice between experience or metaphysics. He need not opt for the empiricism of Locke and Hume without metaphysics or the transcendentalism of Kant without experience. For the Thomist there is no metaphysics without experience, and experience itself naturally leads to the insights of metaphysics. Moreover, the progress of metaphysics is intimately bound up with advances in the natural and social sciences, art and religion. If he is truly a creative philosopher, the Thomist will take all of these into account. Nor will he neglect the important data disclosed by phenomenology and the philosophy of language. All experience, whatever its source, will be grist for his mill.

If this is so, metaphysics will not be a closed system that can be completed within a short time, as Kant and Strawson believed. It is open to endless progress, to an ever deepening insight into being, its modes and causes, especially the first cause, or God.

By way of conclusion I should like to recall an episode in Herman Melville's *Moby-Dick*—that masterpiece of imagination and symbolism.[24] As one of the analysts of the novel says, it speaks "to the modern mind with profound pertinence."[25]

Before the whaling ship, Pequod, has its fateful encounter with that devil of a whale, Moby Dick, it captures two smaller whales—a right whale and a sperm whale. After cutting off their heads, which contain precious bone and whale oil, the whalers first attach the head of the sperm whale to the starboard side of the boat, making it lean perilously to the right. When they fasten the head of the other whale to the port side, the boat regains a somewhat even keel, but it rides low and sluggishly in the water. At this point in his narrative Melville is reminded of the debate in the New England of his day (c. 1850) between the followers of the empiricism of Locke and those who favored the newer transcendentalism of Kant. The two whale heads become in his mind symbols of the two philosophers. The ship itself he takes as a symbol of humanity or the human spirit. He describes the situation of the boat, laden with the two whale heads, in these words: "So, when on one side you hoist in Locke's head, you go over that way; but now, on the other side, hoist in Kant's and you came back again; but in very poor plight. Thus, some minds for ever keep trimming boat. O, ye foolish," Melville exclaims, "throw all these thunder-heads overboard, and then you will float light and right."

To this, the friends of Thomas Aquinas can only say "Amen." He has shown them a better way to trim ship in philosophy!

Pontifical Institute of Mediaeval Studies
Toronto, Canada

NOTES

1. See Sidney Hook, *The Quest for Being* (New York: St. Martin's Press, 1961), p. 147.

2. I. Kant, *Critique of Pure Reason,* Preface to second edition, Bxiv; trans. N. K. Smith (London: Macmillan, 1950), p. 21. Kant describes speculative metaphysics as "that philosophy...which considers everything in so far as it is." B873, p. 661. But he holds that all metaphysical conclusions regarding the nature of things in general are *a priori,* i.e., derived not from experience but from reason itself. See Douglas Dryer, *Kant's Solution for Verification in Metaphysics* (London: Allen & Unwin, 1966), p. 34.

3. I. Kant, *ibid.*, Axx, pp. 13-14.

4. P. F. Strawson, *Individuals. An Essay in Descriptive Metaphysics* (London: Methuen, 1959), pp. 9-10. In his "Imagination and Perception," in *Freedom and Resentment* (London: Methuen, 1974) Strawson begins to move from a more Kantian position to a more Hegelian or existentialist one. He recognized the need of a more fluid notion of conceptuality and understanding. See Colin Flack, "On the Process of Meaning-Creation," *The Review of Metaphysics,* 38 (1985), p. 510, n. 8.

5. Arthur C. Danto, *Nietzsche as Philosopher* (New York: Columbia University Press, 1980), p. 8. Cited in Henry Veatch, "Deconstruction in Philosophy: Has Rorty Made It the Denouement of Contemporary Analytical Philosophy?" *The Review of Metaphysics,* 39 (1985), p. 305.

6. Danto, *ibid.*, p. 9.

7. Arthur C. Danto, *Analytical Philosophy of Knowledge* (Cambridge: Cambridge University Press, 1968), p. 242. Danto's emphasis.

8. *Ibid.*, p. 241. See J. H. Randall, Jr., "Art of Language and Linguistic Situation. A Naturalistic Analysis," *Journal of Philosophy,* 60.2 (1963), p. 50.

9. Richard Rorty, *Philosophy and the Mirror of Nature* (Princeton: Princeton University Press, 1979).

10. Henry Veatch, "Deconstruction in Philosophy...," pp. 315-316.

11. Richard Rorty, *ibid.*, pp. 377-379. See Henry Veatch, *ibid.*, pp. 313-316.

12. Saul Kripke, "Identity and Necessity," in *Philosophy As It Is;* ed. H. and M. Burgyeat (Pelican Books, 1979), pp. 478-513. This is a shorter version of Kripke's "Naming and Necessity" in *Semantics of Natural Languages,* ed. Donald Davidson and Gilbert Harman (Dordrecht: D. Reidel, 1972). Kripke is here taking issue with Quine. See "Identity and Necessity," p. 484.

13. Aristotle, *De Interpretatione,* 9. 19a22. St. Thomas, *In I Peri Hermenias,* lect. 15; ed. Leonine 1 (Rome: Ex Typographia Polyglotta, 1882), p. 72, n. 2; *De Potentia,* q. 5, a. 4.

14. "Esse autem est aliquid fixum et quietum in ente." St. Thomas, *Summa contra gentiles,* I, 20, n. 24.

15. Aristotle, *Nic. Eth.* 6, 6, 1041a7. St. Thomas, *In VI Eth.*, lect. 5; ed. Leonine 47² (Rome: Ad Sanctae Sabinae, 1969), p. 349. 50-63.

16. Aristotle, *Nic. Eth.* 9, 9 1169b13-15. St. Thomas, *In IX Eth.*, lect. 10; ed. Leonine, p. 536. 51-58. Cicero, *De Amiticia,* VI (Loeb Classical Library, 1923), pp. 131-132.

17. Jacques Maritain, *A Preface to Metaphysics* (London: Sheed & Ward, 1943), pp. 49-51.

18. Etienne Gilson, "Remarques sur l'expérience en métaphysique," *Actes du XIᵉ Congrès international de philosophie,* Bruxelles, Aug. 20-26, 1953 (Amsterdam-Louvain: North-Holland Publishing Co., 1953), pp. 5-10.

19. "C'est ici, et sur ce plan défini, qu'à son tour l'expérimentation en matière d'histoire doctrinale s'avère irremplaçable. Elle aide à reconnaître les véritables principes et à en discerner le sens par la vue de leurs conséquences nécessaires. Elle ne fait pas voir, elle conduit au point d'où l'on voit." *Ibid.* p. 9.

20. J. Maritain, *A Preface to Metaphysics,* p. 52. Gilson did not see eye to eye with Maritain on the intuition of being. For Maritain, the metaphysician enjoys an intellectual intuition of being that gives rise to a concept of existence that has not been abstracted from images. See J. Maritain, "Réflexions sur la nature blessée et sur l'intuition de l'être," *Revue thomiste* 68 (1968), p. 20; reprinted in *Approches sans entraves* (Paris: Fayard, 1973), p. 267. Gilson replied that in the philosophy of Thomas Aquinas there is no exception to the rule that our concepts are formed by abstraction from images. See E. Gilson, "Propos sur l'être et sa notion," *Studi Tomistici* 3; Pontificia Accademia Romana di S. Tommaso d'Aquino; Città Nuova Editrice, 1974, p. 16.

21. St. Thomas, *In Boethii de Trin.*, q. 6, a. 2; ed. Decker (Leiden: Brill, 1965), pp. 215-217. Trans. A. Maurer, *The Division and Methods of the Sciences,* 4th ed. (Toronto: Pontifical Institute of Mediaeval Studies, 1986), pp. 76-78.

22. St. Thomas, *ibid.*, q. 5, a. 1, ad 9, p. 172.5-12. *The Division and Methods...,* p. 23. St. Thomas here follows Avicenna. For an excellent study of this passage in Aquinas, see John F. Wippel, "Aquinas and Avicenna on the Relationship between First Philosophy and the other Theoretical Sciences; a Note on Thomas's Commentary on Boethius' *De Trinitate,* Q. 5, art. 1, ad 9," in *The Thomist* 37 (1973), pp. 133-154. Reprinted in John F. Wippel, *Metaphysical*

Themes in Thomas Aquinas (Washington, D.C.: The Catholic University of America Press, 1984), pp. 37-53.

23. Etienne Gilson, *Matières et formes. Poiétiques particulières des arts majeurs* (Paris: Vrin, 1964), pp. 146-147. See Joseph Owens, "Aquinas—Existential Permanence and Flux," *Mediaeval Studies,* 31 (1969), pp. 71-92.

24. Herman Melville, *Moby-Dick or, the Whale,* ch. 73; ed. A. Kazin (Boston: Houghton Mifflin, 1956), p. 259.

25. Edward F. Edinger, *Melville's Moby-Dick: A Jungian Commentary* (New York: A New Direction Book, 1978), p. 5.

PLENARY SESSION — I

Leo Sweeney, S.J., Chairman
Loyola University of Chicago

Substance in Aristotle

by Gerard Verbeke

In his inquiry on the notion of substance Aristotle starts from prephilo-sophical opinions: this way of proceeding is far from being exceptional. Particularly in his research on ethical matters, the author frequently appeals to popular opinions and beliefs as a starting point of his investigation. This method, however, doesn't mean that the Stagirite confines himself to reproducing what people commonly accept as moral rules and maxims: on the contrary, prephilosophical doctrines are carefully studied and submitted to a critical examination.[1] And yet, the author highly appreciates common opinions, particularly when they are very ancient and date back to immemo-rial times in the past; when they never have been abandoned or repudiated, but are constantly adhered to; and when they are universally accepted up to the present period. When the three conditions are fulfilled, common opin-ions must be valuable, their truth value must be very high. If they were mistaken, that would mean that mankind during centuries sticks to errone-ous conceptions regarding important topics of human life and behaviour or regarding metaphysical and anthropological issues. In Aristotle's view such persistent universal mistakes with respect to important matters of human existence are impossible, since they would be in clear contradiction to the teleological theory. If everything in the world aims at the good, how could the whole of mankind persistently live in darkness, ignorance and error with respect to significant matters?[2] According to Aristotle prephilosophical opinions which fulfill the above mentioned conditions are in a sense "natural views": they belong to the work of nature, which always tends towards the good and reaches this goal at least in the majority of the cases.[3] There are of course situations in which nature is prevented from attaining its goal, but such cases are accidental and rather exceptional.

One of these prephilosophical conceptions is related to language, which plays an important part in Aristotle's philosophical reflection. Language has not been shaped by philosophers: it springs from ordinary people who, wanting to communicate with each other, invented articulate sounds and composed sentences.[4] A word like "eudaimonia," analysed in Aristotle's ethics, expresses a prephilosophical view about human happiness and per- fection: it is considered to be a gift bestowed upon some individuals by divine beings. Needless to say, the author has radically transformed the meaning of this term.[5] Equally with respect to the notion of substance, it is quite clear that Aristotle starts from a prephilosophical view borrowed from language: in this case what stimulated the investigation of the Stagirite was the elementary structure of a sentence. Language is very old, it dates back to a very distant past, it is constantly used by various people and is transmitted from one generation to another. So Aristotle was entitled to rely on language and to start his inquiry from linguistic data.

Initiating his investigation, Aristotle immediately establishes a close con- nection and even a coincidence between the question of being and that of substance.[6] In his view the question of being is not new: it was put forward in the past, it is asked in the present days and it will constantly be posed again in the future. It is an everlasting question; people never stop pointing to this embarrassing issue: what is being?[7] At first glance this questioning seems rather amazing: doesn't everybody know the answer to that question? Every- body constantly speaks of being and uses the term implicitly or explicitly in all sentences. One may conclude that being is the most knowable of all concepts; more than anything else, being must be known. And yet Aristotle emphasizes the embarrassing and everlasting nature of this question: it is always present in human mind, it is like an obsession of which man is unable to free himself. Prof. P. Aubenque believes the question of being to be everlasting, because it is never answered in an adequate way; there will never be a definitive solution. According to the same author, the statement of Aristotle should be interpreted in the light of a cyclical concept of time, as it was generally accepted in Greek culture. Some progress may be achieved, a partial clarification of the topic may be attained, but the problem remains and thus the question is formulated again and again in the successive cycles of historical development.[8] I could hardly agree with this interpretation. Of course, Aristotle is quite conscious of the fact that metaphysical research is difficult. In his survey of the various stages which may be distinguished in the development of civilisation, the study of metaphysics is put at the end, as the highest achievement of the human mind; it started later than the study of politics and physics. And also in his *Protrepticus* he stresses that the investi- gation concerning truth, which coincides with metaphysical reflection, is the most recent of all scientific disciplines.[9] But in Aristotle's view the difficulty of metaphysics is not related to the notion of being, but to the highest degree of intelligibility, that which is most knowable in itself. This object is far away from the sensible world and so human mind is hardly able to grasp it. In this respect the author compares our intellectual power to the eyes of a bat, which are blinded by daylight. In the same way our cognitive faculties, being used to deal with sensible things, are in a sense blinded by the most intelligible objects.[10] As to the notion of being, Aristotle is convinced that it has to be clarified and that it can be disclosed. He repudiates some former attempts and then proceeds to his own explanation, which he certainly considers to be adequate and which he vindicates against the theory of Plato.

The first step regarding the clarification of being concerns the meaning of the *question*: in Aristotle's view to ask what is being coincides with asking what is substance; he wants to know whether there is only one substance or many and if many, whether their number is limited or unlimited. The author does not explain why he identifies the questioning about being with the questioning about substance. In order to understand this coincidence, we have to take into account the Greek vocabulary: the term "substance" is a literal translation of ὑπόστασις, which is used also by Aristotle, but not in a technical philosophical sense; "hypostasis" rather refers to the philosophy of Plotinus, where it has a basic philosophical meaning regarding the highest principles, from which all lower levels of reality emanate. If Aristotle had used the term "hypostasis," the transition from being to substance would be less evident: in fact the author uses the term οὐσία, which directly derives from εἶναι (to be), namely from the participium of the verb. The term "ousia" primarily means beingness, the density or fullness of being, and corresponds to the Latin "essentia." The question "What is being?" thus coincides with "What is ousia?" in the sense already indicated: What is properly being, what represents the density of being, or where can we primarily find being?[11]

The question thus formulated corresponds to the teaching of Aristotle in Book IV of the *Metaphysics:* there he explains that "being" is not a univocal term, it is said in many ways without being equivocal, since the various senses in which it is used refer to one single nature. The author makes a comparison between being and two other terms, "healthy" and "medical": in both cases there is a basic meaning, namely health or medical art. Something may be healthy in the sense that it preserves health, or it may produce health, or be a symptom of health or be capable of health. So the term "healthy" is not equivocal, because these various meanings refer to some primary nature, which is health.[12] The same obtains in the case of being: "being" is said in many senses, but they all refer to a common nature, which is substance (ousia). So the question "What is being?" actually coincides with

"What is substance?" because substance is the primary common nature to which all other meanings of being refer.[13]

When Aristotle turns to the treatment of substance, he first deals with the prephilosophical meaning of the notion as it is found in language. In this view substance is the first subject to which all predicates are attributed, whereas it itself is never attributed to something else.[14] In a sentence there is a subject on which the predicates are conferred. It is a common belief that the subject exists in itself, it doesn't exist in something else, whereas the predicates do not exist independently, they belong to a subject of which they are considered to be affections or accidental qualifications. The link between subject and predicates is not always expressed, the verb "to be" may be explicitly or implicitly present and it is not always invested with the same meaning. Some predicates may be necessarily connected with the subject, whereas others are transitory and contingent. It is a view of popular belief that reality corresponds to this linguistic pattern. In the sensible world there are subjects which exist in themselves and there are more or less permanent affections, which are related to subjects and attached to them. People spontaneously accept that the subjects represent a higher degree of being than the affections, because they exist in themselves. A house, a plant or an animal belong to a higher level of being than their colour or their shape. Colour and shape are related to a subject and are dependent upon it for their existence. In prephilosophical thought the correspondence between language and reality is not questioned. Man always endeavours to know and understand the world in which he lives, just as he tries also to know himself. This knowing is not separated from language. Human thinking is not wordless, it is articulated in language; language is not only an instrument used by the mind, as a craftsman uses instruments in order to produce an artifact. Taking into account the Aristotelian teaching on the relationship between body and soul, we must conclude that language and thought are intimately united like matter and form. It would not be adequate to say that man thinks with the help of words, human thinking is actually effected in a linguistic framework.[15] In this context language becomes a very important prephilosophical insight. It dates back to very ancient times, it is always present in the development of culture and it is used and accepted by everybody. Thus the value of language could hardly be put into question. The pattern of a sentence, which is considered to be a faithful expression of reality, must be taken seriously by a philosopher like Aristotle. He could hardly repudiate this universally accepted opinion that there are subjects and affections of subjects and that the first represent a higher density of being and as a result the title of substance will primarily belong to subjects, rather than to affections.[16] In fact Aristotle does not reject this prephilosophical opinion, he rather attempts to correct and improve it.[17]

Let us look more closely at the criticisms which are put forward. The first objection formulated by Aristotle points to a lack of clarity.[18] In a sentence all kinds of predicates may be attributed to a subject. Of course those predicates vary from one subject to another; not all subjects are on the same level of reality, there are, e.g., human beings and inanimate bodies, there are earthly things and heavenly spheres. If substance primarily refers to a subject, the question may be asked which kind of subject is intended. It is not evident that all subjects, whatever their nature may be, are substances. Aristotle is concerned with the multiplicity of beings, he doesn't agree with the doctrine of Parmenides and his followers that being is one and that the multiplicity of distinct individual beings should be denied. Opposing the univocity of the term "being" and maintaining its analogical character, the author is able to argue that there are many beings. But the question still remains to what extent this multiplicity can be justified, particularly with respect to inanimate things. In the case of living beings, there is an organic structure and unity; beings such as plants and animals exist in themselves within the broader totality of the universe. Even artifacts possess some unitarian structure, since they have been produced in conformity with a concept of the mind; in the world of sensible things a house or a statue possesses its specific arrangement, which distinguishes it from the surrounding objects. But the question becomes more delicate if we want to know whether a stone or a piece of wood is a substance. They may be divided into parts and the question arises again whether each of the parts should be considered to be substance.[19] Hence the notion of subject is not clear. If it is applied to sensible things, as is likely in prephilosophical thought, it is true that these beings have all kinds of properties and affections, but it is not always clear which part of sensible reality may be regarded to be a substance.

Moreover, in Aristotle's view substance refers to being in its primary sense; in other words being belongs primarily to substance. This priority is carefully specified by the Greek Master.[20] In the first place there is a chronological priority of substance towards the other categories, because these latter cannot exist separately, whereas substance exists in itself.[21] Colour, quantity or quality do not exist separately; they adhere to a particular subject of which they are the moving characteristics. Of course a substance never exists without quality or quantity, but these characteristics constantly change, whereas substance remains. A similar remark has already been formulated by Pseudo-Alexander in his commentary; the author compares substance to a recipient which every day is filled with different kinds of wine.[22] The problem however is much more delicate: in Aristotle's view substance manifests itself in its accidental qualifications and never exists without them, and yet it is temporally prior to them. When the author declares that substance exists separately whereas accidental properties do not, he does not intend to say that substance exists without any characteristics, but that these latter frequently change, whereas substance remains the same. In the sensible world individual beings, including both substance and accidental qualifications, exist separately, and yet substance is the subject of the accidental properties and in this sense possesses some temporal priority with respect to them.[23] Nevertheless an individual sensible being is always both substance and accidental categories. So what ordinary people believe to be a substance is at once a whole of accidental characteristics.

There is still another priority which belongs to substance, namely logical priority. In the definition of the other categories the notion of substance is always involved. All the other categories refer to substance because they don't exist in themselves, but in a subject which is substance.[24] With respect to this priority, the same difficulty arises as in the former case: doesn't substance refer to accidental categories, since it never exists without them? Shouldn't we recognize the relation of substance and accidents to be reciprocal? As far as we are concerned with sensible substances, we must acknowledge that they never occur without accidental qualifications. But there is even more: if substance primarily means a subject to which predicates are attributed, the definition of substance involves the presence of at least some accidental categories. But in this case what is the meaning of the logical priority intended by Aristotle? If the relation between substance and accidents is reciprocal, it is not of the same nature. Substance exists in itself, it does not exist in the accidental determinations; substance manifests itself in those qualifications, it shows itself in these moving characteristics because they are in a sense derived from it. Some of those determinations are much more closely connected with substance than others: what Aristotle calls ἴδιον or property in the strict sense is always and necessarily linked to a particular substance, it flows from it and uncovers it. Hence there are accidental determinations which are always linked to a substance: and yet substance doesn't exist in them, it certainly doesn't exist in contingent and constantly changing qualifications.[25] As to the accidental determinations, they not only reveal and disclose substance, but they exist in it and could only exist in a subject. So the logical priority of substance doesn't mean that it could exist without accidental qualifications. It is always connected with some accidental categories, but it does not exist in them, whereas the accidental categories only exist in a substance. But what does it mean "to exist in something"? The preposition *in* primarily has a spatial meaning. It signifies that something is located within the boundaries of another thing and is encompassed by them. This spatial meaning could hardly be applied to the case under consideration. What Aristotle has in mind is that accidental categories need some support or subject. A colour must always be the colour of something and the same obtains regarding the other accidental categories. A human being always is invested with some accidental qualifications and yet it doesn't exist in them because these determinations flow from the substance of man and not the other way around. Accidental determinations exist in a substance because they all in a sense derive from it in a closer or more distant way. The properties in the strict sense certainly exist in the substance because they necessarily belong to it, so that this particular substance could never exist without possessing these necessary properties.

A third priority attributed to substance belongs to the level of knowledge. Aristotle points to the fact that we better know something when we understand what it is, e.g., man or fire, than when we grasp its quality, its quantity and its location; and the author adds with respect to these accidental categories that we only understand them when we know what they are.[26] So the knowledge of substance is prior and superior to the knowledge of accidental determinations. Here again some questions arise with respect to the nature of the priority intended by Aristotle. The author does not want to say that we firstly know substances and afterwards the accidental features. As we already explained, a substance manifests itself through its accidental determinations, e.g., through its activity. This method is frequently used by the author in various investigations. The nature of the human soul is examined in this way: in order to disclose its real nature the author starts from a careful inquiry of human knowledge, sensitive and intellectual knowledge. Even regarding the question of the immortality of the human soul Aristotle proceeds in the same way. In order to answer this difficult question, the author wants to know whether there is any activity totally independent of the bodily organism. This question is asked especially with regard to our intellectual knowing, which is the highest human activity. The answer however is negative because even our intellectual knowing depends upon the body because it is always linked to some sensitive perception.[27] Hence Aristotle does not start from his knowledge of the nature of human soul to disclose its activity. On the contrary he starts from the study of human activity in order to uncover its principle, the soul and especially the mind. The study of some accidental features is a normal access to the disclosure of substance. Nevertheless it remains true that the knowledge of substance is superior and more valuable than that of accidental determinations. So the priority intended by Aristotle in this case is one of value.

It is noticeable that Aristotle in this context speaks of substance, not as a mere subject, but as the nature or essence of a being. He emphasizes the distinction between knowing the very essence of a being and grasping only some accidental features. After all these considerations we may conclude that the notion of substance as a subject of accidental categories is not quite clear. The subject itself and also its relation to the predicates which are attributed to it are not sufficiently clarified. In particular it is not clear why a subject should be being in the primary sense. Why does being primarily belong to a subject instead of being recognized to other categories? We could reply that according to Aristotle the other categories in some sense flow from substance. That is true, but then the notion of subject has to be more specified. So from this lack of clarity the author is driven to some further criticism.

The notion of subject is not only unclear, it is moreover insufficient. This statement however may be interpreted in two different ways. The insufficiency may concern the explanation put forward and most commentators have adopted this interpretation. If one declares that substance is primarily a subject of accidental categories, that is not sufficient in the sense that the explanation given is not sufficient; in other words the notion of subject has to be more thoroughly clarified. One has to determine in which sense substance could be considered to be a subject. Within an Aristotelian context the notion of subject may indeed have various meanings. It may first of all refer to individual sensible beings which are compounded of matter and form. In the *Categoriae* the author introduces a distinction between primary and secondary substances. As examples of primary substances are given a horse or a man. In his definition the author stresses the fact that a substance neither is predicated of a subject nor exists in a subject; in other words a substance exists in itself and is never attributed to some subject. According to the *Categoriae* this is the primary and most fundamental meaning of substance.[28] And yet some difficulty arises with respect to this viewpoint. A sensible thing is a compounded being, it is compounded of matter and form. Hence the question whether the components are not prior to the compositum: Aristotle does not deny a sensible being to be a substance.[29] But the question is whether the notion of substance primarily refers to those kinds of beings. In this respect the treatment of substance in the *Categoriae* does not perfectly coincide with the interpretation of the topic in the *Metaphysics*. If the first treatise is an authentic work of Aristotle, some shift may have occurred in Aristotle's thought.[30]

According to the *Categoriae* substance primarily means some independence and some unity in the whole of sensible reality. Of course all sensible beings depend upon each other: a plant or an animal could not subsist without the support of the surrounding world. And yet there is a difference. A plant needs the surrounding world for its own growth and development, whereas the colour of a plant could not even exist without adhering to a particular subject.[31] In this context we may come back to the structure of a sentence: a predicate is attributed to a subject because it really needs the support of a substance in order to exist. The distinction made in language between subject and predicate is supposed to be a faithful reproduction of sensible reality. There are predicates which never exist in themselves as independent beings, and there are subjects which always exist in themselves and show some degree of independence in the whole of reality. A horse never exists as an attribute of something else.[32] In this sense the notion of substance perfectly corresponds to the Greek ὑπόστασις (substance); the question however remains whether a subject really represents the density of being as it is expressed by the term οὐσία.

Prof. R. Boehm in his penetrating analysis of *Metaphysics* VII, 3 believes that not only the explanation is insufficient, but also the notion of subject itself. In other words he maintains that the notion of subject is inadequate to express what Aristotle is looking for.[33] Let us turn back to the initial question, which in the author's mind is an everlasting one, namely what is being? This question is everlasting because everybody has to face it; it couldn't be avoided because it belongs to the very structure of human thinking. Everybody is concerned with being; this notion is always present in our mind, either explicitly or implicitly. Ultimately the only notion we are concerned with, is being. The question: what is being? coincides with: what is substance? As we already declared the transition from being to *ousia* entails no difficulty; it is the same word. But the passage from being to hypostasis or substance is not at all evident; it is not evident that the density of being is found primarily in a subject. In other words the notion of subject seems to be inadequate to express what Aristotle is searching for; he wants to know what is being. If somebody tells him being is a multiplicity of subjects, he couldn't be satisfied, because that notion refers only to a non-specified support of accidental categories.

Finally, if the notion of subject is taken in its ultimate sense, it refers to prime matter, which in Aristotle's view is a component of all sensible things.[34] But prime matter is totally undetermined, it is mere potentiality, it could not exist separately and in itself, it could by no means be taken into account to express the density of being. To the question: what is being?, the reply could not be: being is primarily prime matter.[35] This repudiation doesn't mean that prime matter is unimportant in the composition of sensible things; on the contrary it is a very important factor in Aristotle's interpretation of the physical world. Thanks to prime matter a multiplicity of individuals may belong to the same species, e.g., a multiplicity of human beings, which all possess the same specific characteristics. Moreover substantial changes are made possible, such as coming to be and passing away. The physical world is constantly changing; some of these changes are rather superficial, they touch only some contingent aspects of a thing; others however are much deeper and concern the essential structure of a being. Connected with this constant becoming is the notion of temporality. Physical beings are temporal, they are inserted in a permanent process of becoming, because they bear within themselves a component that is merely potential.

If the notion of subject is understood in the sense of prime matter, then it has to be discarded, because it couldn't express the density of being. And yet Prof. Boehm believes that even this interpretation is not rejected. The density of being may be disclosed in confrontation with non-being; one becomes conscious of the full meaning of being in a kind of dread or anguish in front of non-being. And so the notion of prime matter, because it is insufficient, could reveal the true density of being. This interpretation however is closer to Heidegger than to Aristotle.[36]

The conclusion of our previous inquiry may be formulated in this way: the notion of substance could not refer to prime matter, because it is undetermined and merely potential; nor could it primarily indicate an individual sensible thing, compounded of matter and form, since the elements of a compositum are prior to the whole. In an Aristotelian context the conclusion must be that substance primarily refers to the immanent form.[37] This solution is quite understandable. The essential perfection of an individual sensible being springs from its form, not from matter. The form is determined and corresponds to the specific nature of an individual being. Aristotle declares that substance is a principle and a cause.[38] This statement applies very well to the form, which is at the origin of the essential structure and formal perfection of a being. And yet this doctrine also raises some embarrassing questions: according to Aristotle substance must be determined ($\tau\acute{o}\delta\epsilon$ $\tau\iota$) and separable ($\chi\omega\rho\iota\sigma\tau\acute{o}\nu$).[39] The first specification fully applies to the substantial form; as to the latter there may be some doubt. What Aristotle has in mind is the distinction between substance and accidental categories; these latter couldn't exist separately, they always need the support of a subject to which they are attached. As to the form of sensible things, it is always linked to matter and could never exist on its own, when separated from the other component.

In Aristotle's view the form is an immanent principle in all sensible beings; it doesn't exist in a separate world, in a transcendent reality of which sensible things are only an imitation, a participation and a kind of communion. According to Plato the transcendent forms are purely immaterial, they are immutable and perfect. It is quite clear that in Plato's view the density of being belongs to these transcendent forms. They represent true reality. The sensible world participates in these perfect patterns and imitates them, but after all it is only a shadow of authentic being. The prisoners in the cave were not conscious of the fact that they were looking at shadows, but they actually did. Starting from the imitations present in sensible reality could man ever come to grasp the perfect patterns? Not really; in Plato's view our knowledge of the transcendent forms does not derive from the perception of sensible objects. This perception is only a stimulus that awakens in us a knowledge which is present in the soul from the beginning of human life. It is actually prior to our existence on earth and springs from the immediate intuition of the Ideas, which the soul enjoyed before being joined to the body. As a result of this union with a corporal principle the knowledge of the transcendent patterns was obscured and asleep. In order to become an active knowledge it has to be stimulated either in a dialogue with other individuals or through contact with the sensible world. Anyhow according to Plato knowledge is not an active creation of the mind, it is rather passive intuition or contemplation, whose object is preserved in the mind, so that it can be evoked through a process of reminiscence.[40]

Aristotle agrees with Plato to a large extent. He also maintains that true being primarily and fundamentally belongs to the substantial form, but in his opinion this form is not transcendent, but immanent. It is really present in each sensible being. Moreover man is able to grasp the form, starting from sensible perception. The reason is that, in the first place, the form is present in sensible beings; moreover human knowing is considered to be an active process in which thanks to the role of the creative intellect (ποιητικόν) sensible images are made intelligible. Whatever the status of this creative mind may be, whether it is an individual power or the same for all humans, it operates an important transformation since it produces intelligible objects from sensible images.[41] Aristotle rejects the transcendent character of the substantial forms, because these separated patterns are a useless reduplication of sensible things, they are like sensible objects to which the specification "in itself" has been added. Next to concrete acts of justice, courage or temperance, there would be justice in itself, or courage in itself, and the particular moral acts would only be some finite participation of the corresponding perfect patterns. These models are useless for human behaviour. Man always acts in a particular context, in constantly changing circumstances, and he has to discover what is truly good in this varying context. Man couldn't be helped in his daily behaviour by looking at a transcendent form.[42]

As a result of his criticism Aristotle believes substantial forms not to be separate from sensible things, but to be immanent. This immanent form is what Aristotle calls ousia or substance. It is determined, prior to the whole of matter and form, it represents the density of being and primarily deserves the name "being." And yet this solution immediately raises a new problem. The form of sensible beings could not exist separately, it is always linked to prime matter, whereas substance in Aristotle's view must be separable. Of course, prime matter is totally potential, all perfection of a sensible being springs from the form. Nevertheless neither matter nor form could ever exist independently from each other. Should we conclude that the form of a sensible thing may not be called substance, because it is unable to exist separately?

In order to answer this question, we have to take into account the general method of Aristotle in his metaphysical inquiry. He starts from what is immediately intelligible for us and proceeds gradually to what is intelligible in itself. In fact what is most knowable for us, namely sensible reality, is less knowable in itself. It is a starting point of metaphysical reflection, because it is immediately accessible, but it raises many questions; according to Aristotle's vocabulary it is an object of amazement.[43] The main questions arise from the instability of sensible things. Their existence is precarious, they come to be and pass away, they are inserted in a permanent process of generations and corruptions. In his *De generatione et corruptione* the author asks the question whether this constant becoming is a necessary process; anyhow it is always present in the sublunary world.[44] Beings which come to be, since they did not always exist, bear within themselves the potency of non-existing, and this potency must at some stage be actualized. Moreover sensible beings are not simple, but compounded: the most fundamental composition is that of prime matter and form; the coming to be and passing away of sensible things is explained on the basis of this composition. Furthermore sensible things are constantly changing and evolving: they are permanently influenced by the movement of the heavenly bodies and are incorporated in the temporal process of the universe, which never started and will never come to an end.

In Aristotle's view all movement or change is a transition from potency to act, which requires a cause that couldn't coincide with the moving thing. The ultimate cause of this process is the divine substance, which is eternal, unmoved, separated from sensible reality, without parts and indivisible, impassible and unchangeable. This supreme substance is the ultimate final cause of the permanent becoming that occurs in the universe. It constantly moves as an object of love and desire. It also represents the highest level of intelligibility: beings are intelligible according to their logical priority and to their degree of simplicity. The first substance is totally simple, uncompounded and it is prior to all other beings, since it is their final cause.[45] On the level of sensible reality substance refers to the immanent form, which is the principle of intelligibility, the source of all perfection and the origin of all activity. In the sensible world the form is necessarily linked to prime matter, not because it is substance, but because it is sensible. The highest substance is pure Act and is not linked to any material component. So in the light of the First Act we understand that substance coincides with the formal principle, even in the case of sensible beings where it is necessarily linked to prime matter. The accidental features are also being but only in a secondary sense, whether they be necessary or contingent characteristics. The density of being belongs to the form, not to matter nor to accidental categories. Between Plato and Aristotle there is regarding substance a fundamental agreement and an equally fundamental disagreement. Both philosophers agree that the formal principle represents the density of being, on the level of individual beings as well as with respect to the universe; the universe is an orderly whole, a harmonious cosmos. Each being is intelligible thanks to its form, and this also obtains with respect to the whole. The form is a principle of perfection, of activity and intelligibility. The disagreement between Plato and Aristotle concerns the valuation of sensible reality. To the question whether sensible beings could be the totality of being, both authors will give a negative reply. Yet the valuation of sensible reality is more positive in Aristotle than it is in Plato, because the substantial form is immanent and may be known thanks to experience and to the decisive intervention of the active intellect.

So to the question: what is being or what is substance?, the reply of Aristotle may be formulated in the following way: on the level of sensible reality which is immediately knowable to us, substance is the formal principle of individual beings; on the level of the highest intelligibility, substance is pure act or pure form without any link to a material component.

Starting from a prephilosophical linguistic pattern Aristotle arrives at a truly metaphysical interpretation of being and substance.[46]

Katholieke Universiteit Leuven
Leuven, Belgium

NOTES

1. One of the ancient maxims regarding moral conduct was "Nothing too much." Man has to avoid any kind of excess: he ought to be conscious always of being mortal, he never should go beyond the frontiers of his condition and should carefully dismiss any act of pride (ΰβρις). The background of this rule is a mythological belief according to which the gods are jealous of humans and don't tolerate any excess in their conduct. The same idea is adopted and largely elaborated in Aristotle's ethics: virtue is considered to be a mean between two possible extremes (in medio virtus). Nevertheless the background of the ancient maxim has been radically transformed: in Aristotle's view envy of the Divine Substance makes no sense.

2. Cf. G. Verbeke, *Philosophie et conceptions préphilosophiques chez Aristote,* in: *Revue philosophique de Louvain,* 59 (1961), 405-430. In his *Eudemian Ethics* (I, 6, 1216b17) Aristotle writes that everybody is able to afford a personal contribution to the discovery of truth: this discovery is not reserved to a select group of talented people; every human mind is oriented to the same goal. Philosophical inquiry is a business in which all humans are involved.

3. Cf. *Rhet.*, B9, 1387a16: τὸ ἀρχαῖον ἐγγύς τι φαίνεται τοῦ φύσει. According to Aristotle what is very ancient is close to what is by nature. The meaning is obvious: what is by nature is generally effected; this is necessary, if the universe has to exist indefinitely. If some common opinions are very ancient and are still agreed on, they are comparable to the work of nature.

4. In Aristotle's view man is by nature a political being. One of the arguments put forward is related to language: among animals man is the only one to utter articulated sounds, allowing him not only to communicate with other humans, but also to disclose ideas and notions and to reach with other people a common understanding, which makes a political society possible. Without

a common agreement on justice, political life couldn't be possible (*Pol.* I, 2, 1253a9-18).

5. According to the term εὐδαιμονία, the destiny of man depends upon the favour of some higher beings (δαίμονες). This view was widely spread in Greek culture: human happiness is considered to be a matter of good luck; it is subdued to fate and to various higher powers which irresistibly determine the course of man's existence. In Aristotle's opinion everybody is the author of his own destiny: happiness and perfection are the result of human behaviour (*Eth. Nic.*, I, 7, 1097b22-1098a20).

6. *Metaph.* VII, 1, 1028b4: τί τὸ ὄν, τοῦτό ἐστι τίς ἡ οὐσία. According to the context the question has been suggested because of a fundamental disagreement: some philosophers declare that there is only one substance, whereas others maintain that there are many. Among the latter some state that there are a limited number of substances, whereas others say that their number is unlimited. The Eleatics had vindicated a monistic interpretation of reality as a result of their univocal notion of being. In their view non-being could never be predicated of being; it would be erroneous to declare that one being "is not" another one.

7. *Metaph.* VII, 1, 1028b2: καὶ δὴ καὶ τὸ πάλαι τε καὶ νῦν καὶ ἀεὶ ζητούμενον καὶ ἀεὶ ἀπορούμενον, τί τὸ ὄν.

8. According to P. Aubenque the problem of being could never be solved, because the term "being" has an indefinite number of meanings. The table of categories is confined to a limited series, but it is unfinished and has been arbitrarily closed. The essential duty of ontology is to distinguish the various meanings of being. This work could never be brought to an end: "C'est parce que l'être a plusieurs sens, et un nombre indéfini de sens, que l'on n'en a jamais fini de poser la question: Qu'est-ce que l'être?" (*Le problème de l'être chez Aristote. Essai sur la problématique Aristotélicienne*, Paris, 1962, p. 189; p. 250).

9. *Aristotelis Fragmenta Selecta*, ed. W. D. Ross (Oxford, 1955), *De philosophia*, fr. 8 (Philop. *In Nicom. Isagogen*, I, 1); *Protrepticus*, fr. 8 (Iambl., Comm. Math. 26): νεώτατον οὖν ὁμολογουμένως ἐστὶ τῶν ἐπιτηδευμάτων ἡ περὶ τὴν ἀλήθειαν ἀκριβογία.

10. Cf. G. Verbeke, *Démarches de la réflexion métaphysique*, in *Aristote et problèmes de méthode* (Symposium Aristotelicum). Louvain-Paris, 1961, p. 111-112. Aristotle wonders whether there is only one being or many. In his view there are many beings: at each time they are limited in number, but if one considers past, present and future beings, their number is unlimited, since the world never came to be and will never pass away (*Metaph.* VII, 1, 1028b4). The question put forward is not about the *meanings* of the term "being," but about the multiplicity of particular beings.

11. W. Marx, in his work, *The Meaning of Aristotle's Ontology* (The Hague, 1954, p. 32) suggests to translate οὐσία as "substantiality": "Since it has been shown that Aristotle used the word ousia as a determinant, it might be preferable to translate it *substantiality*, as differentiated from *substance*." Unfortunately neither substance nor substantiality corresponds to the original meaning of οὐσία.

12. *Metaph.*, IV, 2, 1003a33-b4.

13. *Metaph.*, IV, 2, 1003b4-19. Aristotle is mainly concerned with the question whether the study of being belongs to one single discipline. If the term being has various meanings, one may conclude that each of them will be investigated by a distinct discipline. Aristotle however maintains that this multiplicity of meanings doesn't prevent the topic from being treated by one discipline, since the various meanings refer to one single nature, which is substance (δῆλον οὖν ὅτι καὶ τὰ ὄντα μιᾶς θεωρῆσαι ᾗ ὄντα). Therefore a philosopher has to concentrate his inquiry on substance and since there are many substances, he has to disclose their principles (τὰς ἀρχὰς) and causes (τὰς αἰτίας).

14. *Metaph.*, VII, 3, 1028b35-1029a2: μάλιστα γὰρ δοκεῖ εἶναι οὐσία τὸ ὑποκείμενον πρῶτον. All predicates refer to the subject, like all meanings of being refer to substance. As to the notion of subject, it is immediately explained within the context of a proposition (καθ' οὖ τὰ ἄλλα λέγεται, ἐκεῖνο δὲ αὐτὸ μηκέτι κατ' ἄλλου); VII, 13, 1038b15.

15. *De anima*, II, 1, 412a27: according to this teaching human soul is the *first* entelechy of a physical body that possesses life in potency. If soul is the first entelechy, the other component must be entirely potential. Hence the organic structure of the body also springs from the psychic principle. In this way the unity of man is secured and there is no activity in which the material component is not involved.

16. In the *Categoriae* (5, 2a11) Aristotle introduces a distinction between first and second substance. First substance is never attributed to a subject nor does it exist in a subject, whereas species and genus are second substances. Species however is more substance than genus, since it is closer to a concrete being (2b7). In this context the criterion of substantiality is independent existence; substance exists in itself, it doesn't exist in something else. In his moral doctrine Aristotle also maintains that the highest level of ethical perfection is characterized by self-sufficiency. According to a similar criterion something becomes more being when it exists in itself, when it has some degree of self-sufficiency.

17. *Metaph.*, VII, 3, 1029a9: δεῖ δὲ μὴ μόνον οὕτως. This short remark means that Aristotle does not merely repudiate the doctrine according to which substance primarily refers to a subject that exists in itself and of which all kinds of attributes are predicated. This definition is considered to be a first and rough description of what substance really means (τύπῳ): it is mainly based on a prephilosophical linguistic pattern. So it is valuable, but it has to be completed. In this particular context R. Boehm believes the usual interpretation of τύπῳ to be wrong: "Im gegenwärtigen Zusammenhange jedoch steht ganz und gar nicht eine unbestimmte 'Typisierung' einem wohlbestimmten, genauen Begriff gegenüber, sondern das Gepräge, welches das Wesen zu einem solchen prägt, ist abgehoben von der blossen Bezeichnung dessen, was Wesen heissen kann" (*Das Grundlegende und das Wesentliche*. Zu Aristoteles' Abhandlung "Ueber das Sein und das Seiende" (Metaphysik Z). Den Haag, 1965, p. 58). This explanation does not conform to the Aristotelian vocabulary and does not fit into the method of proceeding from a prephilosophical notion of substance to its philosophical clarification.

18. *Metaph.*, VII, 3, 1029a10: αὐτό τε γὰρ τοῦτο ἄδηλον.

19. Dealing with this topic, Aristotle states that most of the things considered to be substances, are actually potencies (δυνάμεις). He mentions parts of animals, and also earth, fire and air. These things lack unity. Hence they couldn't be regarded as substantial beings (*Metaph.*, VII, 16, 1040b5-16).

20. *Metaph.*, VII, 1, 1028a30: ὥστε τὸ πρώτως ὄν καὶ οὐ τὶ ὄν ἀλλ' ὄν ἁπλῶς ἡ οὐσία ἂν εἴη. This statement should be understood in the light of the original meaning of *ousia*: in Aristotle's view *ousia* constitutes the beingness of all beings.

21. *Metaph.*, VII, 1, 1028a33: τῶν μὲν γὰρ ἄλλων κατηγορημάτων οὐθὲν χωριστόν, αὕτη δὲ μόνη.

22. Cf. *Aristotle's Metaphysics*. A Revised Text with Introduction and Commentary by W. D. Ross. Oxford, 1924, II, p. 160.

23. It is not quite clear why this priority is called temporal: what Aristotle seems to have in mind is that substance manifest itself in its accidental qualifications, whereas these latter always presuppose a subject to which they belong. Of course what is called temporal priority is basically a priority in nature (κατὰ φύσιν).

24. *Metaph.*, VII, 1, 1028a35: ἀνάγκη γὰρ ἐν τῷ ἑκάστου λόγῳ τὸν τῆς οὐσίας ἐνυπάρχειν.

25. Cf. G. Verbeke, *La notion de propriété dans les Topiques*, in: *Aristotle on Dialectic. The Topics* (Third Symposium Aristotelicum), ed. G. E. L. Owen, Oxford, 1968, p. 257-276. In his daily life man is constantly confronted with various accidental categories: they don't exist in themselves, but belong to a particular substance or an individual being, which manifests itself in those accidental attributes: ὅπερ ἐμφαίνεται ἐν τῇ κατηγορίᾳ τῇ τοιαύτῃ τὸ καθ' ἕκαστον (VII, 1, 1028a27).

26. *Metaph.*, VII, 1, 1028a36-b2. In the first place and in an absolute way definition belongs

to substance, and in a secondary way only to the other categories (VII, 4, 1030b4-7; 5, 1031a7-14).

27. Cf. G. Verbeke, *Comment Aristote conçoit-il l'immatériel?* in: *Revue philosophique de Louvain,* 44 (1946), p. 205-236.

28. *Categoriae,* 5, 2a11-19.

29. *Metaph.,* VII, 3, 1029a30-34. In Aristotle's opinion a compositum could not be prior to its components. With respect to sensible beings the components are matter and form. Regarding the material factor the author writes that it is more or less clear. As it is totally undetermined, it could not constitute the beingness of beings. So Aristotle has to concentrate his inquiry on the immanent form: αὕτη γὰρ ἀπορωτάτη. Having dismissed the compositum and the material principle, the author has to examine carefully whether and how substance may be identified with the formal component.

30. Cf. S. Mansion, *La doctrine Aristotélicienne de la substance et le traité des Catégories,* in: S. Mansion, *Etudes Aristotéliciennes* (Recueil d'articles). Louvain-la-Neuve, 1984, p. 337-340.

31. Aristotle states that seemingly (δοκεῖ) substance belongs most evidently to bodies and their parts (*Metaph.,* VII, 2, 1028b8-13); the author refers to sensible experience and common opinions. This view has to be examined and critically analyzed.

32. S. Mansion, *La première doctrine de la substance: la substance selon Aristote,* in: *Etudes Aristotéliciennes,* p. 365: "la substance aristotélicienne est un être *subsistant, déterminé, substrat* de modalités d'être non substantielles, les accidents."

33. R. Boehm, *Das Grundlegende und das Wesentliche,* p. 49: "Ganz im Gegenteil 'scheint' Aristoteles aus der erwiesenen Unzulänglichkeit des Wesensbegriffs des Zugrundeliegenden, aus der offenbaren 'Unmöglichkeit,' mit diesem Begriff zu fassen, was das Wesen ist, die Konsequenz zu ziehen, diesen Wesensbegriff preiszugeben und zur Erörterung des Wesensbegriffs des Seins-was-es-war überzugehen."

34. *Metaph.,* VII, 3, 1029a2: τοιοῦτον δὲ τρόπον μέν τινα ἡ ὕλη λέγεται. In his further exposition Aristotle declares that matter could not be identified with substance: ἀδύνατον δέ (1029b27), because it couldn't exist separately and it is undetermined. In his view those characteristics seem to belong mainly to substance (ὑπάρχειν δοκεῖ μάλιστα τῇ οὐσίᾳ).

35. In Aristotle's view prime matter doesn't possess a definite structure. Hence not even negations may be *per se* attributed to matter, because any *per se* attribution implies within the subject some definite structure (*Metaph.,* VII, 3, 1029a25).

36. R. Boehm, *Das Grundlegende und das Wesentliche,* p. 206: "Der Vorrang des Wesensbegriffs des Zugrundeliegenden *als* eines unzulänglichen gründet im Wesen der Metaphysik selbst. Er gründet letzlich in einem die Frage der Metaphysik erst hervorzufinden eigentümlichen Vorrang des "Nichts" vor allem wesentlichen Sein von Seienden."

37. *Metaph.,* VII, 3, 1029a5-7; VII, 11, 1037a29: ἡ γὰρ οὐσία ἐστὶ τὸ εἶδος τὸ ἐνόν. This statement corresponds to the aporematic question formulated in *Metaph.,* III, 5 (1002 a27): διαφεύγει τί τὸ ὂν καὶ τίς ἡ οὐσία τῶν ὄντων. The author wants to know what exactly constitutes the beingness of beings. Aristotle's reply is unambiguous: substance and quiddity (τὸ τί ἦν εἶναι) are identified; Socrates and the quiddity of Socrates coincide (*Metaph.,* VII, 6, 1031b31).

38. *Metaph.,* VII, 17, 1041a9; thanks to the immanent form matter becomes something determined (VII, 17, 1041b27-28: τοῦτο γὰρ (scil. οὐσία) αἴτιον πρῶτον τοῦ εἶναι).

39. *Metaph.,* VII, 3, 1029a27-30. In Aristotle's view a common predicate could never be a substance: οὐδὲν γὰρ τῶν κοινῶν τόδε τι σημαίνει, ἀλλὰ τοιόνδε, ἡ δὲ οὐσία τόδε τι; VII, 13, 1038b8.

40. In this respect the difference between Plato and Aristotle is very significant. In Aristotle's view each individual creates his intelligible objects, starting from sensible experience; in this process the role of the active intellect, which may be unique and transcendent, is essential.

Plato doesn't introduce such an active principle; in his view intelligible objects could never derive from sensible data.

41. *De anima,* III, 5, 430a14-19. There is a connection between Aristotle's doctrine of substance and his theory of knowledge. Starting from sensible experience it is possible to grasp the nature of material beings, since the formal principle does not belong to a transcendent world, but is immanent and determines from within the structure of each thing. On the other hand sensible knowledge is not separated from thought. In the process of knowing there are not two successive stages, one of sensitive perception and one of thinking; such interpretation would be in disagreement with the unity of man. Sensitive activity itself is penetrated by intellectual insight.

42. Cf. G. Verbeke, *La critique des Idées dans l'Ethique Eudémienne,* in: *Untersuchungen zur Eudemischen Ethik* (Akten des 5. Symposium Aristotelicum), herausg. Paul Moraux und Dieter Harlfinger. Berlin, 1971, p. 135-156. Dealing with the doctrine of transcendent Ideas, Aristotle doesn't hesitate to call it absurd. To accept next to the sensible world a higher reality which totally corresponds to the first one, except however that Ideas are eternal, doesn't make sense. In Aristotle's view those who maintain such Ideas are like people who believe in the existence of gods, but consider them to be similar to humans (*Metaph.,* III, 2, 997a34-b12). Ideas also are like sensible beings to which the qualification "in itself" has been joined (*Metaph.,* VII, 16, 1040b30-34).

43. *Metaph.,* VII, 3, 1029b7-12; II, 1, 993b9-11.

44. *De gen. et corr.,* II, 11, 337a34-338b19. In a world without beginning and without end, what happens always must be necessary: if it were not, there would be a potency which is never actualized. In Aristotle's view such a hypothesis must be excluded: so the constant becoming of the universe is not a contingent process, it is necessary since it always occurs.

45. *Metaph.,* XII, 7, 1073a3-13.

46. According to J. P. Dougherty: "There is nothing in contemporary science which forces us to abandon Aristotle's analysis. If we raise Aristotelian questions we still get Aristotelian answers" (*Essays Honoring Allan B. Wolter,* ed. by W. A. Frank and G. J. Etzkorn. St. Bonaventure, N.Y.: Franciscan Institute Publications, 1985, p. 129).

PLENARY SESSION — II

Thomas D. Langan, Chairman
University of Toronto

Substance Is Not Enough. Hegel's Slogan: From Substance to Subject

by Kenneth L. Schmitz

Often enough, Hegel's philosophy is first encountered through its slogans. And it must be admitted that Hegel and Hegelians have invented not a few, even if their critics have invented even more. These slogans are sometimes the product of compressed technical jargon, as when the system is said to be "the concept in and for itself," or when it is summed up by others (in a rather too Fichtean manner) as the dialectical process of thesis, antithesis and synthesis.[1] At other times the summation is hardly more than metaphor, as when Hegel himself speaks of the "speculative Good Friday," or "the Owl of Minerva." Among these slogans is one that we find in the Preface to Hegel's first major published work, the *Phenomenology of Spirit*:[2]

> In my view, which can be justified only by the exposition of the system itself, everything turns on grasping and expressing the True, not only as *Substance,* but equally as *Subject* [das Wahre nicht als *Substanz,* sondern eben so sehr als *Subjekt*].

The term "substance" has received several nuanced meanings in Hegel's philosophy, but they can be traced back to the ambivalence that is rooted in the history of the term itself. From the *Metaphysics* of Aristotle—who remained for Hegel *the* philosopher—we may be permitted to reduce the usage of the term "substance" [*ousia*] to three foci:[3] (1) There are those uses which stress the *subsistence* of substance, the capacity to exist separately, in and through itself. Various locutions express this meaning, such as "first substance" [*prote ousia*] and "this individual of a certain kind" [*tode ti*], and by transference, this meaning is extended to non-individual referents, and to

52

the constituent parts of a substance. The Latin usage, for the most part, expresses this subsistence by the term *secundum se* or *ens per se* [*kath'auto*].[4] (2) Closely related to the insistent identity inherent in such a self-subsistent being is the second focus of the term "substance": namely, that "substance" stands for the true nature or *essence* of the thing in question, what is essential. This is the formal sense of the term; it is the root of the definition that expresses what the thing is as such [*to ti en einai, quod quid erat esse*]. The Latins coined the terms *essentia* and *quidditas* in order to express this formal meaning of *ousia*. (3) The third focus is also found in Aristotle: substance is that in the thing that is *fundamental and stable*. Inasmuch as the substance exists in itself and is essential to the whole being (i.e., to the composite), and inasmuch as it is that which remains as long as the thing itself remains—substance is the permanent reality that underlies the altera- tions of state or accidental modifications that come to the substance through the influence of others. Although the Greek term *ousia* can stand for such stable reality, another term, *'upokeimenon,* was also employed to indicate a stable "substrate" [cf. the Latin *subjectum* and *substerno, -stratum*]. Like the term "substance," its use was by no means restricted to substances in the full and primary sense of individual subsisting beings. Among the Latins, the term *substantia* came to be used for all three of the above senses, although its very etymology seems to have drawn it towards the notion of "substrate."[5] Philosophical Latin generally followed this rendering; and, as the more formal structure of Aristotelian metaphysics gave way from the fourteenth to the seventeenth centuries, the term came more and more, without ever wholly losing its other meanings, to bear the passive meaning of: that which underlies the accidents of the composite as their support.

It is possible to sum up Hegel's general sense of substance by citing four pressure points posed by the concept of substance. I cannot pretend to respect the nuances and details of these four points, and will instead merely name them, describe them briefly and associate them, loosely, with four philosophers: (1) There is, first of all, the insistence of Aristotle that the primary instances of substance are individual and limited. But Hegel points out that, under the influence of the Christian doctrine of creation, the Greek principle of limit came to be transformed, from the positive reality of form or shape into the negative sense of the finite. Now, finitude differs from simple limitation; for the same content—let us say, the nature of man as rational animal—may be looked at in two ways: positively as limited or negatively as finite. Looked at in itself as limited or bounded, it is taken positively alongside other limited contents. When looked at in the second way, however, i.e., from the point of view of the positive Infinity of the Creator, this limited content or entity is seen to lack complete being in itself and to have being fully only in and through Another. Understood in this second way, the significance of such a finite being is essentially negative, since its warranty lies beyond itself, and beyond the whole order of finite beings;[6] for in calling such a being "finite" we invoke its relation to the infinite. Of course, as with most things that Hegel learned by way of Aristotle, this sense of the limited-become-finite is not only a sign of the inadequacy of the finite but also a sign of its promise. The first sense of substance, then, is: *individuality, limitation and finitude.* (2) There is, secondly, the drift of the term "substance" towards the meaning of "substrate"; so that the aspect of underlying and providing support for accidental states receives the principal emphasis. Moreover, this capacity to be determined by accidents tends to be viewed more and more as something passive—as, for example, by Locke[7]—so that the term "substance" drifts even further towards the meaning of *potentiality, materiality* and, more generally, of *indeterminacy.* (3) Kant also takes the term "substance" to signify the *substratum* that underlies alterations of state and generally all modifications that occur in relation to a permanent substrate. But he gives prominence to the aspect of relation, and specifically to the relation of *inherence,* emphasizing the role of substance as that in which the states or modifications come to rest.[8] (4) It is left to Spinoza in modern times to recover the active sense of substance along with its universality and unity.[9] Hegel finds much affinity with Spinoza's view of substance, especially in its recovery of the active sense of relation, and specifically the category of self-relation. Indeed, he finds in Spinoza's concept of substance as *self-determining* [*causa sui*] the last barrier thrown up in the face of what he takes to be the adequate central concept of philosophy, viz., the concept of subject in the sense of subjectivity or spirit.[10]

In short, then, the four pressure points of the problematic of substance for Hegel are: (1) Aristotle and limit-become-finitude; (2) the indeterminacy, potentiality, passivity or materiality associated with the term by Locke and others; (3) the completion of the concept of substance with the help of the category of relation, specifically the relation of inherence, as highlighted by Kant; and finally, (4) the restoration of the dynamism inherent in self-subsistence to the concept of substance by returning to it the feature of causal activity, as in the philosophy of Spinoza.

By halving the four pressure points to two we can state in the starkest terms the persistent anomaly endemic to the traditional concept of substance: it is what Hegel calls the contradiction of indeterminacy and determinacy, for both are demanded at once by the potential and actual moments of the traditional concept. Substance exists in and through itself and is somehow complete, and yet it is an indeterminacy that receives its completion only by further determination from others.

Now, Hegel's complaint against the adequacy of "substance"—his warning that it cannot be the first and last name to be given to what is real—may be put as follows: Why after so many centuries is this anomaly in the term itself still unresolved?—the anomaly of a first principle that must remedy its own indeterminacy, that must realize its *own* potentiality, *at the hands of others?* Is there not some unfinished business here? And must we not look elsewhere than to substance in order to finish that business? Especially since, because it concerns first philosophy, that "business" is nothing less than the business of philosophy itself, which must put its fundamental concepts in the right order if it is to give a coherent and adequate account of the nature of reality and of its own enquiry into that reality. Surely, it cannot be that what is essential and primary in reality must wait upon that which is secondary and derivative for its completion, as substance must wait upon accidents; nor can it be that what is supposed to be being *itself* must wait upon that which is *other* than it in order to receive its fully determinate constitution. The traditional answer to this anomaly is to trace the origin of those substances which are determined or completed by accidents to those which are not, i.e., to those which do not require accidents in order to be determinate and actual. These latter substances are called "separated substances," "pure intelligences," and "spiritual substances," and the highest such substance or substances are divine. But if these are not to remain merely indeterminate, they must be the sources of their own determinacy and actuality. Aristotle's answer—to which we will return—was that they are the pure self-thinking substances. However, this introduces a separation between spirit and matter that is unacceptable to Hegel and indicates to him the need to go beyond substance to what he calls "subject."

One can trace Hegel's analysis of the problem of substance in its purest terms in the so-called "Greater Logic."[11] His analysis stretches over three books: the first, the objective "Logic of Being," takes up the traditional understanding of substance and the traditional metaphysics based upon it; the second, the objective "Logic of Essence," traces out the modern exploration of the geography of the mind; leading finally in the third book to the subjective "Logic of the Concept," that is, the logic of the properly Hegelian sense of subjectivity and Spirit.

In the logic of being, in the chapter on *determinate being,* he establishes the need of limit to pass over into finitude and of finitude to pass over into the infinite. But the nature of this limiting determinacy is such that its outreach exceeds its grasp. I mean that the tendency to conceive being in the shape of finitude casts a shadow well beyond finitude proper; for long after the concept of the infinite has been reached, the finite habit of thinking prolongs the negative rule of finitude over all of the categories of what Hegel calls the "Logic of Being." Indeed, what appears at the very end of the "Logic of Being"—much of whose backdrop is provided by Aristotle's metaphysics of substance—is the stubborn shape of finitude in the form of thinghood [*Etwas*].[12]

What is this stubborn shape of finite determinacy that Hegel thinks must be overcome? It consists in a certain understanding—or, to speak in terms of Hegel's full-fledged speculative philosophy, a misunderstanding—of the nature of identity. This intransigency consists in taking identity to be a core of sheer self-sameness retained against all threats, invitations, relationships and influences. It is the mistaken notion that something can remain what it is *only* through its ultimate indifference to others. It insists that at the heart of the self-same there is resistance to the power of others, an unreduced, besieged fortress of identity. This siege mentality is, for Hegel, what lies at the root of the traditional, metaphysical understanding of substance. Now, if it is true that substance can preserve its own identity only *against* otherness, this means that its relations to all forms of otherness—to other things, but also to its *own* accidents, since they are the effects of others—will be external; they will lie "outside" its privileged substantial core. In physical terms, that externality is defined through spatial location and boundaries, and more dynamically, through temporal sequence. But, to speak metaphysically as well, *all* relations will be understood to lie "outside" the metaphysical nodal point, which—even if affected in a certain sense[13]—will hold itself in reserve, untouched, unaffected, indifferent and self-same.[14] This is to say that the issue lodges in the meaning of relation. If relation is taken to be "connection" [*Beziehung*],[15] then the self-sameness will remain unreduced; but if unreduced, no fundamental unity can be achieved in reality: the best that can be said will be that reality is a collection of unreduced individuals. It will follow, too, that knowledge cannot achieve the unity of a system, since its components will be related in the same external way.

Now, for Hegel this is not good enough. For if knowledge cannot attain to systematic unity, it cannot attain to either absolute universality or unconditional necessity in its conclusions. But to settle for relative universality is to remain with what is partial, and to settle for conditioned necessity is to reach no further than contingency. Hegel is enough of a Kantian—he would rather say, enough of an Aristotelian—to demand of the rational enterprise that it attain justified truth in the form of necessary, universal cognition. But if our knowledge falls short under such strictures, so would reality itself. For, if reality is a collection of unreduced and irreducible items, there is no universe to which we can address such terms as "being," "unity," "totality," "world," and the like. The project of first philosophy would itself be stillborn. When one looks back at Hegel's critique of what he calls the "logic of being" and which he identifies with the more or less traditional metaphysics of substance, Hegel is saying that such a metaphysics is not really a *meta*physics at all, since it remains caught in the web of external and transitive relations that are characteristic of physical things and the alteration of states in nature.

A word of explanation is needed about the way in which Hegel understands the relation between substance and its accidents, as well as its relations to other substances. In the ordinary sense of substance, substance receives its accidents through the action of another upon it. Now, such an alteration may be physical in the proper sense of the term, i.e., it may occur in time and place. On the other hand, it may be "metaphysical," i.e., it may be an alteration or modification occurring in an analogous way at an allegedly spiritual level of being. As far as Hegel is concerned, however, whether the entity undergoes a properly physical alteration or, whether it undergoes a supposedly mental or spiritual change of state, the manner in which the reception of a new state is traditionally understood does not differ radically from the process of physical reception. In the vocabulary of pop-science, we might say that the understanding of such an ontological process is "modelled" upon the spatio-temporal processes of physical things, and kept within the "semantic horizon" of thinghood. But this "model"—as even the traditional metaphysics tried to show by its invocation of an immaterial, spiritual order—is too restrictive, since it does not let consciousness come forward into its own true nature. It keeps consciousness and its spiritual principle under the leading strings of the object understood after the manner of a reality that lacks consciousness.

The traditional metaphysics—kept as it was in the leading-strings of thinghood—failed to appreciate the true nature of spirituality and thought of it as *immateriality*. Nevertheless, its very proclamation of an *immaterial* order is a sign of its recognition of an inner necessity to go beyond the "logic of being" so conceived. Moreover, this need is indicated by the already-mentioned, suggestive anomaly that has plagued the concept of substance since its inception. The Greeks explored the rational character of being. Hegel credits them with the origination of philosophy itself, just because they showed forth the objective intelligibility of being, by showing how it could be brought to concepts and thereby made susceptible to a rational account. Their faith in the rationality of things underlay that love of wisdom which has given its name to philosophy.

Hegel remarks that the great discovery of modern thought, on the other hand, has been the recognition that the subject—consciousness—is essential to and constitutive of reality itself and not only of knowledge. It cannot be left out of an account of the object, any more than it can be left out of an account of knowing. Now, the modern thinkers—from Descartes to Kant and Fichte—explored this insistent nature of thought, and demanded that consciousness itself be brought within the horizon of philosophy as an explicit, constitutive principle, so that the love of knowledge for which we honour the Greeks could in our own day realize itself in the philosophical form of the system of scientific knowing.

His observation about the shift from Greek objectivity to modern subjectivity is confirmed by a quite general trend away from substance as a primary principle of explanation. We see this trend in the move from entity to law in early modern science,[16] occurring as it did in the initial stages of the abandonment of the Aristotelian fourfold causality, and of the rejection or subordination of entitative principles.[17] We see it also in the move from substance to function, and in such other forms as process philosophy, phenomenology, existentialism and hermeneutics.[18] We must ask, then, why has substance retreated in favour of other categories, such as *law, function* and *process*? Or again, why has substance been displaced by such concepts as *relation, context* and *system*? Hegel's answer is: that substance has had to retreat in order to let subjectivity—he calls it "subject"—come forward.

It does not come forward at once, however, and only by stages is its approach heralded. In what he calls the "Logic of Essence" [*Wesen*], Hegel appropriates what he has hailed as the peculiarly "modern" discovery: that consciousness must be made an equal partner in the elaboration of both the nature of reality and our knowledge of it. Since he thinks that Kant has raised this discovery of subjectivity to its pinnacle—with all of its promise and all of its unresolved problems—the categories associated with Kant play a large role in the "Logic of Essence." Hegel parades them before his readers, though not in Kant's order: appearance and reality (though Hegel speaks of knowable essence where Kant speaks of the unknowable thing-in-itself),[19] the laws of thought (identity, difference, opposition and contradiction), the explanatory structure of ground and consequent, the concept of totality and world, of whole and part, of contingency and necessity, of possibility and actuality, and finally of substance, causality and reciprocity.

Now, if the first book of his *Logic* developed the categories of being with the help of a running critique of the older metaphysics of substance, the second book develops the categories of essence with the help of a running critique of the newer metaphysics of subjectivity. For these categories of essence are meant to supply what we might call—with caution—the epistemological supplement to the logic of being (i.e., to the ontology), since they provide the explanatory framework by which the meaning and truth of what has gone on in the sphere of being can be brought to expression. Now, to *explain* a situation is to disclose what is there and why it is there, and to do it by introducing into the situation a relation that illuminates it but does not alter it. Once we leave the sphere of being we leave the sphere of mutation in the ordinary sense, and if we speak of the development of categories of essence we now use the word "development" in a new sense. A term borrowed from the philosophy of the schools may help: the relations (or connections) in the sphere of being are brought about by *transitive* actions— actions that alter the being of the recipient: the mutability of Plato's material world, and the mobility of Aristotle's physical world—whereas the categories of essence enter the sphere of being without introducing any further change into it; they are *intransitive* relations. It is clear, then, that in the "Logic of Essence" Hegel gives the terms "relation," "determination" and "development" a quite new meaning.[20]

According to the conventional wisdom that has prevailed among many philosophers in recent centuries, these new relations are usually looked upon as "only mental," "purely subjective," "mere constructions of reason," and therefore as entirely external to reality itself, and consequently unreal. As Hegel remarks: they are supposed to be "external to being and irrelevant to being's own nature."[21] Hegel, on the contrary, insists that they are inherent in the very development of reality itself. Of course, if we do not suspend the conventional wisdom which considers the categories of explanation to be unreal, then we will view Hegel at this point as one more subjective idealist simply imposing his mental constructions upon a recalcitrant reality.[22] But for Hegel there is even more at stake here than recognizing the importance of the modern discovery of subjectivity and the essential role of consciousness in the determination of reality. It seems to me—though he does not say this explicitly, and may not even have formulated it to himself in these terms—that Hegel goes beyond transitive relations of mutation to an order of intransitive relations just because he recognizes the necessity and the reality of what the older metaphysics called spirituality, even if it misconceived its true nature.

His bridge for incorporating the spiritual principle into reality, however, is a long one. My word "incorporation," of course, still suggests mutation, whereas Hegel's own terms for this process are: "speculation," "show," "reflection," and "appearance."[23] These metaphors express his intention more exactly, just because their primitive meanings suggest an expansion or development which is a mirroring of what remains the same and—insofar as it is faithfully mirrored—without alteration or distortion. For, of course, the issue is still the nature of identity. What recommends substance in the first place as the privileged bearer of being is its abiding *ownness* [its *perseity*] and its consequent capacity to provide a more or less *stable support* for the accidental determinations it receives from others. Both of these features of substance derive from its character as the enduring selfsame. On the other hand, what tells against substance in Hegel's judgment is that the character of substantial identity [Being-in-itself, *Ansichsein*] takes its stand in the siege mentality [*Verstand*][24] that defends identity as a fortress under siege from without. It has not reconciled itself to otherness. With the introduction of a spiritual principle, which Hegel here calls "essence" and reflection," a certain doubling breaks open the content, and a new integration begins to take place with a new sense of identity. For the same content

[*Being* and its states] that exists at the "push-and-pull" level of the processes of ontological determination is at the same time rendered more explicit at the level of the processes of essential (dare I say, epistemic?) determination. The fortress of self-identity is, so to speak, taken from within, without an assault upon the outer walls. But this "within," this "internalization" [*Erinnerung*],[25] is no mere "inside" matching a spatial "outside." It is the process of truth-gathering; for the concretion or collection brought about by the push-and-pull of ontological processes is now re-collected [*erinnert*]. This re-gathering does not alter the processes of physical being, but it is nonetheless a genuine development, a bringing to light of the meaning and truth of the content. It is, if I may appropriate another word from the ancient metaphysics, a *spiritual* development, an unmoving procession in the life of spirit, the process of rendering being intelligible. It is not, of course, the Latin *spiritus,* spirit without embodiment; it is the Germanic *Geist,* the spiritual principle in the Hegelian sense, viz., that which is the embodied energy and higher life of the one world.

The "Logic of Essence" provides the long bridge between the traditional concept of substance and the Hegelian concept of subject. This middle section of the *Science of Logic* displays a series of categories which are "essential" in Hegel's sense of the term, i.e., they are not merely ontological: they recapitulate and bring to light the true meaning of ontological processes. Thus, the term "ground" [*Grund*] is not a mere cause, immediately and directly inducing an alteration in some other thing; for, although it does incorporate the concept of cause within it, "ground" is that which explains and justifies the nature of the very process of origination and development as such. Even the category of "existence" [*Existenz*] stands for no mere brute fact, nor even for the ontological process of emergence; but rather for well-grounded and explicit states of affairs. The category of "appearance" [*Erscheinung*] does not refer merely to a psychological event, but also to that which occurs in nature, as when the first signs of spring appeared even before there were human beings to perceive them; that is to say, even before life had reached the state at which it was able to ponder upon the joy of fresh growth. But even more, the category of "appearance" gives a self-validating account of the phenomenon of manifestation in general. Indeed, the very category of "actuality" itself [*Wirklichkeit*] is at once more than a merely mental idea and more than a merely real thing.[26] All of these categories of essence recapitulate the physical and metaphysical processes of being; but they are themselves filled with the energy of spiritual life. They are epistemic developments in a special sense, for they make explicit the complex and concrete totality within which the ontological processes arise and within which the categories of ontology are situated. The categories of being are rendered more intelligible and more concrete, just because they are taken up into the spiritual dimension of reality by way of the categories of essence.

So far I have traced out Hegel's criticism of the traditional understanding of substance and its primacy. It may be surprising, then, to find that Hegel explicitly introduces the category of substance only at the end of the "Logic of Essence," that is to say, at the very threshold to his logic of subjectivity. That means that he introduces substance as the highest and most developed category in the "Logic of Essence." To be sure, the concept of substance that re-appears has been converted to Hegelianism. Still, it is surprising that even such a convert should assume its place just short of the categories that form the logical crown of the Hegelian system; I mean the categories of the Absolute Spirit: that is, the categories of Subjectivity, the Concept, and the Idea.[27] And yet it is the very virtues of the concept of substance that raise it to such a lofty philosophical position, even though its inability to be completely converted eventually bars it from entrance to the inner courtyard of the Hegelian temple.

The rejuvenated category of substance makes its appearance, then, in the last section of the *Logic of Essence,* in the form of a concept very much like Spinoza's *Substance.*[28] The term has long since overcome any restriction to finitude, and now takes its place as the provisionally supreme designation of infinite fundamental self-existent reality. Hegel's treatment of the category of substance occurs here under the general rubric of "The Absolute Relation"; but the term used to designate the new sense of relation is no longer that which means an external "connection" between relatively independent, nodal terms [*Beziehung*]. Such an external relation has given way to relation understood as absolute totality, and the difference is great enough to warrant another term: *Verhaeltnis.*[29] The new relation is the primary actuality, the system as a whole, within which the terms themselves are embedded and through which they receive their meaning, value and reality. Speaking precisely, then, Hegel does not so much take up the traditional concept of substance as he does the "relation of substantiality" [*das Verhaeltnis der Substantialitaet*].

Substance understood as absolute relation is, up to this point, the most self-subsistent shape taken by the system in all of its universality. It is no longer mere being by itself [*perseitas*], but absolute substance existing in and through and from itself alone [*Aseitas*]. For all that, however, the substantial relation still stands in need of further development. As Hegel sees it, Spinoza is not yet in possession of a sufficiently active, articulated and integrated concept of substance to give expression to the unity of the whole of reality. That is why the Spinozistic modes either remain external to substance in preserving their distinct character or lose their distinctness by collapsing back into substance as their only ground of being.[30]

What Spinoza recognized is that substance is inherently necessary and

infinite. What is needed in addition, however, is the appropriate development of substance as active self-relation, for this too is inherent in its
perseity.[31] And indeed, Spinoza intuitively grasped this self-relation inasmuch as he identified substance with self-cause [*causa sui*]. Hegel, too, finds
in the category of causality the basis for a determinate and active form of
self-relation, and he introduces the causal concept in order to develop a
more adequate dynamic of substantial self-relation.[32] Ordinarily, we accept
the fact that accidental states and incidental modifications come about in a
substance through active causation by other beings; but a deeper consideration will show us that the relation of inherence characteristic of the accidents of a substance are, so to speak, "owned" by the substance: the
substance possesses its accidents and states as *its* own. Moreover, they take
their very being as accidents from the self-subsistent being of the substance;
it is the only being they have. And so, while initially we think of accidents as
pointing to other beings as their principal causes, their most proper cause is
the very substance which has appropriated them. In this sense, then, we
must situate the external modifying influence of other beings within a more
fundamental unity: and this is substance understood as that which determines itself by translating its relations to others into its relation to itself. The
spiritually significant property of substance, then, is self-relation precisely as
self-determining; and this is to recognize as primary to substance not merely
a passive substrate but also the active energy that is the very subsistence of
substance and the ground of its determinations. Moreover, if substance is
the name given to the whole system insofar as it is both the substrate of its
own self-determination *and* the active energy that is its self-determining, we
have reached the concept of a self-determining totality.

Nevertheless, this active self-determination that is characteristic of the
relation of substantiality still falls short of the full account of reality. The
causal translation of other-relatedness into self-relating substance cannot
complete itself at the level of substance and cause, because even the converted Hegelian category of substantial relation still retains the shadow of
unreduced otherness. Unqualified self-identification and absolute systematic integration cannot be brought about within the category of substance, for
even in its most sublimated and spiritual form it still remembers the unequal
duality of substance and accident; nor can it be brought about through
causality, which even in its most sublimated form still remembers the duality
of cause and effect, of agent and patient, of source and recipient. The
insufficiency of the whole essential order manifests itself in a sort of sublimated dualism that is intrinsic to the epistemic structure of explanation; for
at its root is the correlativity of what is to be explained [*explanandum*] and
the activity of explaining [*explanans*].[33]

This *correlativity* shows that the full reconciliation of the category of

relation to that of identity remains unfinished. Only *subjectivity* can enter-
tain and hold within itself the rich concrete complexity of relationships that
gives to all aspects of reality their own place and function, while it yet retains
its own self-sameness. The sign of such a rich integration is already at hand in
the activity and life of consciousness. For only consciousness can "go out" to
the other (what we would call "intentionality," other-relatedness), can "lose"
itself in that other (what Hegel calls "objectivity," the very hallmark of
knowledge), and yet be able to return to itself enriched by its relation to
otherness (what Hegel calls "reflection"), and hold these together in a fully
concrete, fully integrated totality (what Hegel calls "subjectivity," and which
further realizes itself in the Concept, the Idea and the System). To recapitulate, then, in terms of identity and identification: (1) consciousness has
self-existence (simple identity in itself); (2) consciousness relates to an other
(intentional or objective identity), (3) consciousness returns to itself (self-
consciousness or reflective identity), and yet (4) consciousness preserves
this totality of difference and identity within its own self-sameness (speculative identity). Hegel calls the full process "speculation." It reaches its
unobstructed self-determination as the self-developing system of all reality
and all knowledge. This alone is spirit, and it lies beyond the merely external
relatedness with which traditional substance is afflicted,[34] and even beyond
the correlative unity of the Hegelian substantial relation. Only in the expand-
ed Hegelian sense of subjectivity, which no longer stands over against the
object but takes it up into its own life, even while respecting its true reality,
only in that wholly active process is all otherness recognized yet subsumed,
its resistance cancelled from within yet without destroying its determinateness. Only then does spirit finally come home to itself. At home with itself,
substance in both its passivity and its activity is there, but more concretely
than it could be if its resistance to otherness were the ultimate identity and
its stubborn self-sameness were the last word.

    In following Hegel through his long journey beyond substance and to
subjectivity I have rejected the interpretation that would consign his thought
to a mere idealism, whether called subjective or absolute. It seems to me that
more is at stake in his dissatisfaction with substance: it is nothing less than
(1) his attempt to safeguard the spiritual dimension of reality and of life from
the materialist tendencies hidden in the original ambiguity of the concept,
but (2) it is also his rejection of the efforts of traditional metaphysics to
forestall those tendencies by propounding a doctrine of immaterial substance, and (3) it is also his attempt to rescue the spiritual dimension of
reality and life from its imprisonment within the confines of modern sub-
jectivism and the consequent reduction to relativism and scepticism.

    My attempt to present Hegel in this light should not obscure my own
reservations, though I can only mention here what I take to be the deficiencies

of his attempt; an attempt, nonetheless, which I consider to be the most serious metaphysical retrieval since the High Middle Ages and on a level with the great Aristotle himself. I agree with his rejection of false transcendence, set as it is over against and beyond immanence; but there is another kind of transcendence (of which the great mediaeval thinkers knew) that releases finite beings from being dominated by their systemic functions.[35] This release can be seen and established, however, only in and through the reality of gift, where the finite recovers again the moment of affirmation: in the very act of saying yes to the gratuity of creation and to the contingency of its being and its world. But that freedom requires a doctrine of *creatio ex nihilo* which Hegel steadfastly rejected as philosophically meaningless.[36] If Hegel has shown us a way beyond what he calls ontological determinations, and has insisted upon the reality of the spiritual dimension, we may yet disagree with him on the nature of that spirituality. I would argue that it is an "inwardness" at whose centre is the divine mystery, the excess of light that opens up intelligibility itself, never to be closed again.[37] So that the chain which binds meaning to necessity is broken, and the truth itself made free without ceasing to be intellectual and rational. Hegel's critique of substance, however, can illuminate the crisis that faces a metaphysics of being, and can serve as prelude for finding a way beyond the crisis, a way forward that is continuous with the way back.

Trinity College, University of Toronto
Toronto, Canada

NOTES

1. Hegel prefers locutions, such as "affirmation," "negation," and "negation of the negation"; the second term being the properly *dialectical* moment, and the third being the properly *speculative* moment, i.e., the moment of sublation [*Aufhebung*]. See Grégoire, *Etudes Hégéliennes. Les Points Capitaux du Systeme,* Louvain: Institut Supérieur de Philosophie, 1958, p. 55, fn. 1.

2. *Phaenomenologie des Geistes* (1807), 6th edn. Joh. Hoffmeister, Hamburg: F. Meiner, 1952, p. 19. English translation by A. V. Miller, Oxford: Clarendon, 1977, para. 17, pp. 9-10. For the critical edition of the text, see: *Gesammelte Werke,* ed. O. Poeggeler, Hamburg: F. Meiner, 1968ff.; Bd. 9, ed. W. Bonsiepen and R. Heede, 1979.

3. See, for example, *Metaphysics* Book Z (VII), c. 3, 1028b33-36: "The term 'substance' [*ousia*] is spoken of, if not in more, still in four main senses; for the essence [*to ti en einai*] is thought to be the substance of an individual [*ousia dokei einai 'ekastou*], and the universal [*to katholou*], and the genus [*to genos*], and fourthly the underlying subject [*to 'upokeimenon*]." (Ed. W. Jaeger, Oxford: Clarendon, 1957, p. 130; tr. H. Apostle, Grinnell, 1966, p. 206.) Cf. *Categories,* c.5, 2allff.

4. In his presidential address in this volume, John Wippel makes precise the position of St. Thomas Aquinas. If I have understood him correctly, *ens per se* is, for St. Thomas, not the

definition of substance, since the definition is taken from the quiddity; nevertheless, the two terms are equivalent in the sense that whatever is *ens per se* is substance, though that which is substance is not, by virtue of its being substance, that which is *ens per se*. Something is *ens per se* by virtue of its *being* in the full and primary sense [*esse*].

5. The differentiation of the senses of the term can be seen in Boethius' reflection upon the Conciliar theological debates. He played a prominent role, of course, in fixing the technical Latin vocabulary for philosophy and theology, and he steered the term "substance" towards the third meaning. Thus, in *Contra Eutychen*, sec. III (*The Theological Tractates*, tr. by H. F. Stewart and E. K. Rand, London: Heinemann (Loeb), 1962, pp. 88ff.), he distinguishes between the family of terms stemming from *ousia* and those stemming from *'upostasin* (cf. *'upokeimenon*): "For a thing has subsistence [*subsistit*] when it does not require accidents in order to be, but that thing has substance [*substat*] which supplies to other things, accidents to wit, a substrate [*subjectum*] enabling them to be; for it "substands" those things so long as it is subjected to accidents....Particulars [*individua*] have not only subsistence but substance [*non modo subsistunt verum etiam substant*]....For Greece is not, as Marcus Tullius playfully says [*Tusc. Disp.*, ii, 15, 35], short of words, but provides exact equivalents for *essentia, subsistentia, substantia* and *persona—ousia* for *essentia, ousiosis* for *subsistentia, 'upostasis* for *substantia, prosopon* for *persona*. But the Greeks called individual substances *'upostaseis* because they underlie the rest and offer support and substrate to what are called accidents; and we in our term call them substances as being substrates [*quasi subpositas*]— *'upostaseis*...."

6. This is the meaning of his play upon the German term *das Endliche:* the destiny of finite beings is that they cease to be, "the hour of their birth is the hour of their death," "non-being constitutes their [very] nature and being," etc. See *Science of Logic*, tr. Miller, New York: Humanities, 1969, pp. 129-154; *Wissenschaft der Logik*, ed. G. Lasson, Hamburg: F. Meiner, 1966-67, 2 vols.; I, pp. 116-145.

7. *An Enquiry Concerning Human Understanding*, Bk. I, c. 4, # 18; II, 13, ## 18-19; III, 6, ## 1-51.

8. Immanuel Kant, *Critique of Pure Reason*, the First Analogy, A182/B224.

9. *Ethics*, Bk. I, Def. I, III, VI and VII.

10. Cf. K. L. Schmitz, "Hegel's Assessment of Spinoza," *The Philosophy of Baruch Spinoza*, Studies in Philosophy and the History of Philosophy, vol. 7, ed. by R. Kennington, Washington, D.C.: The Catholic University of America, 1980, pp. 229-243.

11. In addition to the Lasson edition (cited in fn. 6), the critical edition of the *Wissenschaft der Logik* is to be found in *Gesammelte Werke*, Hamburg: F. Meiner, 1968ff.

12. *Science of Logic*, Part I: The Objective Logic; Book I: The Doctrine of Being; Section 1: Determinateness (Quality); Chapter 2: Determinate Being [*bestimmtes Sein, Dasein*]. Determinate being assumes its first shape in the category, "Something" [*Etwas*], and this soon passes over into "Another" [*ein Anderes*], into the "Finite" [*das Endliche*] and into the "Infinite" [*das Unendliche*]; but even after the spurious forms of infinity are overcome, the logic of finite thinghood does not loosen its grip until—only at the very end of the first book—the total collapse of being, with all of its predicates and all of its external relations, into *Indifferenz*. This utter negation then leads us into Book II: The Doctrine of Essence.

13. *Science of Logic*, Bk. I, sec. 1, c. 2: Constitution [*Beschaffenheit*], tr. Miller, p. 125 (ed. Lasson, vol. I, p. 112).

14. For the total collapse just mentioned (in fn. 12), and for the category of absolute indifference [*Indifferenz*], see Bk. I, sec. 3, c. 3, especially "Transition to Essence" (tr. Miller, p. 390; ed. Lasson, I, 398).

15. First introduced technically in the form of a negative, external connection with another thing [*Sein-fuer-Anderes*]. See *Science of Logic*, Bk. I, sec. 1, c. 2B: Something and Other (tr. Miller, p. 119; ed. Lasson, I, p. 106).

16. Cf. Hegel's own treatment of the concept of physical law, e.g., in *Phenomenology*, cc. 3 and 5, and *Science of Logic*, Bk. II, sec. 2, c. 2: The Law of Appearance. He concludes, however, that the concept of law is not adequate to what is expected of it in the sciences.

17. K. L. Schmitz, "Analysis by Principles and Analysis by Elements," *Graceful Reason, Essays in Ancient and Medieval Philosophy Presented to Joseph Owens, CSSR*, ed. L. P. Gerson, Toronto: Pontifical Institute of Mediaeval Studies, 1983, pp. 315-330.

18. Cf. Ernst Cassirer, *Substance and Function* (1910), tr. W. and M. Swabey, New York: Dover, 1953; and the primacy of relation, context and system in such varied thinkers as Buber, Heidegger, De Saussure and R. Barthes.

19. Cf. K. L. Schmitz, "Hegel on Kant: Being-in-itself and the Thing-in-itself," *The Philosophy of Immanuel Kant*, Studies in Philosophy and the History of Philosophy, vol. 12, ed. R. Kennington, Washington, D.C.: The Catholic University of America, 1985, pp. 229-251.

20. In his editorial remarks introducing the "Logic of Essence" Hegel signals the new order of relations by reminding us that the term "essence" [*Wesen*] derives—not, as the Latin *essentia*, through the construction of the present participle [*essens*] from the verb "to be" [*esse*]—but from the past participle [*gewesen*] of the German verb "to be" [*sein*], taken as "timelessly past being" [*zeitlos vergangenes Sein*]. And he signals the break with the transitive or mutational categories of being by insisting that in the new order of essential relations "otherness and relation-to-other have been completely sublated [*das Anderssein und die Beziehung auf anderes schlechthin aufgehoben worden ist*]....Its determining [i.e., the intransitive process of *essential* determination as contrasted with the transitive determination which brings about the alteration that is characteristic of the order of being in the first book]...is neither a becoming nor a transition [*kein Werden noch Uebergehen*], nor are the determinations themselves an *other* as other, or relations *to other* [*so wie die Bestimmungen selbst nicht ein Anderes als anderes, noch Beziehungen auf anderes sind*]." (*Science of Logic*, Bk. II, the prefatory remarks, tr. Miller, pp. 389-390; ed. Lasson, I, pp. 3-5.)

21. "...die dem Sein aeusserlich sei und dessen eigene Natur nichts angehe." (*loc. cit.*)

22. N. Rotenstreich expresses Hegel's point well: "Thinking has to be absorbed in Being and Essence. It cannot remain in a subject whose position is that of a merely external observer overlooking the game of dialectic. Thinking must eventually inhere in the position attained by the dialectic: thinking is mediation, the stage we arrive at is mediated by thinking, so that the stage we arrive at has the character of thinking. This is another statement of the shift from substance to subject. This mode of realization is for Hegel 'speculation.'" (*From Substance to Subject: Studies in Hegel*, The Hague: Nijhoff, 1974, p. 107.)

23. *Science of Logic*, Bk. II, sec. 1, c. 1: *Wesen, Schein, Reflexion, Erscheinung* and more generally, *Spekulation*.

24. To Hegel, the technical term *Verstand*, "understanding," designates the analytical principle of differentiation, in that it separates out one item from another. The term *Vernunft*, "reason," on the other hand, is the speculative principle that re-integrates what appears to be separate, thereby transforming a mere collection into a genuine totality whose members are related intrinsically and which is itself self-related. It would not be simply wrong to regard such a process of re-integration (the Hegelian sublation or *Aufhebung*) as the translation of separations into distinctions; and in this it is not wholly unlike the traditional metaphysics. At least insofar as the latter takes as its task: to recognize what is *really* and not merely mentally distinguished in a being, without thereby losing the *reality* of the original and ultimate unity of the being. Of course, the radical difference between Hegel and traditional metaphysics makes the comparison a rather remote analogy: "not wholly unlike."

25. *Science of Logic*, Bk. II, prefatory remarks (tr. Miller, p. 389; ed. Lasson, II, p. 3). Miller's rendering of the German word for remembering or recollecting [*Erinnerung*] by "inwardizing" is as happy as his rendering of *Schein* by "illusory being" is unhappy. "Show" retains the

ambiguity of the German term, as that which both makes manifest ("Show me") and/or creates illusion ("Mere show").

26. These are the principal categories of the "Logic of Essence," and they mediate between the traditional concept of substance (developed in "The Objective Logic of Being") and the Hegelian concept of subject (arrived at in "The Subjective Logic of Concept").

27. *Science of Logic,* vol. II: "The Subjective Logic or The Doctrine of the Concept" (tr. Miller, pp. 573ff.; ed. Lasson, II, pp. 209ff).

28. *Science of Logic,* Book II, sec. 3, c. 1: "The Absolute," including the remark on Spinoza and Leibniz (tr. Miller, pp. 530-540, ed. Lasson, II, pp. 157-169).

29. Towards the end of his discussion of "the world of appearance and the world-in-itself"—we might say: his discussion of the distinction between manifest appearance and hidden or implicit reality—Hegel passes over from speaking of the relation between the two concepts as a "connection" [*Grundbeziehung, wesentliche Beziehung*], implying a residual externality *between* the terms, to speaking of the relation as a primary totality within which the *relata* are embedded and constituted. For this latter sense of *relation as totality* he uses the term "*Verhaeltnis.*" He had already used the term in the "Logic of Being," but there it was to designate the category of numerical ratio in which it is not the numbers by themselves that are primary nor the distinction between them that is real but rather the relationship itself. See *Science of Logic,* Bk. I, sec. 2, c. 3 (tr. Miller, p. 314; ed. Lasson, I, 322). With the sublation of the distinction between appearance and reality Hegel arrives at what he calls "the essential relation," that is "the relation of whole and parts," in which parts are *parts* only as parts of a whole, and a whole is a *whole* only if it has parts; that is, the distance between one side of the relation (e.g., reality) and the other side (e.g., appearance) has been closed. See (*op. cit.,* Bk. II, sec. 2, c. 3 (tr. Miller, p. 512; ed. Lasson, II, 136).

30. See Laura Byrne, *Hegel's Critique of Spinoza,* Dissertation, University of Toronto, 1987 (unpublished).

31. Indeed, Spinoza even recognized the essentiality of thought, for he pronounced it to be one of the two essential attributes of substance of which we know. Hegel's criticism is that thought is not related explicitly and concretely either to substance or to extension. The immediate *identity* of thought with substance in the definition left their *identification* a mere assertion.

32. It is not incidental that Hegel places at the end of his most complete exposition of the system (i.e., at the end of the *Encyclopedia*) the Greek text from Aristotle on self-thinking thought ‹*Metaphysics* Bk. Lambda, c. 7, 1072b18-30›, which he appropriates for his own purposes in a free and bold manner. Aristotle grasped that the highest reality was intelligence, though he was unable to incorporate otherness into its knowledge: it was self-thinking thought. N. Rotenstreich, *op. cit.,* pp. 59-60 and ff., describes the implied appropriation: "It is the object of speculation to conceive all objects, whether of pure thought, of nature or of Spirit, in the form of thought, and thus to conceive of the unity of their differences....Reason...is substantive or self-reflective in the sense propounded by Aristotle in his concept of *noesis noeseos.* What Aristotle applied to the first mover is applied by Hegel to the whole of reality. Reality is imbued with reflection because reality is the Idea....The subject matter of philosophy is the world, and self-knowledge is the subjectivity of the world. The whole world is the self-explication of the *noesis noeseos.*"

33. Cf. Rotenstreich, *op. cit.,* pp. 15-16 and 20: "The category of substance is lodged within the sphere of essence, which means that it still bears traces of dualities that have not yet been fully overcome; or, it bears traces of the traditional distinctions, made in terms of content and status, between substance and its accidents....Thus the full identity between substance and accidents is not realized since the nominal and formal traces of previous distinctions are still retained....But substance cannot be viewed as identical with the Absolute, since the Absolute

68 *The Metaphysics of Substance*

has to be viewed as overcoming all duality. Within the sphere of dualities and correlations, the Absolute would be merely one of the correlates and not the actual fullness....The advantage of the concept of subject over the category of substance lies [in the fact that]...subject is intrinsically related to content....This [intrinsic] relation...removes the residue of duality and mere correlation which cling to the category of substance."

34. Hegel speaks of the external relation to another [*Sein-fuer-Anderes*] as an affliction inseparable from "being-in-itself" [*Ansichsein*]: "mit Sein-fuer-Anderes behaftet ist." (*Science of Logic*, Bk. I, sec. 2, c. 2Bb (tr. Miller, p. 122; ed. Lasson, I, p. 110. Also tr. Miller, p. 124; ed. Lasson, I, p. 112))—Speaking of the distinction between "what is still *in itself*" [*an sich*] and "what is *posited*"[*gesetzt*], he remarks quite generally: "This is a distinction which belongs only to the dialectical development [*dialektische Entwicklung*] and which is unknown to metaphysical philosophizing [*das metaphysische Philosophieren*], which also includes the critical philosophy [of Kant]; the definitions of metaphysics, like its presuppositions, distinctions and conclusions, seek to assert and produce only what comes under the category of *being*, and that, too, of *being-in-itself*"[nur Seiendes und zwar Ansichseiendes], (tr. Miller, p. 122; edn. Lasson, I, 109).

35. Cf. K. L. Schmitz, "La transcendance coincidente: fondement de l'interrogation religieuse," *Urgence de la Philosophie*, Québec: Université Laval, edd. T. De Koninck and L. Morin, pp. 591-598.

36. Cf. K. L. Schmitz, *The Gift: Creation*, The Aquinas Lecture, Milwaukee: Marquette University, 1982.

37. Cf. K. L. Schmitz, "The Conceptualization of Religious Mystery: An Essay in Hegel's Philosophy of Religion," *The Legacy of Hegel*, ed. J. O'Malley *et. al.*, The Hague: Nijhoff, 1973, pp. 108-137.

SECTION I — ARISTOTLE

Lawrence Dewan, O.P., Chairman
College Dominican, Ottawa

Aristotle's Notion of Theology and the Meaning of Οὐσία*

by Walter Patt

This paper has three sections. In the first section, the problem presented is whether or not Aristotle is justified in claiming that the science of separate and unchangeable being is universal. The second section deals with Ph. Merlan's solution to the problem, to which an objection is made. The third section offers a different solution, based upon a distinction between two meanings of οὐσία.

I. *The Problem.* Bk. E, ch. 1, of Aristotle's *Metaphysics* contains a well-known argument which suggests the identification of theology with the science of being as such. Aristotle says that the first science treats of the separate and unchangeable (χωριστὰ καὶ ἀκίνητα), in contrast with physics and mathematics (*Met.*[1] 1026 a 13-16). As is clear from the enumeration of the three theoretical philosophies, the first science may be called "theology," since the divine exists in such a nature (i.e., among the separate and unchangeable) if it exists at all (*Met.* 1026 a 18-21). For Aristotle, the first science, dealing with the separate and unchangeable, in the last analysis is theology or theological philosophy. Moreover, Aristotle says that an unchangeable οὐσία would be prior (i.e., to natural οὐσίαι) if it exists. Philosophy (which here seems to be synonymous with the science of the separate and unchangeable) then is first, and it is universal (καθόλου) because it is first. This science would investigate being as such, what it is as well as that which belongs to being as such (*Met.* 1026 a 29-32).[2]

*A grant from the "Deutscher Akademischer Austauschdienst" during the academic year of 1985-1986 made it possible for me to write this article. Dr. Daniel Dahlstrom and Dr. Bonnie Kent have improved my English in many ways.

In short, if any unchangeable οὐσία exists, the corresponding science will be both the first of all sciences and the universal science of being as such. If we assume that the realm of unchangeable being for Aristotle includes the divine, we can infer that theology (which is the culmination of the science of separate and unchangeable being) is identical with the universal science of being as such.

The obvious question, raised by Aristotle himself (cf. *Met.* 1026 a 23-25), and much debated ever since:[3] Is first philosophy, taken as the science of the separate and unchangeable or as theology, universal or particular in character? The science of separate and unchangeable being apparently deals with a particular kind of being, not with being in general. If first philosophy is identical with the science of separate and unchangeable being, is it just as particular as it would be if it were identical with physics?

II. *Merlan's Solution.* Many interpreters rejected the identification of the science of being as such with theology as suggested in E 1. However, an affirmative and ingenious solution to the problem has been proposed by Ph. Merlan.[4] According to his reading, in Γ, E 1, and K 7, ὄν ᾗ ὄν does not mean an abstract characteristic which is expressed by a concept, and καθόλου does not mean an abstract universal. Rather, ὄν is καθόλου in that it is an element common to all existents. (As Merlan stresses, καθόλου here should be translated as "common," not as "general" or "universal.") Ὄν ᾗ ὄν, in general another term for χωριστὸν καὶ ἀκίνητον (separate and unchangeable), indicates an entity which is nothing but being, an entity not composed of existence and something else. While any entity composed of existence and something else is somehow determined (limited), an entity which is only being must be undetermined (unlimited), and cannot be a particular thing. In fact, it must be the most positive entity, as Merlan points out. This entity is the divine.

Accordingly, Aristotle's first philosophy, as Merlan understands it, is a καθόλου science in two regards. First, it deals with ὄν ᾗ ὄν, that is, with being as it is καθόλου (undeterminately or unlimitedly) present in the highest entity, the divine. Secondly, it deals with being as it is καθόλου present in any existent, or is common to all existents. If "being as such" is another phrase for the separate and unchangeable (divine) being, the science of being as such is basically theology, concludes Merlan. Insofar as Aristotle assumes that there is a realm of being above the realm of natural being, Merlan sees him as part of the Platonic tradition.

The ingenuity of Merlan's solution consists in his attempt to establish the universal character of Aristotle's science of separate and unchangeable being by showing that this kind of being, at least in the case of the divine, is universal. This kind of being is universal, argues Merlan, inasmuch as it is pure, undetermined being. However, this seems to be an un-Aristotelian interpretation of Aristotle's notion of the separate and unchangeable. Aristotle does not characterize the separate and unchangeable as nothing but being, as undetermined and unqualified being. Furthermore, it is unclear whether Aristotle ever conceives ὄν ᾗ ὄν as a subsisting entity. Merlan, it seems to me, has interpreted Aristotle's notions in a Thomistic way. He renders ὄν ᾗ ὄν as *esse tantum*, presupposing that it designates an entity whose quiddity *is* its *esse*. He then equates separate and unchangeable (divine) being with *esse tantum*, thereby arriving at the notion of *ipsum esse subsistens*. Thus, Merlan intriguingly combines *metaphysica generalis* and *metaphysica specialis*. For him, the science of a certain kind of being *is* the science of being as such.

III. *A Different Solution.* While not accepting Merlan's Thomistically inspired solution, I propose a solution that still affirms the universal character of the science of separate and unchangeable being, or its identity with the science of being as such. This solution is spelled out in a discussion of two pairs of questions, one of which is discussed in *Met.* E 1, the other in K 7. Although the authenticity of Bk. K, chs. 1-8, has been contested by A. Mansion,[5] I shall try to show that the two questions in K 7 correspond with the two questions asked in E 1.

The two questions in E 1 are:

(1) Which science is first philosophy: physics or the science of separate and unchangeable being? (Cf *Met.* 1026 a 27-30).
(2) Is first philosophy universal in character, that is, is it identical with the science of being as such? (Cf. *Met.* 1026 a 23-25; 30-32).

The two questions in K 7 are:

(1) Which science is the science of being as such and as subsistent: physics or the science of separate and unchangeable being? (Cf. *Met.* 1064 a 28-b 6).
(2) Is the science of being as such universal in character? (Cf. *Met.* 1064 b 6-14).

We focus on these questions in turn.

In *Met.* 1026 a 10-22, Aristotle presents three theoretical philosophies which differ from each other according to their objects. Physics deals with that which is subsistent (χωριστά)[6] but not unchangeable (οὐκ ἀκίνητα). Some branches of mathematics deal with that which is unchangeable (ἀκίνητα), yet perhaps not subsistent (οὐ χωριστὰ δὲ ἴσως) but in matter (*Met.* 1026 a 13-15). If there is something eternal and unchangeable and separate (from matter), it will be the object of a science prior to physics and mathematics (*Met.* 1026 a 10-13). In fact, the science dealing with separate

and unchangeable being for Aristotle is the first science (*Met*. 1026 a 15-16)—
if indeed an entity of such nature exists. This science would be first philosophy or the most honourable science because it treats of the most honourable
object. If the divine exists at all, it exists in such a nature (*Met*. 1026 a 19-22),
that is, as a separate and unchangeable entity. The science dealing with
separate and unchangeable being is primarily theology, and Aristotle mentions theological philosophy as one of the three theoretical philosophies
(*Met*. 1026 a 18-19).

   This division of theoretical philosophy seems to be merely formal. It does
not imply that something separate and unchangeable exists. Rather, the
predicates "separate" (or "subsistent"), "unchangeable," "not subsistent,"
"not unchangeable" are used to indicate the three branches possible within
theoretical philosophy. Theology is a real science only if the realm of the
separate and unchangeable is actual.

   So the question remains: Which science is first philosophy? Aristotle
presents the disjunction: If there is no substance besides the natural substances, physics is the first science; but if there is an unchangeable substance, this substance is prior (to natural substances), and the corresponding
science is first philosophy (*Met*. 1026 a 27-30).

   Interestingly enough, this disjunction is not tripartite, but bipartite. Mathematics for Aristotle cannot be first philosophy. As Merlan has pointed out,
mathematics for Aristotle ultimately was not a philosophical discipline
because its objects are not substances but rather exist merely by virtue of
abstraction. Therefore interpreters of Aristotle were right in calling Aristotelian theology "metaphysics," and not "meta-mathematics."[7] According to
this reasoning, mathematics for Aristotle is no candidate for first philosophy
because mathematical objects have no existence independent of our intellect, or are not χωριστά. For Aristotle, the subject matter of first philosophy
is actual substances.

   No decision is made here as to which science will finally be first philosophy. But Aristotle's discussion of the theoretical philosophies and their
objects leaves no doubt that for him the realm of the separate and unchangeable is the highest type of being. In fact, we can distinguish between three
meanings of being in the passage at hand: (1) "being" in a wide sense which
includes mathematical objects, i.e., unchangeable but perhaps (according to
Met. 1064 a 33: certainly) nonsubsistent entities (which, according to *Met*.
1026 a 9-10, can at least be looked upon as subsistent for the sake of investigation); (2) "being" in a stronger (and more restricted) sense: that which is
subsistent (χωριστόν in a weak sense), but not unchangeable (natural substances); (3) "being" in the strongest (and most restricted) sense: that which
subsists separately from matter (χωριστόν in a strong sense) and is unchangeable (the divine, primarily). Thus, *subsistence* is a necessary, *un-*

changeability a sufficient condition for true being. One might ask whether in Aristotle's *Metaphysics* there is a fourth sense of being which would cover that which is neither subsistent nor unchangeable. For Aristotle, what cannot exist on its own and is subject to change is a mere συμβεβηκός (accident), not a true being, and it seems that he would not admit a particular science of accidents.

The second question in E 1, as to whether first philosophy is universal in character or merely deals with a particular kind of being, is answered in the affirmative: First philosophy is universal in this fashion just because it is first (καὶ καθόλου οὕτως ὅτι πρώτη *Met.* 1026 a 30-31). This statement obviously is connected with the conditional clause discussed above. Only if there is an unchangeable (and presumably separate) substance, is the corresponding science first philosophy and the most universal science. Apparently, first philosophy for Aristotle can only be the universal science if it is the science of the separate and unchangeable, and not physics. Thus, the little word οὕτως would be important, indicating that only in this fashion, that is, on the condition that the science of separate and unchangeable being is first philosophy, is this first philosophy the universal science.

But the obvious question then is: Why could first philosophy not be universal if it were identical with physics, that is, if there were no realm of being above the realm of natural substances? In answering this question, we should look at Aristotle's justification for the universal character of first philosophy. The justification is presented in two words: ὅτι πρώτη. First philosophy is universal because it is first. But it is first because it studies the highest possible kind of being, the separate and unchangeable which includes the divine. (According to Aristotle, that science is first which studies the most dignified type of being; cf. *Met.* 1026 a 21-22.) Aristotle seems to imply that on any other level (i.e., on the levels of natural substances and mathematical objects) being is not fully realized, or that on those levels beings are beings in a weaker sense. Now, if physics in fact is first philosophy (just because no separate and unchangeable substance exists), in some sense it is still not the first science and is not universal because the science of a higher kind of being can still be conceived. Physics would be first philosophy by virtue of a fact, but it would not be the highest possible philosophy. On the other hand, the science of separate and unchangeable being is universal in that it studies being in the strongest sense of the word, which somehow includes being in weaker senses.

The result of E 1, then, seems to be: Aristotle obviously assumes that separate and unchangeable being is the highest kind of being, or is being in the fullest sense of the word. If entities of such nature exist, the science dealing with them is first philosophy and the universal science of being as such. Aristotle indeed states that first philosophy, taken as the science of separate and unchangeable being, has to study being as such, what it is as well as that which is proper to it as being (*Met.* 1026 a 31-32). The science of separate and unchangeable being, which primarily is theology, turns out to be the universal science of being as such.

The first question in K 7 is whether the science of being as such and as subsistent (χωριστόν, here again in the broader sense) is to be posited as identical with physics, or rather as a different science (*Met.* 1064 a 28-30). Since the question concerns the science of being as such *and as subsistent*, mathematics is not mentioned as a candidate for this science. What follows is a division of theoretical science (cf. *Met.* 1064 a 30-35) similar to that in *Met.* 1026 a 13-16. Although the author of K 7 does not explicitly say that a being of subsistent (in the narrow sense: separate) and unchangeable nature is a being in the true sense of the word, or that the science of such a being is the science in question, the context seems to imply as much. (1) The author asserts that such nature (of being), if it exists, is the first and most dominant principle, the divine entity having such a nature (*Met.* 1064 a 36-b 1). (2) He asserts that the science dealing with the most dignified entity (i.e., with the divine) is the best science (*Met.* 1064 b 4-5). (3) The possible science of separate and unchangeable being is introduced as a third science, different from physics and mathematics (*Met.* 1064 a 33-34).

Supposing that one of the three sciences mentioned is the science of being as such and as subsistent, we may infer that the author of K 7 intends to answer the above question in two ways: negatively, by rejecting physics as a candidate for that science; positively, by maintaining that only the science of the separate and unchangeable can be identified with the science in question. We here take the phrase "being as such and as subsistent" (ᾗ ὂν καὶ χωριστόν: *Met.* 1064 a 29) to indicate being in the true sense of the word. Natural things, subsistent but not unchangeable, only fulfill the necessary, not the sufficient condition for being considered beings in the true sense. In the eyes of the author of K 7, separate and unchangeable being is true being.

But the author apparently considers the divine the highest entity in the highest realm of being, and hence the highest of all beings. In *Met.* 1064 b 3-5, he stresses that the theoretical sciences are the best kind of science, and that theology is the best among the theoretical sciences because its subject matter is the most dignified entity.

Our discussion of the first question in K 7 has the result: The science of being as such and as subsistent is not conceived as universal ontology; it is primarily theology.

The second question in K 7 is whether the science of being as such is to be posited as universal (καθόλου) or not (*Met.* 1064 b 6-8). At first glance, this question is confusing. Which science could be more universal than the science of being as such? The question makes sense only if we do not regard that science as the science of being in general, but rather as a science dealing with a particular kind of being. In fact, the example of mathematics in *Met.* 1064 b 8-9 points to the difference between a general science and particular sciences.

As in 1026 a 27-31, there is a disjunction. If there is no realm of being above the realm of natural substances, if subsistent and changeable being is the highest in existence, then physics is the first of the sciences. But if there is a substance of separate and unchangeable nature, the corresponding science must be different from and prior to physics, and it must be universal just by being prior (*Met.* 1064 b 9-14).

Again, mathematics (which deals with non-subsistent entities) is not part of the disjunction. Again the author seems to suggest that the first science can be universal only if it is identical with the science of separate and unchangeable being. The implication again seems to be that this is the highest possible kind of being, somehow including all the weaker senses of being. If—due to the fact that no separate and unchangeable substance exists—physics is the first science, a kind of being can at least be thought of which is not the object of physics and is being in the fullest sense. Therefore, if physics is the first science, the first science is not universal. To study being as such for the author of K 7 means to study being in the strongest sense of the word, thereby encompassing every weaker sense of being; it means to study the separate and unchangeable. And again, the science of separate and unchangeable being is considered to be real only if an entity of such nature exists. "First philosophy" (E 1) and "science of being as such" (K 7) are equivalent terms, since both sciences are subject to the alternatives, physics or the science of separate and unchangeable being. Thus, K 7 is in exact parallel with E 1 in this regard.

The following sketch might clarify the situation:

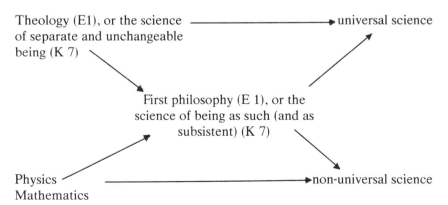

Theology (E1), or the science of separate and unchangeable being (K 7) ⟶ universal science

First philosophy (E 1), or the science of being as such (and as subsistent) (K 7)

Physics
Mathematics ⟶ non-universal science

In the column on the left, we find the sciences that are possible candidates for first philosophy or the science of being as such and as subsistent. Among these Aristotle does not really count mathematics. If theology is first philosophy (in other words, if the science of separate and unchangeable being is the science of being as such), first philosophy (the science of being as such) is universal. If physics is first philosophy (in other words, if physics is the science of being as such), first philosophy (the science of being as such) is not universal.

Conclusion. For Aristotle, the separate and unchangeable οὐσία is the highest type of οὐσία, since it has the highest degree of being which includes all lower degrees of being. To study the separate and unchangeable οὐσία therefore means to study being in the full sense of the word, or being as such. This investigation is universal in that it somehow implies the investigation of being in the weaker senses. However, Aristotle does not appear to conceive the separate and unchangeable οὐσία in terms of an entity which is nothing but being. Moreover, it is doubtful whether Aristotle would allow for the notion of *esse subsistens*. The different conception of the science of being as such presented in Bk. *Γ*, chs. 1-2, and Bk. K, ch. 3, could not be discussed here.

J. Owens pointed to an ambiguity in the meaning of οὐσία as the word is used in Aristotle's *Metaphysics*.[8] Οὐσία has a concrete and an abstract meaning. Sometimes it means the individual *being*, sometimes its *beingness*. (The German language preserves this distinction with the terms "Seiendes" and "Seiendheit.") Adopting this distinction, we may state as a result that the science of separate and unchangeable being (which primarily is theology) has a particular as well as a universal character. Insofar as this science treats of separate and unchangeable beings ("Seiende"), it certainly is particular, just as physics, which deals with natural substances, is a particular science. Insofar as this science inquires into the beingness ("Seiendheit") of separate and unchangeable entities, it is universal, since proper to that beingness is the highest degree of being, encompassing all other (lower) degrees of being.

The Catholic University of America
Washington, D.C.

NOTES

1. All references to Aristotle's *Metaphysics* follow the edition: *Aristotelis Metaphysica*, rec. W. Jaeger, Oxford, 1957.

2. Other possible renditions of this dense passage will not be discussed here.

3. Valuable criticism of some positions regarding this question: H. Wagner, "Zum Prob-

lem des Aristotelischen Metaphysikbegriffs," Id.: *Kritische Philosophie. Systematische und historische Abhandlungen*, hg. v. K. Bärthlein u. W. Flach, Würzburg, 1980, pp. 249-60. W. Jaeger, *Aristoteles. Grundlegung einer Geschichte seiner Entwicklung*, Berlin, 1923, pp. 223-28, maintains that the exposition of the science of the highest being in E 1 is not compatible with the exposition of the universal science of being as such in *Γ*. He assumes that the exposition in E is earlier and Platonic in character, the exposition in *Γ* more Aristotelian. A. Mansion, "Philosophie première, philosophie seconde et métaphysique chez Aristote," *Revue philosophique de Louvain* 56 (1958), p. 180, stresses that the first philosophy is not simply identical with the science of being as such, and that it can rather be looked upon as a culmination of this science.

4. For the following argumentation, see Ph. Merlan, *From Platonism to Neoplatonism*, The Hague, 1960, 2nd ed., pp. 173f., 178, 179. Id., "On the terms 'Metaphysics' and 'Being-qua-Being,'" *The Monist* 52 (1968), pp. 190-92.

5. A. Mansion, "Philosophie première...," pp. 214-20.

6. As W. Jaeger, *Aristoteles,* p. 225 with n. 1, stresses, χωριστόν does not always indicate that which is separated from matter, but can also mean "self-subsisting material entity." Cf. also Jaeger's emendation in 1026 a 14: χωριστὰ instead of ἀχώριστα (*Aristotelis Metaphysica*, p. 122).

7. Cf. Ph. Merlan, "On the terms...," pp. 182-84.

8. J. Owens, *The Doctrine of Being in the Aristotelian "Metaphysics." A Study in the Greek Background of Mediaeval Thought*, Toronto, 1963, 2nd ed., p. 139.

Aristotle on Substance and Predication: A Mediaeval View

by Mary C. Sommers

In chapter four of Book I of the *Posterior Analytics* Aristotle begins a discussion of the things on which demonstration depends. And as preliminary, he determines the meaning of the expressions κατὰ παντὸς to be said "of every case," καθ' αὐτὸ to be said "in itself" and καθόλου to be said "universally." Aristotle's concern in treating of the first and third expressions is to fix their precise meaning in relation to demonstration, since the terms have a broader usage. But in relation to the second expression καθ' αὐτὸ, the question arises, does all of Aristotle's discussion pertain properly to demonstration or only part and, if so, what part? This question is answered variously by his mediaeval commentators.[1]

Aristotle distinguishes four different ways in which something can be said to be "in itself" (καθ' αὐτὸ) and, correspondingly, four ways in which a thing is not said to be "in itself," but "incidentally" (συμβεβηκός).[2] About the first two ways there is no dispute. Each is a characteristic of propositions which occur in demonstrations. A is said to belong to or to be predicated of B "in itself" in the first way, if A belongs "in the account which says what" B is or the definition of B. In this way 'line' is predicated of 'triangle.' In the second way, A is said to be predicated of B "in itself" if B "belongs in the account which makes clear what" A is or the definition of A. 'Straight' and 'curved' are predicated of 'line' in this way. The fourth way is a Gordian knot which will not be gnawed at here.

The third way in which something is said to be "in itself" seems, initially at least, not to be a propositional qualification at all, let alone a quality peculiar to demonstrative propositions.[3] We are alerted to the different status of the third way by the absence of the verb ὑπάρχειν, "belonging to" or "being predicated of" another, which is the operative idea in the other ways.[4] Aristotle, then, is not necessarily talking about a relationship of predication between two things. The contrast between "incidental" and "in itself" which is drawn here is that of those things which are not said (λέγεται) of "some underlying subject" (ὑποκειμένου) and those which are. For example, "what is walking" is "something different walking" and "what is white" is something different being white. A substance, on the other hand, and what "signifies some this, is just what it is without being something else."[5] Socrates or the horse, therefore, is said to be "in itself," since it is not in something

78

else. But when we say "what is walking" or "what is white" we signify two entities, one of which is in the other. Walking *is* what it is through being in Socrates; white is what it is through being in the horse.

The language Aristotle uses in describing the third mode of καθ᾽ αὑτὸ leads us back to the second chapter of the *Categories*, where he distinguishes between those things which are said (λέγεται) of a subject and those which are not.[6] Nothing which is "numerically one" is ever "said of a subject," whether it is one in the category of substance, "the individual man or individual horse" or in any of the remaining categories, "the individual knowledge-of-grammar" or "the individual white."[7] Those things, therefore, which can be said of a subject are without numerical unity, namely, the species and genera either in the category of substance ("man") or of the other categories ("knowledge").[8] In the *Categories* substantial individuals are differentiated from those in other categories as those which are "neither in a subject nor said of a subject."[9] Now it is clear that in the *Posterior Analytics* those things which are "not said of some underlying subject"[10] are limited to individuals in the category of substance; for only one of these could be "just what it is without being something else."[11] Things, therefore, which are to be καθ᾽ αὑτό in the third way are identifiable with the πρώτη οὐσία of the *Categories*.[12]

The mediaeval tradition of commentary, accordingly, has distinguished this third way from the others as a *modus essendi*, rather than a *modus praedicandi*.[13] Here καθ᾽ αὑτό or *per se* "idem est quod 'solitarie'":[14] to exist "in itself" rather than "in another." This amounts to a distinction between primary substance and its accidents although, as Thomas Aquinas points out, secondary substance, which is not "in itself" in this way, is not an accident.[15] But does the third way of calling something "in itself" have only a metaphysical dimension or is it related to propositions and so to demonstration?

On this point, the mediaeval commentators are divided. Averroes flatly denies that this sense of *per se* is "useful for demonstrative propositions." Robert Grosseteste draws no connection between *per se* as a *modus essendi* and predication, nor does Thomas Aquinas in any explicit way. On the other hand, the Ps.-Scotistic commentary and the *Quaestiones* on the *Posterior Analytics* by Walter Burley both posit a connection between *per se tertio modo* and demonstration. The subject of a demonstration considered by itself, not as compared to a predicate, is said to be "in itself" since it is a *per se ens et subsistens*.[16]

Modern commentary too has debated the relation between the *per se* existent, or primary substance, and predication in Aristotle's logic. This debate has been aided materially by the existence of new, literal translations in the Clarendon series of the *Categories* (by J. L. Ackrill) and the *Posterior*

Analytics (by Jonathan Barnes). While W. D. Ross, who produced the critical edition of the *Analytics*, explains that the inclusion of the third mode of *per se* (and the fourth) is "for the sake of completeness,"[17] more recent opinion, led by Jonathan Barnes and D. W. Hamlyn, has held that this mode of *per se* has an important function in Aristotle's theory of predication as a whole.[18] Some commentators have even held that the connection between primary substance and predication which Aristotle describes is that the primary substance is the *only* valid subject of which predications can be made. In contrast, neither Walter Burley nor the Ps.-Scotus mentioned above as endorsing the connection between primary substances and demonstrative propositions limit valid predications to those made concerning primary substances. Following their lead, it can be argued that while Aristotle does draw the connection, he does not intend nor is he compelled by this connection to make primary substance the only valid subject of predication.

It is in chapter twenty-two of Book I of the *Posterior Analytics* that the entity introduced and described in chapter four (with reference to the *Categories*) is connected unmistakably with predication.[19] Here Aristotle makes a distinction between predication ἁπλῶς and predication which is only predication incidentally (κατὰ συμβεβηκὸς), which the ancient commentators denominated respectively "natural" and "unnatural" predication. 'The log is white' is an example of natural predication; 'What is white is a log' is an example of unnatural predication. In the first example, 'white' is predicated of 'log' as log, and not because log is something else; in the second example, 'log' is predicated of 'white' not as white but because white is something else. 'White' is not the underlying subject of which 'log' is said, rather 'log' can only be said of 'white' insofar as 'white' is also said of some underlying subject. We can conclude, then, that a predication is natural when the subject through itself can receive the predicate; and predication is unnatural when the subject cannot receive the predicate through itself, but only through another.

Finally, putting together chapters four and twenty-two of Book I, certain comparisons can be achieved. 'What is white' (τὸ λευκὸν) is said to be συμβεβηκὸς in comparison with a primary substance, e.g., a log, which is καθ᾽ αὑτό. The sentence 'What is white is a log' is said to be a predication κατὰ συμβεβηκὸς in comparison with the sentence 'The log is white' which is predication ἁπλῶς. A proposition, then, which has as its subject something καθ᾽αὑτὸ in the third way will have natural predication; one which has a subject which is συμβεβηκὸς will have unnatural predication. It is clear from these comparisons that the third way in which something can be said to be "in itself," or καθ᾽αὑτὸ, is specifically concerned with the subject terms of predicative sentences. One of the two types of non-predicates outlined in the second chapter of the *Categories* is shown to have a characteristic which fits it to be subjected to predicates. And since it is through propositions with natural predication that "demonstrations demonstrate," the connection of primary substance, or a being $\kappa\alpha\theta'\,\alpha\grave{\upsilon}\tau\grave{o}$ in the third way, with demonstration, becomes explicit.

Now not all $\kappa\alpha\theta'\,\alpha\grave{\upsilon}\tau\grave{o}$ predications in the sense of "natural predications" predicate essentially, that is, where the predicate is contained in the $\lambda\acute{o}\gamma o\varsigma$ of the subject or vice versa.[20] These two further senses of $\kappa\alpha\theta'\alpha\grave{\upsilon}\tau\grave{o}$ outlined in I, 4, separate predications like 'Man is white,' which are natural or $\kappa\alpha\theta'\,\alpha\grave{\upsilon}\tau\grave{o}$ in the broad sense from those like 'Man is an animal' or 'Man is wisdom-loving,' which are $\kappa\alpha\theta'\,\alpha\grave{\upsilon}\tau\grave{o}$ in the strictest sense.

If Aristotle builds his theory of predication and, even more important, of *per se* predication on which demonstration depends, on the notion of a $\kappa\alpha\theta'\,\alpha\grave{\upsilon}\tau\grave{o}$ subject of predication, does this entail that only particular substances can validly accept predicates? According to D. W. Hamlyn, since only particulars have "independent existence," are $\kappa\alpha\theta'\alpha\grave{\upsilon}\tau\grave{o}$, "predication is possible of them alone."[21] For Aristotle, according to Kwame Gyeke, "every predicate...implies a substrate...which is an individual."[22]

Now for neither of these commentators does this imply (1) that Aristotle does not use predications which have universal terms as subjects, such as 'Megalopsychia is intolerance of insults';[23] or (2) that Aristotle had a fully developed notion of what Strawson calls the "incompleteness" of universal or concept-introducing expressions[24] or the reducibility of predications made of them to those made of particular subjects. But each finds that Aristotle's insistence on "the buck stops here" character of primary substances makes them the ultimate subject of any predication. This, Gyeke claims, puts Aristotle in general agreement with the modern logicians who explain every universal or concept-introducing expression as "essentially predicative"[25] and so inadmissible as logical subjects. According to Gyeke, therefore, the statement 'Megalopsychia is intolerance of insult' should be formalized as $(\exists x)$ $(Mx \bullet Ix)$: there exists some x, Alcibiades or Achilles or Ajax, who is both a $\mu\epsilon\gamma\alpha\lambda\acute{o}\psi\upsilon\chi o\varsigma$ and intolerant of insult.[26] The alternative interpretation is that while Aristotle's inquiry into megalopsychia begins with individuals, he nevertheless wishes to discuss this characteristic apart from its historical instances and, therefore, uses the abstract noun rather than the adjective plus a proper name; 'Big-souledness' rather than the 'big-souled Alcibiades.'

George Englebretsen argues that it is a distortion of Aristotle to use the existential quantifier since the notion of an x which is just a 'thing,' not a 'some thing' is repudiated by him in the *Posterior Analytics*.[27] The distortion is, furthermore, an unnecessary one, according to this commentator, since the contemporary dogma of the impropriety of universal terms as logical subjects is breaking down.[28] I would add that it seems excessive to insist that a paradigmatic case like the predication of the genus or an accident of the particular substance ('the man is an animal' or 'the man is white') become an exclusive rule.

First of all, Aristotle's treatment of those interesting statements like 'the musical is white' or 'the white one is a log' is nothing like excommunication. It is clear from the *Topics* I[29] that expressions like 'the sitting one' or 'the talking one' are useful, illuminating, and commonly signify substances as do proper names like 'Socrates.' However, their common signification could be misused to identify substances and accidents. These expressions which are not $\kappa\alpha\theta'\alpha\dot{\upsilon}\tau\dot{o}$ (or *per se*) can nevertheless be subject terms in real predications according to Thomas Aquinas in his commentary on *Posterior Analytics* I, 22, but not in those which function in demonstrative syllogisms.[30] Aquinas interprets Aristotle, correctly, I think, to say that *for the purposes of demonstration* predication will be restricted so that "that which is *after the manner of* 'white'" will be taken "on the part of the predicate, and that which is *after the manner of* 'wood'" will be taken "on the part of the subject" (my emphases).[31] Predication for Aristotle, then, is not limited to attributions to particular substances. Predication $\kappa\alpha\tau\dot{\alpha}\ \sigma\upsilon\mu\beta\epsilon\beta\eta\kappa\dot{o}\varsigma$ is predication, although not explicable as such on its own, but only with reference to predication $\dot{\alpha}\pi\lambda\hat{\omega}\varsigma$.[32]

Furthermore, if Aquinas is correct, it is not only primary substances which are proper subjects of predication in predications $\dot{\alpha}\pi\lambda\hat{\omega}\varsigma$. Not only 'wood' but that which is "after the manner of 'wood'" can be a subject in these predications. This interpretation finds support in the relation between primary and secondary substances outlined in the *Categories*.

The 'said of' relationship which characterizes certain "beings" in chapter two is shown in chapters three and five to ground a hierarchy of logical predications, both within the genera and among the differences of the genera. We are told at the beginning of chapter three that "whenever one thing is predicated of another as of a subject, all things said of what is predicated will be said of the subject also. For example, 'man' is predicated of the individual man and animal of man, so animal will be predicated of the individual man also."[33] While both species and genera "reveal the primary substance," the most informative answer to the question "what is it" is that the species be "said of" the individual.[34] For Aristotle, in contrast to Plato, the relationship between genus and species is dependent upon the individual.[35]

The aptitude of the species to stand as a subject of predication is its "nearness" to the primary substance.[36] It is because the primary substances are subjects ($\dot{\upsilon}\pi o\kappa\hat{\epsilon}\iota\sigma\theta\alpha\iota$) "for all other things" that all other things are either said of them or are in them. "But as the primary substances stand to other things so the species stands to the genus," it is the subject ($\dot{\upsilon}\pi\acute{o}\kappa\epsilon\iota\tau\alpha\iota$) of the genus.[37] Again, the secondary substances together, species and genus, stand as subjects to "everything else." So "everything else" is predicated of secondary substances, assuming of course that they are the types of being that can be said of another, i.e., universals of categories other than substance.[38]

Now it is certainly the case that the statement 'man is animal' is true because Socrates is an animal and that the statement 'some animal is grammatical' is true because Priscian is grammatical.[39] But this does not alter the fact that 'animal' is said of 'man' not of 'Socrates,' and 'grammatical' is said of 'animal,' not of 'Priscian.' What functions like primary substance with respect to something else can, for Aristotle, have this 'something else' said of it.

In the Ps.-Scotistic commentary on the *Posterior Analytics* it is laid down as a "general condition" for the validity of all *per se* predications in whatever mode that the "subject be apt to be subjected (*natum subicii*) and the predicate apt to be predicated (*natum predicari*)."[40] This condition is simply making into a formula Aristotle's discussion at *Posterior Analytics* I, 22, of predication ἁπλῶς and κατὰ συμβεβηκὸς. To be a predication in the strictest sense the subject must receive the predicate through itself, not in virtue of some underlying subject. The formula seems to have been enunciated in order to analyze propositions which have the form of a *per se* mode of predication, but which could produce false conclusions if used in an argument, like 'animal est homo' or 'risibile est homo.' This aptitude for being a subject or a predicate is not something absolute, but is always defined with respect to something else. For example, "'risible' is not apt to be subjected with respect to 'man'; for a property is apt rather to be predicated than to be subjected with respect to a subject."[41] But it is possible, nevertheless, for a proposition with an accident as subject to be *per se*. 'Risibilitas est hominis' is *per se* in the first way because the predicate is contained in the definition of the subject and, according to this commentator, it also obeys the general condition that the subject be an apt subject with respect to its predicate, which the first proposition does not. In 'risibile est homo,' 'risible' does not receive the predicate 'man' *qua* risible, but *qua* Socrates or Plato, that is, insofar as 'man' is said of 'Socrates' or 'Plato.' But in the proposition 'risibilitas est hominis,' the subject 'ability to laugh' or 'sense of humor' accepts the predicate through itself, because it is in virtue of just what it is that it is 'of man' or 'human.'

If Thomas Aquinas and Ps.-Scotus have read Aristotle rightly, the discussion of ἁπλῶς predication in I, 22, does not conclude that all valid predications are of particular substances or are reducible to ones made of particular substances. The chapter can certainly bear the construction they place on it. The basic point of the chapter is an argument against infinite chains of predication, and so against reciprocal predication. While not denying the validity of statements like 'The one standing over there is the murderer,' Aristotle would argue that 'the man is standing' and 'the standing is a man' cannot be equally proper predications. This would allow for an infinite regress up and down in predications in demonstrative syllogisms, i.e., nothing could be proved. Within this context, Aristotle distinguishes, first, between a strict and loose sense of predication and then between predications which involve essential predicates and those which do not. This schema rests upon two extremes: one, which cannot be, strictly speaking, a subject, 'the walking thing,' because it can receive no predicates through itself but receives them incidentally in virtue of some underlying subject; the other, which cannot be a predicate, a "this something," e.g., 'this man,' and which receives all predicates through itself because it is the sort of thing which underlies everything and nothing underlies it. But if the metaphysical distinction between the mode of being of primary substances and that of its accidents grounds Aristotle's discussion of the proper and improper subjects of predication, must these be identified? To assume that they must is to make a category mistake of the first kind described by Joseph Owens in his article "Aristotle on Categories."[42]

It is because a particular substance is metaphysically "in itself" that every predicate attributed to terms signifying "some this" constitutes predication ἁπλῶς. And it is likewise the metaphysical status of an accident which cannot be except it be something else, which makes terms like τὸ λευκὸν, which signify this ontological dependence unable to receive predicates except incidentally or κατὰ συμβεβηκὸς. Nevertheless, these distinctions are analogous, not identical. Logical entities should not be confused with their metaphysical grounding. Thomas Aquinas and the Ps.-Scotistic commentator do not make this confusion. This leads them to define proper subject terms not as those signifying particular substances, but as those which stand to their predicates as particular substances stand to everything: as subject. They allow that terms which signify things which are not "in themselves" metaphysically can be such as logical subjects inasmuch as they are not said of an underlying subject with respect to a particular predicate.

The mediaeval designation of καθ' αὐτὸ or *per se*, in the third way as a *modus essendi* rather than as a *modus praedicandi,* is basically correct, despite the fact that this obscures its connection with predication. For καθ' αὐτὸ in this sense describes a mode of being without reference to which 'man is white' and 'white is man' are equally proper ways of speaking. It is not, strictly speaking, a predicable relationship like the other modes of καθ' αὐτὸ, but it is the *sine qua non* for all other "natural" predicable relationships. In its logical function it can be made into a formula as the Ps.-Scotus has done, to posit a relation between subject and predicate prior to any other relation of καθ' αὐτὸ. If the "general condition" is met that the subject receives the predicate through itself and not through another, then the predication is καθ' αὐτὸ or *per se*, not κατὰ συμβεβηκὸ, or "incidental" *as predication.*

To read Aristotle's discussion of καθ' αὐτὸ in the third way, first as connected with καθ' αὐτὸ predication and, second, as constituting the ground but not the range of these predications has several advantages.

1) The unity of the discussion of the four modes of καθ' αὐτὸ in I, 4, is equivalent to that of the discussion of κατὰ παντὸ, and καθόλου; not a catalogue, each mode is pertinent to demonstrative propositions.

2) The undeniable fact that Aristotle considers species and genera to be proper subjects of predication is acknowledged and given a place in Aristotle's theory of predication. If Aristotle is concerned, against Plato, to extend valid predication to particulars and to ground demonstrative science in the experience of them, he does not go so far as to exclude species and genus as subjects of predication.

3) This reading does not force a construction on propositions like 'megalopsychia is intolerance of insult' which is neither what in ordinary discourse is intended by it, nor what Aristotle seems to mean by it, unless compelled to inexorably by some commentators on account of his commitment to the independence of primary substances.

4) However, this reading can still satisfy what D. W. Hamlyn has rightly called the *sine qua non* of predicating one thing of another for Aristotle: "that this other should be capable of being picked out unambiguously, without reference to anything else."[43] Hamlyn thinks that this can only happen when predications are made of particular substances and says that Aristotle has followed the consequences of his principles to "the extremes." It is Hamlyn, however, who has gone to extremes, and he needs the mediaeval commentators to put him right.

University of St. Thomas
Houston, Texas

NOTES

1. Albertus Magnus, *Liber Primus Posteriorum Analyticorum* tr. 2, c. 9 (*Opera Omnia* I, ed. A. Borgnet, Paris, 1890), pp. 44-45. Averroes, *In libros Posteriorum*, I, t.c. 32 (*Aristotelis cum Averrois Commentariis* v. I, Venetiis Apud Iunctas, 1562; rpt. Frankfurt/Main: Minerva G.m.b.H., 1962), f. 76v D-E: 1&2 *simpliciter*, 4 *per accidens*; Robert Grosseteste, *In Aristotelis Posteriorum Analyticorum* I, 4 (1514 ed.) f. 5rb: 1&2; Ps.-Scotus, *Quaestiones in Libros Posteriorum Analyticorum Aristotelis* I, qq. 16 & 31 (*Opera Omnia I. Duns Scoti* I, ed. L. Wadding, Lyons, 1639; rpt. Hildesheim: Georg Olms, 1968), p. 367, p. 395a: 1, 2, 3; Thomas Aquinas, *In Posteriorum Analyticorum Expositio* I, 1.10, nn. 82-89 (ed. Spiazzi, Taurini, 1964), pp. 180-81: 1, 2, 4; Walter Burley, *Quaestiones Super Librum Posteriorum*, q. 7 (ed. M. C. Sommers, Diss. U. of Toronto 1982) 7.10: 1-4.

2. Aristotle, *Posterior Analytics* I, 4, 73a 34- 73b 24 (ed. W. D. Ross, Oxford, Clarendon Press, 1949; corr. 1965; trans. Jonathan Barnes, Oxford, Clarendon Press, 1975). All translations of the *Posterior Analytics* in this paper are from Barnes.

3. *Post. Anal.* I, 4, 73b 5-10.

4. The verb which is used, λέγεται, can also mean 'being predicated of,' v. Bonitz, *Index Aristotelicus* (Berlin, Reimer, 1870; rpt. Berlin, De Gruyter, 1961), p. 789a. What is significant is that the verb ὑπάρχειν appears in some form in each of the other three ways, and not here.

5. *Post. Anal.* I, 4, 73b 7-8.

6. Aristotle, *Categories* 2, 1a 20-b9 (ed. L. Minio-Paluello, Oxford, OUP, 1946; corr., 1956; trans. J. L. Ackrill, Oxford, OUP, 1963). All translations of the *Categories* in this paper are from Ackrill.

7. *Ibid.*, 1b 6-9.

8. *Ibid.*, 1a 20-23, a 29-b3.

9. *Ibid.*, 1b 3-6.

10. *Post. Anal* I, 4, 73b 5-6.

11. *Ibid.*, b8.

12. *Cat.* 2a 11-14.

13. Averroes, *In lib. Post.* I, t.c. 33, *ed. cit.*, f. 73v D-E; Grosseteste, *In Arist. Post. Anal.* I, 4, *ed. cit.*, f. 5ra; Thomas Aquinas, *In Post. Anal. Exp.* I, l. 10, n. 87, *ed. cit.*, p. 181; Ps.-Scotus, *QQ. in Lib. Post. Anal.* I, q. 31, *ed. cit.*, p. 394b; Burley, *QQ. super Lib. Post.*, q. 7, *ed. cit.*, 7.10.

14. Burley, 7.10.

15. Thomas Aquinas, *In Post. Anal. Exp.* I, l.10, n. 87, *ed. cit.*, p. 181.

16. Ps.-Scotus, *QQ. in Lib. Post. Anal.* I, q. 31, *ed. cit.,* p. 395a; Burley, *QQ. super Lib. Post.,* q. 7, *ed. cit.*, 7.10.

17. *Post. Anal., ed. cit.*, p. 519.

18. *Post. Anal., trans. cit.*, pp. 115-118; D. W. Hamlyn, "Aristotle on Predication," *Phronesis* 6 (1961), pp. 110-125, esp. p. 122.

19. *Post. Anal.* I, 22, 83a 14-17; *trans. cit.*, p. 116.

20. *Ibid.* I, 4, 73a 34-73b 5.

21. Hamlyn, p. 125.

22. Kwame Gyeke, "Aristotle and a Modern Notion of Predication," *Notre Dame Journal of Formal Logic* 15 (1974), p. 618. On this point v. H. Veatch, "St. Thomas' Doctrine of Subject and Predicate," *St. Thomas Aquinas Commemorative Studies II* (ed. A. A. Maurer, Toronto, 1975), pp. 421-22.

23. Cf. *Post. Anal.* II, 13, 97b 15-25.

24. P. F. Strawson, *Individuals* (Doubleday Anchor Books, 1963), p. 193, quoted in Gyeke, p. 616.

25. Cf. G. Frege, *Translations from the Philosophical Writings of Gottlob Freg* (ed. P. Geach and M. Black, Oxford, 1960), pp. 48-50, quoted in Gyeke, p. 616.

26. "It is, of course, possible to analyse the statement...by the universal quantifier rather than by the existential quantifier (x) $(Px \supset Vx)$....But Aristotle would use the existential quantifier since he is already committed to the actual existence of the primary substance, without which nothing else is. But, it should be noted, whichever quantifier is preferred the fact still remains that some individual object, potential or actual, is presupposed as the possessor, or subject of inherence, of the property...." Gyeke, p. 617.

27. *Post. Anal.* II, 7, 92b 14ff.

28. George Englebretsen, "Aristotle on the Subject of Predication," *Notre Dame Journal of Formal Logic* 19 (1978), pp. 614-616. Englebretsen is referring to the "rehabilitation" of the subject-predicate theory of logical syntax in the "new syllogistic" of Fred Sommers v. Sommers, "On a Fregean Dogma," *Problems in the Philosophy of Mathematics*, I (ed. I. Lakatos,

Amsterdam, 1967), pp. 47-81; Englebretsen, "Some Alleged Semantic Correlations," *New Scholasticism* 59 (1986), pp. 490-500.

29. Aristotle, *Topics* I, 7, 103a 29-39 (trans. W. A. Pickard-Cambridge, Oxford, OUP, 1928; rpt. 1971).

30. Thomas Aquinas, *Commentary on the Posterior Analytics* I, l. 33 (trans. F. R. Larcher, O. P., Albany, NY, Magi Books, 1970), pp. 110-111; *ed. cit.*, I, l. 33, nn. 281-2, p. 266.

31. *Ibid.*, p. 111. Aquinas' phrase, *per modum albi (ligni)* reflects the vulgate translation of the *Posterior Analytics* which uses *tamquam album* and *sicut lignum* (*Arist. Lat.* IV, 2, p. 46, 11. 5-6) to render ὡ̓ς τὸ λευκὸν, ὡ̓ς τὸ ξύλον (I, 22, 83a 17-18).

32. K. Gyeke makes this point in "Aristotle on Predication: An Analysis of *Anal. Post.* 83a," *Notre Dame Journal of Formal Logic* 20 (1979), pp. 191-5, but he does so in the context of taking issue with Aristotle. He takes Aristotle's remark that such statements as "that large thing is a log" may not be predication at all (μησαμῶς κατηγορεῖν) as referring to predication in general. It is, however, an adjudication for demonstrative predications only.

33. *Cat.* 3, 1b 10-15. On the problem of 'said of subject' and 'in a subject' in the *Categories* v. G. E. L. Owen, "Inherence," *Phronesis* 10 (1965), pp. 97-105; J. M. E. Moravcsik, "Aristotle on Predication," *Philosophical Review* 76 (1967), pp. 80-96; G. B. Matthews and S. M. Cohen, "The One and the Many," *Review of Metaphysics* 21 (1968), pp. 630-655; R. E. Allen, "Individual Properties in Aristotle's Categories," *Phronesis* 14 (1969), pp. 31-39; James Duerlinger, "Predication and Inherence in Aristotle's *Categories*," *Phronesis* 15 (1970), pp. 179-203; Barrington Jones, "Individuals in Aristotle's *Categories,*" *Phronesis* 17 (1972), pp. 107-123 and "An Introduction to the First Five Chapters of Aristotle's *Categories*," *Phronesis* 20 (1975), pp. 146-172.

34. *Ibid.* 5, 2b 29-31; 8-10.

35. Cf. G. E. L. Owen, "The Platonism of Aristotle," *Articles on Aristotle I: Science* (ed. J. Barnes et al. London: Duckworth, 1975), pp. 21-26. Ps.-Scotus is clearly aware that the special status given the substantial individual in *per se tertio modo* is an anti-platonic doctrine. *Q.Q. in Lib. Post. Anal.*, q. 31, *ed. cit.*, p. 395b.

36. *Cat.* 5, 2b 7-8.

37. *Ibid.*, 15-20.

38. *Ibid.*, 3a 1-3.

39. Cf. *Ibid.*, 2a 34-2b 6.

40. Ps.-Scotus, *QQ. in Lib. Post. Anal.*, qq. 16 & 23, *ed. cit.*, p. 367b, p. 378b.

41. *Ibid.*, q. 16, *ed. cit.*, p. 367b.

42. Joseph Owens, "Aristotle on Categories," *Review of Metaphysics* 14 (1960-1), pp. 83-86.

43. Hamlyn, p. 125.

SECTION II—MIDDLE AGES

Stephen Brown, Chairman
Boston College

Substance in Arabic Philosophy: Al-Farabi's Discussion

by Thérèse-Anne Druart

Philosophers writing in Arabic often use the term "djawhar" as equivalent to the Greek term "ousia" to designate substance. One may wonder why some translators from Greek or Syriac into Arabic selected this particular term and why philosophers adopted it.[1] Translators did not coin the term "djawhar"; they borrowed it from ordinary language. For "ordinary" Arabic speakers of the time, "djawhar" means "gem" and "ore" and can be used metaphorically in various ways. The two basic meanings of "gem" and "ore" do not seem obviously connected to the philosophical notion of substance. Al-Farabi (870-950),[2] one of the first philosophers writing in Arabic, dedicates some pages of his *Book of Letters*[3] to an elucidation of the term "djawhar." According to Muhsin Mahdi's divisions of the text, this analysis of "djawhar" or substance constitutes chapter 13 of part one, i.e., sections 62 through 73.[4] As al-Farabi's discussion of "djawhar" seems to be the first serious Arabic study of substance, it can help us not only to understand al-Farabi's metaphysics but also the metaphysics of his most famous successors Avicenna and Averroes.

In this paper I shall present an analysis of this passage as well as some reflections on its philosophical importance and originality.

In the *Book of Letters*, al-Farabi discusses different philosophical notions.[5] His method is to lay down first the ordinary meaning or meanings of the term, i.e., to explain how and for what "ordinary" people use the term and then to explicate the philosophical notion. The same method applies to his examination of "djawhar." First, he gives the different "ordinary" meanings of the term, including its metaphorical usages. In so doing, he introduces some kind of logical order into these ordinary usages. He then relates the ordinary meanings and usages to the philosophical notion. The chapter,

which is carefully constructed and designed, emphasizes a parallelism between ordinary and philosophical usages and shows great consistency in terminology. This chapter has certainly been well thought through and shows
originality. It does *not* simply repeat Aristotle. Rather it makes the philosophical notion of substance intelligible for any one who uses Arabic. It also
gives some hints of how various philosophers, all anonymous except for
Aristotle, conceive of substance. It does not really present al-Farabi's own
notion of substance but rather explains general philosophical usages. In fact
on some issues it is not easy to determine whether al-Farabi himself shares
the views he expresses.

As I do not know of any translation or study of this chapter, I shall spend
some time summarizing it.

The common usages of "djawhar" (sections 62-66)[6] are grounded into two
basic literal meanings:

1. gem, i.e., stones, such as hyacinth and also pearls, both of which are
considered precious and valuable. Al-Farabi cannot resist indicating at once
that the value of gems is purely conventional since they have no *ontological*
value or perfection. People admire them only for their color and their
external appearance, despite the fact that glitter is low on the scale of
ontological worth. Metaphorically, therefore, ordinary people call a person
they admire for what they deem valuable a "djawhar" among "djawhars,"
i.e., a gem among gems.[7]

2. ore, from which one will extract gold, silver, iron or copper—the ore
being in some way the "matter" or "materials" for the metals.[8] Metaphorically,
Zayd (the Arabic substitute for the traditional Greek "Socrates" used in
logical examples) is said to be of good "djawhar" when his lineage, tribe or
parents are good, i.e., of good manners and morals. Common people, as
al-Farabi calls ordinary people, mean by this ordinary metaphorical usage
that a person derives from a "source material," so to speak, of parents,
lineage or tribe, just as metal originates from ore. So children of parents who
are good either by nature or by habit, are expected to be good as well.[9] Again
some one is said to be of good "djawhar" when his or her natural disposition
is good, i.e., good actions come easily to him or her.[10] A person's disposition
is to the person as the sharpness of the sword is to the sword. In such a view,
the disposition functions as the form in philosophical sense. But perfected
forms can only appear in matters suitably disposed. Therefore the natural
disposition, referred to by "djawhar," is the quiddity (*to ti esti*) of the human
being, i.e., what makes him or her a human being in act. Common people
assume that quality material causes quality thing. For instance, good wood
produces a good bed and good warp and woof made from flax, cotton or
wool will result in a good piece of cloth. All of these are examples of matter
or materials. The materials or matter (and here al-Farabi is interweaving the

ordinary and philosophical meanings of matter or material) constitutes either a part or the whole of a thing's quiddity.[11]

In sum, al-Farabi establishes two "common" usages of the term "djawhar": 1. the stones or gems commonly considered most precious; 2. the quiddity of a thing; that by means of which it has its quiddity; and that which constitutes its essence, be it matter, form, or both together. This second usage is a generalization from "ore" considered as matter for metal. Al-Farabi ends by claiming that in ordinary usage "djawhar" may be absolute, i.e., "djawhar" per se, presumably in the case of the gems, or relative, i.e., "djawhar" for something else, presumably "djawhar" as ore as well as its metaphorical usages as matter or cause and quiddity of something.[12]

This section on ordinary usages in the *Book of Letters* is a striking example of philosophical rationalization of linguistic usages. Here al-Farabi, using basic Aristotelian notions such as form and matter, manages to derive metaphorical from literal usages. A basic classification of "djawhar" as absolute or relative is discretely inserted at the very end of the analysis. Already al-Farabi hints that most of the views of ordinary people are mistaken. For instance, what they value most is gems because of their colorful glitter whereas gems are really of poor ontological worth. They also assume that someone is "made from" his parents, tribe, etc., as from a material when obviously al-Farabi—or would it be more accurate to say a philosopher?—knows better. Building upon his own self-serving interpretation of ordinary language, al-Farabi next sets out to explain the philosophical meanings of "djawhar" or substance (sections 67-73).

At once he classifies the three basic philosophical meanings of this term into the categories of absolute "djawhar" and "djawhar" for something else.[13] The first meaning is the "this" (*tode ti* in Greek) that is not in any way *in* a subject, i.e., the individual particular substance or thing. This of course is absolute "djawhar." The second kind of philosophical "djawhar" is any predicate that makes known the quiddity of such a "this," i.e., a particular "djawhar." Such predicates are the genus, species and differentiae in the category of substance. This is universal "djawhar," the category of substance. It too is absolute "djawhar" since a thing and its intelligible are one and the same, except that the intelligible is the thing only in so far as it exists in the soul and not outside of it. The third and last philosophical division of "djawhar" is that which makes known the quiddity of any thing falling under all categories other than substance and that which makes known that which constitutes its essence. This of course is "djawhar" for something else.[14]

Al-Farabi next examines more closely the two kinds of absolute "djawhars" and explains why they are classified as absolute and why philosophers call them "djawhar." They are absolute because they are independent from all other categories, whereas all other categories depend on the "this" that is not in a subject and on the category of substance. Therefore the category of substance or "djawhar" is ontologically more perfect, more valuable and more worthwhile than all the other categories. Hence philosophers, considering that this "this" and its category are to all other categories as the stones or gems are to anything else in common views, saw fit to transfer to them the name "djawhar."[15] Yet even among absolute "djawhars" there is a hierarchy. The "this" that is *not* in a subject is ontologically more perfect and valuable than its universals and is prior to them. As al-Farabi tells us: "Aristotle calls the 'this' that is not in a subject, primary 'djawhar' and its universals secondary 'djawhars' since the former exists outside the soul while the latter happen afterwards in the soul."[16] Al-Farabi then simply refers the reader to all other points made by Aristotle in the *Categories*.[17]

As for the third philosophical meaning of "djawhar," i.e., relative "djawhar," it derives its name from what "ordinary" people call "djawhar" for something else, such as the "djawhar" of gold, i.e., the ore, the "djawhar" of Zayd, and the "djawhar" of this cloth.[18]

Having explained how the three philosophical meanings of "djawhar" derive from ordinary Arabic usages, al-Farabi refines some points. He considers in what way every kind of particular or universal may or may not be called a "djawhar." Universals in the category of substance are "djawhars" in two ways: as absolute "djawhar" and as "djawhar" for any "this" that is not *in* a subject. Yet, this "this" itself is "djawhar" only in one way, i.e., as absolute "djawhar." The universals of all other categories are only relative "djawhars." As for the "this" *that is in a subject* it is not a "djawhar" in any way.[19]

Having classified and clarified the philosophical meanings of "djawhar" in the framework of the categories, al-Farabi addresses the metaphysical issues which arise from this requirement. His comments here are somewhat influenced by Aristotle's *Metaphysics*. He tells us that one calls the heavens, the celestial bodies, earth, air, water, fire, animals, plants and human beings "djawhars"[20] since they are either a "this" that is not *in* a subject or they make known what such a "this" is. In the same way one calls "djawhar" any thing that is thought to make known what a "this" that is not *in* a subject is or what any of its species is.[21]

Leaving aside these fairly Aristotelian views—though relative substances are not present in Aristotle—al-Farabi next lists other entities that some philosophers (un-named) have thought to be more worthy of the name "djawhars" than the "this" that is not *in* a subject. All these philosophers, al-Farabi notes, think that what makes known what a thing is is what constitutes that thing and also is the cause for this thing's coming to be an essence and a "djawhar" at all. This cause then is not *merely* "djawhar" but rather is more worthy of this designation than anything else. This reasoning leads different philosophers to give substantial priority to different things that make known the quiddity of what Aristotle called primary "djawhars." Some award the highest status to universals, i.e., *genera* or *differentiae*. Others argue for bodies and solids. Some explain bodies and solids by means of length, breadth, and depth, and will therefore privilege these three. Others claim that highest rank be accorded to points since they cause length, breadth, and depth or are prior because they are indivisible. Still others claim that bodies are made of indivisible parts which therefore they consider most "djawhar." Any one who thinks that a "this" that is not *in* a subject is something by means of its matter and that this matter is one—for instance, water, fire, earth, air, etc.—will call this one matter "djawhar" and will deem it more worthy to be absolute "djawhar" as well as "djawhar" for what arises from it. This kind of position leads to various forms of substantial monism which naturally posit only one "djawhar." On the other hand, those who claim that the matter of individual things is a multiplicity—be it finite or infinite—will posit a multiplicity of "djawhars." Finally, some say that individual things happen to be essences by means of the conjunction of matter and form. They will then call "djawhar" both matter and form or whatever thing they deem to be the matter or form and will consider these more worthy to be "djawhar" than the "this" or the species of the "this."[22]

This passage in the *Book of Letters* which presents a review of basic metaphysical positions on substance reminds one somewhat of Aristotle's review of the history of philosophy at the beginning of his *Metaphysics*, in book I, ch. 3 to 6. It also calls to mind Aristotle's queries about what should be considered substance in *Metaphysics*, book VII, ch. 2. Following Aristotle's metaphysical steps, al-Farabi must now discuss whether or not the term "djawhar" can be applied to a divine substance. He tackles this task in a rather obscure fashion.

Recalling well-known Aristotelian views in the *Categories*, al-Farabi reminds us that the individual particular "djawhar" is not a predicate nor is it *of* a subject. Also it is not a "djawhar" for anything else.[23] Yet everything else is predicated *of* it either as predicate *of* the subject or *in* the subject.[24] So the "this" that is not *in* a subject, i.e., the particular substance, is the *ultimate subject* for all categories, though it itself does not have a subject.[25] Having listed all of these qualifications for the particular substance that is to be subject for all the categories, al-Farabi argues that if such a substance is more worthy to be absolute "djawhar" than that which makes known what this substance is, then the one which is not *of* a subject and is *not* in any way subject for anything else will still be more worthy to be "djawhar" since it would be ontologically more perfect and more valuable. Al-Farabi adds that "demonstration shows that there exists an essence of such description"[26] which therefore is more worthy to be "djawhar." Such being is a "djawhar" that is outside of the categories since it is not predicated of anything else nor is it a subject for anything. But, says al-Farabi, one restricts the *appellation* absolute "djawhar" to that which is not *in* a subject or *of* a subject when it is a "this," a sensible object, and when it is a subject for the categories.[27] A being that is beyond the categories, since it is not a subject for anything else, is ontologically more perfect and worthier to be a "djawhar" than the particular substances, yet properly speaking such a being should not be called "djawhar." For al-Farabi, the proper philosophical usage requires confining the term "djawhar" to that which is in the realm of the categories.

Al-Farabi does not offer any precise explanation of the mysterious being that is beyond the categories, i.e., beyond the realm of natural science, though he has already spoken of such a being much earlier and will return to it later on.[28] But in the *Philosophy of Aristotle*, al-Farabi makes the following comment on Aristotle:

> Therefore he had to investigate also whether the substances of the heavenly bodies consist of a nature or a soul or an intellect, or something more perfect than these. These matters are beyond the scope of natural theory. For natural theory includes only what is included in the categories; and it has become evident that there are other instances of being not encompassed by the categories: that is, the Active Intellect and the thing that supplies the heavenly bodies with perpetual circular motion.[29]

So, according to al-Farabi, such beings were already discovered by Aristotle. In his own metaphysical works, for instance, *The Political Regime or the Principles of Beings*,[30] al-Farabi makes it clear that there is an immaterial first cause, the First, from which emanate nine secondary immaterial causes followed by the Active Intellect. The First is equated with God. The First, the nine secondary causes and the Agent or Active Intellect are all beyond the categories.

In the final section[31] of his discussion of "djawhar," al-Farabi sums up his reflections. "Djawhar" is said philosophically in two ways: 1. the ultimate subject; and 2. the quiddity of something. But if someone uses the term in a lax manner and claims that "djawhar" may be said of that which is neither *of* a subject nor *in* a subject and is neither a "this" nor a subject for anything that is among the categories—and one can prove there is such a being—then there will be three kinds of "djawhar" or substance: 1. that which is beyond the categories; 2. the individual particular substance or thing; 3. the quiddity of anything from among the categories. Then again "djawhar" must be subdivided into absolute "djawhar" and "djawhar" for something else. The text ends with this distinction which is the first one introduced in the passage and which concludes the examination of the "ordinary" usages of "djawhar."

In his examination of the philosophical meanings of "djawhar," al-Farabi at times uses technical terminology without explanation. For instance, the reader must already know what "to be said *of* a subject or *in* a subject" means. Aristotle explains it in the *Categories*, ch. 2, and al-Farabi spells it out in another text, his *Paraphrase of the Categories*.[32] Al-Farabi also assumes that the reader knows what is meant by particular "djawhar" and universal "djawhar." In the *Categories*, ch. 3 and 5, Aristotle contrasts the individual particular substance to the genus and the species but does not use the term "universal." Yet in his paraphrase of this passage, al-Farabi emphasizes the contrast in using technical terms for both the individual and the universal.[33] So in the *Book of Letters*, the passage on "djawhar" presupposes that the reader is already acquainted with some of Aristotle's views in the *Categories* as interpreted and presented in al-Farabi's own paraphrase.

Yet the text is far from restricting itself to some remake of the *Categories* and the *Metaphysics*. It links philosophic and "ordinary" usages; it shows how philosophers in some way develop distinctions already dimly perceived by "ordinary" speakers; it also adds a survey of various philosophical conceptions of substance. It queries whether one can properly call "djawhar" or substance a being that would be beyond the realm of the categories. Aristotle does not deal much with this question.

One feature of the text which strikes the reader schooled in Aristotle is that al-Farabi provides a metaphysical interpretation to an Aristotelian logical distinction. In the *Categories*, ch. 5, the distinction between primary and secondary substances is grounded in their various functions for predication. Secondary substances may be predicated of primary ones but the reverse is not true. Al-Farabi, on the other hand, grounds this very same distinction in various degrees of ontological worth as we saw in a passage of the *Book of Letters*.[34] Even in his paraphrase of the *Categories*, al-Farabi gives metaphysical force to this same distinction:

> Individual substances are said to be *primary substances* and universal ones *secondary substances* because individual substances are more worthy to be substances since they are ontologically more perfect than their universals, in as far as they are more fitted to be ontologically self-sufficient and more fitted to be ontologically more independent from anything else since their constitution does not require a subject...As for the universals qua universals, their constitution requires the individual substances.[35]

The reader will recall that the notion of ontological worth was the first philosophical concept to be mentioned in the passage just analyzed. There al-Farabi rejected the "commoner's" high valuation of gems arguing that these gems were in fact of little ontological worth.[36]

Last but not least, al-Farabi neatly sidesteps a major issue in Aristotelian scholarship.[37] Aristotle's views on substance in the *Categories* are incompatible with his account of substance in the *Metaphysics*. For instance, in the *Categories*, secondary substances are genera and species of primary substances. They are therefore universals as al-Farabi himself points to, as we have seen. Yet, in *Metaphysics*, VII, 13-16, Aristotle argues carefully and at length that universals *cannot* be substances and, in VIII, 1, he draws the implication that genus *cannot* be substance.[38] The incompatibility between these views can be solved, either by denying the authenticity of the *Categories* as Suzanne Mansion did,[39] or by claiming that Aristotle changed his views, as Michael Frede recently did.[40] Al-Farabi's own solution is to hide the problem. He simply skips the controversial chapters in *Metaphysics*, VII and VIII, though he uses *Metaphysics*, V, 8, and the beginning of VII. Why al-Farabi adopts this unusual solution is probably another example of his rather devious treatment of Aristotle and of his duplicity. But this is another story.

Georgetown University
  Washington, D.C.

NOTES

1. General studies of the term "djawhar's" philosophical meanings include: 1. Sohleil M. Afnan, *Philosophical Terminology in Arabic and Persian*. Leiden: Brill, 1964, pp. 99-102, which also examines two other Arabic words sometimes used for substance; 2. S. van den Bergh, in the article on "djawhar" in the *Encyclopaedia of Islam*, 2nd ed., vol. II, 1957, pp. 493-494. Neither study refers to the text which I shall analyze.

2. The famous *Epistle of Definitions (Risalat fi'l-Hudud)*, attributed to al-Kindi (d. ca 870), which is probably anterior to Farabi's text, includes a definition of "djawhar" (n. 12, p. 16, Arabic text; p. 31, French translation; and p. 43, commentary, in al-Kindi, *Cinq Epîtres* (Centre d'Histoire des Sciences et des Doctrines. Histoire des Sciences et de la Philosophie arabes). Paris: Editions du CNRS, 1976). This definition is brief, fairly obscure and uses a terminology different from al-Farabi's.

3. *Alfarabi's Book of Letters (Kitab al-Huruf)*, Arabic text ed. with an introduction and notes by Muhsin Mahdi (Recherches, serie 1: pensée arabe et musulmane, vol. xlvi). Beirut: Dar el-Mashreq, 1969.

4. *Ibid.*, pp. 97-105. Henceforth I shall refer only to section numbers.

5. For a study of one of these, namely, the notion of being ("mawdjud"), see: Amina Rachid, "Dieu et l'être selon al-Farabi: le chapitre de "l'être" dans le *Livre des Lettres*," in *Dieu et l'être. Exégèse d'Exode 3, 14 et de Coran 20, 11-24.* Paris: Etudes Augustiniennes, 1978, pp. 179-190.

6. I shall of course leave aside the issue of the linguistic correctness of al-Farabi's analysis of "ordinary" usages of "djawhar" as well as of the historical accuracy of the transfer from "ordinary" to "philosophic" language.

7. Section 62.

8. End of section 62.

9. Section 63.

10. Section 64.

11. Section 65.

12. Section 66.

13. The same classification is worked out at the beginning of the *Book of Letters*, section 5, p. 63.

14. Section 67.

15. Section 68, particularly p. 102, 1. 3-4.

16. Section 68, p. 102, 1. 7-9.

17. Aristotle distinguishes first substance from secondary substances at the beginning of the fifth chapter of the *Categories*, i.e., 2a11-19. The whole of this chapter studies substance which is the first category. Al-Farabi wrote a paraphrase of the *Categories*. The Arabic text along with an English translation has been published by D. M. Dunlop, "Al-Farabi's Paraphrase of the *Categories* of Aristotle," *Islamic Quarterly*, 4 (1958), 168-197 and 5 (1959), 21-54. A more critical edition of the Arabic text has been published by Nihat Keklik, "Abu Nasr al-Farabi'nin Katagoriler Kitabi," *Islam Tetkikleri Enstitüsü Dergisi*, 2 (1958), EK pp. 1-48.

18. Section 69.

19. Section 70 up to p. 103, 1. 5.

20. One finds the same list of "djawhars," except for the human being, in Aristotle's *Metaphysics*, Book VIII, beginning of chapter 1.

21. Section 70 from p. 103, 1. 5 to the end.

22. Section 71.

23. Cf. *Cat.*, ch. II, 1a20-1b6 and *Met.*, V, ch. 8, 1017b13-15.

24. Cf. *Cat.*, 5, 2a34-2b5.

25. Cf. *Cat.*, 5, 2b37-3a1. One finds the expression *ultimate subject* applied to substance in *Met.*, V, 8, 1017 b 23-25 where Aristotle distinguishes two basic meanings of substance, the first one being "the ultimate subject, which is no longer predicated of anything else." See also, *Posterior Analytics*, I, 22.

26. Section 72, p. 105, 1. 3.

27. Section 72.

28. Section 17, p. 69 and section 92, p. 119.

29. Mahdi's translation in his *Alfarabi's Philosophy of Plato and Aristotle*, revised ed. (Cornell Paperbacks). Ithaca, N.Y.: Cornell University Press, 1969, n. 99, p. 129; Arabic ed. by Muhsin Mahdi, Al-Farabi's Philosophy of Aristotle (Falsafat Aristutalis) (Committee on research in Arabic philosophy, Text Series, n. 1). Beirut: Dar Majallat Shi'r, 1961, p. 130, 1. 9-14.

30. Arabic ed. by Fauzi M. Najjar, *Al-Farabi's the Political Regime (Al-Siyasa al-madaniyya also known as the Treatise on the Principles of Beings)*. Beirut: Imprimerie catholique, 1964, first part, pp. 31-69.

31. Section 73.

32. English transl. and Arabic ed. by Dunlop, *op. cit.*, *Islamic Quarterly*, 4 (1958), 183-186 and 169-171; Arabic ed. by Keklik, *op. cit.*, 12-16.

33. English and Arabic by Dunlop, 184-185 and 170-171; Arabic by Keklik, 13-14.

34. Section 68, p. 102.

35. Arabic by Keklik, 14-15; Arabic by Dunlop, p. 170; the emphasis is mine.

36. Section 62.

37. See, for instance, Michael Frede's "The Title, Unity, and Authenticity of the Aristotelian *Categories*," in his *Essays in Ancient Philosophy*. Minneapolis: University of Minnesota Press, 1987, pp. 11-28, which retraces the history of the problem. See also, his "Substance in Aristotle's *Metaphysics*," *op. cit.*, pp. 72-80.

38. 1042a21-22.

39. "La première doctrine de la substance: la substance selon Aristote," *Revue philosophique de Louvain*, 44 (1946), 349-369, and "La doctrine aristotélicienne de la substance et le traité des Catégories," in *Proceedings of the Tenth International Congress of Philosophy*. Amsterdam, August 11-18, 1948. Edited by E. W. Beth, H. J. Pos and J. H. Hollak. Amsterdam: North-Holland Publishing Co., 1949, pp. 337-340. Both articles have been reprinted in Suzanne Mansion, *Etudes aristotéliciennes. Recueil d'articles*, ed. by J. Follon. Louvain-la-Neuve: Editions de l'Institut Supérieur de Philosophie, 1984, pp. |203|-|303|.

40. See the two articles referred to in n. 37.

The Route to Substance in Suarez's *Disputationes Metaphysicae*

by Michael B. Ewbank

When Francisco Suarez's *Disputationes Metaphysicae* were printed in Salamanca in 1597, some 17 years prior to his retirement and 27 years after his career's initiation, the author was fully conscious that he was making available a unique source instrument which, in his judgment, would present all major metaphysical disputations subjected to an expositive method.[1] Suarez, perhaps, was not the first scholastic theologian to offer a systematic treatment of metaphysics as has been often assumed.[2] However, such by no means diminishes the importance of his work in having influenced how subsequent thinkers would understand this discipline.[3] Indeed, Suarez's impact on European thinkers in the seventeenth century has led some to conclude that it was he who originated the distinction between 'metaphysica generalis' or 'ontologia' and 'metaphysica specialis,' and that if anyone deserves to be accused of having committed 'Seinsvergessenheit,' it is he.[4]

The influence of his notion of substance is but one aspect of his doctrine, but it too may have been a latent influence on subsequent metaphysical speculation. After all, Suarez was an advocate of a definition of substance which is well known: "complete substance [is] one being 'per se' and absolute in its genus"; even more clearly, "being 'per se' constitutes substance and being 'in alio' constitutes accident."[5] Moreover, Suarez's acceptance of this definition is not exceptional among scholastic theologians, and he is not unaware that it is but an etymological description.[6] After all, this description of substance derived from Aristotle's texts had been commonly referred to by prior thinkers. Aquinas, for instance, never questions the validity of affirming that substance is 'proprie et per se ens.'[7] However, he offered an important qualification to this description, which we shall consider later.

In examining Suarez's procedure to arrive at his notion of substance, it is well to recall his order of development in the *Disputationes*. The initial section of the work is a lengthy synopsis or detailed index of Aristotle's *Metaphysics* in which he makes frequent references to the following disputations so that the reader may preview his order of development.[8] Before arriving at 'disputatio' 32 for the first significant treatment of substance, one progresses through the following disputations: the concept of being (2); the transcendentals (3-11); the causes of being (12-27); the division of being into infinite and finite (28); the first uncreated Being, whether it exists (29); and what it is (30); the distinction of 'esse' and essence in finite being (31); and finally, the division of created being into substance and accident (32). In focussing upon cardinal issues Suarez considers prior to his analysis of sustance, it is advisable to seek out his determinations where he speaks on his own behalf as a metaphysician, and not as a reporter of the positions of others.[9]

In the initial 'disputatio' Suarez had concluded that the proper object of metaphysics is 'ens inquantum ens reale.' By 'ens' Suarez means not only actually existing beings, but also things that may exist.[10] Since the "essence and unity of a thing are identical or are intrinsically united," one can define metaphysics as "the science which considers being as being, or insofar as it abstracts from matter according to 'esse.'"[11] In order to avoid ambiguity, Suarez utilises what he terms the 'vulgaris distinctio' between formal and objective concept in the following 'disputatio.'

The formal concept is the act or word with which the understanding conceives a thing or common notion; and the objective concept is the thing or notion which, properly and immediately, is known or represented by means of the formal concept.[12] The formal concept of being, thus, unites what is distinct in reality, and is the simplest of all concepts into which all others are resolved. However, to the formal concept of being there corresponds an objective concept which possesses a certain unity inasmuch as all things are similar.[13] The ultimate origin of this concept is somewhat obscure, in that it in some manner presupposes the existence of real immaterial beings or realities as established, although in other contexts it is this very concept that is necessary to attain knowledge of the existence of immaterial things.[14]

As an act of the mind, the formal concept enables the intellect to know either individual things or many things under a common aspect. In the instance of 'ens in quantum ens,' however, the object of the one formal concept is not an act of the intellect, nor an individual being or plurality as such, but rather a plurality only insofar as its members agree in the fact that they are. Comprising one common objective concept of being, it is the consideration of this agreement which designates the object of metaphysics, which is concerned with real things, although not as individuals.[15] Moreover, since 'being' as a noun designates whatever is not a mental fiction or chimera but rather what is true in itself and apt really to exist, and thus it includes 'being' as a participle which signifies "the act of existing as exercised" in an actual existent, it is 'being' as a noun which is metaphysics' objective concept, and upon which analogy is founded.[16] It is 'being' as a noun which, in Suarez's view, bonds together the inequality and commonality of beings. Such is the case, even though it is in fact an extrinsic denomination.[17] This, perhaps, reflects Suarez's tendency to restrict genuine existence to the real order, implying thus, that intentional being is extrinsic to things, and is an extrinsic denomination of the thing known.[18] Regardless, being as a noun is able to fulfill this role because it signifies, in John Doyle's words, "the lowest common intrinsic denominator," that of "non-repugnance or non-contradiction."[19]

It is appropriate that Suarez consider his doctrines regarding objective vs. formal concept and 'being' as substantival vs. 'being' as participial prior to his consideration of substance. Set within the framework of these considerations is a determination of the first division of being. As the arbitor of various positions, Suarez interfaces the judgments of Scotus and that of the 'Thomistae.' After noting that Scotus determined the first division to be between finite/infinite, Suarez brings Soncinas' interpretation of Aquinas into the discussion with his assertion that the first division is between 'ens per se' and 'ens per accidens,' or the one and the many.[20]

Suarez here approaches Scotus' position by dividing being first into 'ens a se' and 'entes ab alio' by insisting that the first division is that which distinguishes created and uncreated being. He recognizes that the divisions of created/uncreated, 'ente' by essence/'ente' by participation, or pure act/ potential mode, coincide under diverse negative concepts and express the same diversity of being. However, created vs. uncreated has a priority even to the division of being into substance and accident because "it possesses a more immediate diversity."[21] Similarly, the division of created vs. uncreated is prior to the division of being into absolute and relative.[22]

An analysis of the 'passiones entis' or transcendentals follows in 'disputatio' 4. Of these, the 'one' or unity is acknowledged as "intimately related to entity and presupposed in a manner by the other passiones" because the latter consist in a certain 'comparatione seu habitudine' of distinct things which cannot be understood without unity.[23] Basically following Aristotle (IV Meta., 3), Suarez concludes that unity adds nothing positive, neither of reason nor real, although it does add to being a negation in the manner of privation.[24] No being which is real or within formal consideration of reason fails to be comprehended within unity.

Suarez must establish that the unity in his univocal notion of being is greater than the unity found in any generic concept, since a univocal concept is equally indifferent to all its inferiors.[25] However, in regard to the notion of being, difference in rank and order of actualization does not derive from the essence of an entity alone. For instance, in reference to substance and accidents, the concept of being is of itself already directed to an order of precedence among its inferiors. As Suarez states:

> The formal content of being (ratio formalis entis) does not descend (descendit) to substance and accident in a fully equal degree, but in a

certain order and in a relation which it (ratio) demands of itself: that is, the 'ratio formalis' is actualized in the substance absolutely and then in the accident with reference to substance.[26]

Apparently, Suarez is offering an appropriation of Scotus' description of being as contracted in its inferiors, although Suarez's tactic is to imply that if one considers being inasmuch as it comprises the diverse contents of beings (ut includit proprias rationes inferiorum), it is analogous, for as such it comprises the order of individual things in relation to one another; but if being is considered not as comprising the diversity of its inferiors, it is not analogous, nor is it univocal, for in each a reference must be given to being's inferiors.[27] A somewhat similar explanation applies to the determination of being, whether to infinite or finite, although each of these determinations as compared to being taken simply is less abstract.[28] Such indicates Suarez's focus, and serves as background for discussing substance as uncreated and created.

Since "uncreated substance is by itself substantially and essentially subsistent," created substance, in contrast, may be either complete or incomplete. If it is the former, it is said to subsist in act, although "not formally and precisely in virtue of its essence, but through a mode or act of its essence, and therefore, substantial nature...is not an act essentially subsisting, but [an act subsisting] by an aptitude."[29] However, if it is incomplete it neither subsists perfectly nor completely, but rather enters into composition, such as one finds in matter and form.[30]

Form, thus, in Suarez's purview is primarily a "simple and incomplete substance, which as the act of matter, constitutes with it the essence of the composite substance," and as such, it is primarily a physical principle that is the 'forma partis' which does not express the whole essence.[31] In contrast, the 'forma totius' is equivalent to the essence and includes the composite's matter, and as such, this is what is abstractly considered in metaphysics, for it is not, strictly speaking, a physically structuring principle.[32]

In considering whether the substantial form is the principle of individuation in material substances, Suarez adverts to Aristotle's affirmation (II *De anima*, 1) that form is that which constitutes the 'tóde ti' or 'this something.' Regarding this, Suarez asserts that the principal foundation for this judgment is the fact that "the principle of individuation ought to be that which intrinsically constitutes 'this' substance and is in the highest manner proper to it." Such cannot be matter alone, but rather the form principally.[33]

Suarez at this point refers to St. Thomas (*De anima*, 1, ad 2), and he subsumes Aquinas' affirmation that "unumquodque secundum idem habet esse et individuationem" within his own "idem est principium unitatis quod entitatis."[34] Suarez's point is not that form is the plenary principle of the individuation of material realities if one refers to their total entity.[35] Rather, it is in speaking formally that a focus upon form is sufficient for the denomination of the individual. In other words, while one may make a conceptual distinction between the common nature and the individual, it is the latter unity which is the basis of the former, and which requires no distinction between itself and the former to be real.[36]

Since, therefore, "the fundament of unity cannot be distinguished from the entity itself," the principle of individuation can "not be either existence or subsistence."[37] One need not look for any other principle outside the singular substance's entity or the intrinsic principles of which its entity are composed since:

> In effect, if one such substance considered physically is simple, it is individuated of itself and by its simple entity; and if it is composed, for example, of matter and form, the principles of its unity as of its entity are the matter, the form, and their union, and thus they are themselves what, taken within the individual are principles of its individuation. On the other hand, those, by being simple, will be of themselves individuals.[38]

Entity itself, therefore, is the principle of individuation. Just as individual unity taken formally can add nothing positive and real to individual entity, since it has the same 'ratio' as all unity, neither can the positive fundament of this unity add anything positive, physically speaking, to the entity denominated one and individual.[39]

In Suarez's portrayal of individuation, matter is recognized as being 'pure potency,' with the reservation that 'pure' should not be understood as excluding "entity and actuality 'secundum quid,'" which is necessary by reason of pure potency." However, what is excluded is every function other than that of passive potency, and the notion of complete or simple act taken absolutely.[40] To give greater precision to this, Suarez distinguishes 'esse in actu' and 'esse actum,' or 'being in act' vs. 'being act.' One can say that matter is in act since this means that matter is within the nature of things and exists. In contrast:

> that matter is act is at least ambiguous, for absolutely, this signifies that it is an acting act, or certainly that it is an act absolutely; and because of this, it cannot be admitted at all without some restricting addition, namely, that it is an imperfect and relative entitative act.[41]

Such is to say that while matter is not an acting or informing act, nor an act which is perfect, this does not prove that it is not an incomplete yet entitative act.

In following Suarez's reasons, one may legitimately wonder whether his elucidation excludes a view of matter as an incomplete substance endowed with a proper partial existence that is distinct from that arising from form.[42] Further, one must then ask whether this understanding does not jeopardize a portrayal of the real unity of composed substance. Suarez hinges his understanding of the unity of substance on a refined doctrine of modality. Substantial mode is present when such establishes the constitution of the substance to which it occurs, and accidental mode is present when what occurs presupposes the completely constituted substance, and affects this in a further manner.[43]

By 'modes,' Suarez means that in created things, in addition to their 'entities,' there are real modes that are positive and which modify said entities by conferring on them something beyond their complete essence as individual and existing. Strictly, modes cannot exist as entities, but they can only modify in reality either substantially or accidentally, although human understanding can establish conceptual modes. As Suarez describes it:

> This is clear from induction. For in quantity, for example, which inheres in a substance, two aspects may be considered: one is the entity of quantity itself, the other is the union or actual inherence of the quantity in the substance. The first we call simply the reality of quantity, comprising whatever pertains to the essence of the individual quantity as it is found in reality, and remains and is preserved even if quantity is separated from its subject. It is impossible to preserve this thing which is this numerical quantity without including the essence of quantity with its intrinsic individuation and actual existence....The second, the inherence, we term a mode of quantity, although not in the general sense in which every quality is usually called a mode of substance...nor is 'mode' used in the general sense in which every contracting or determining principle is usually termed the mode of the thing contracted.... [Nor] is this word taken in the ample meaning in which every determination or limitation affixed to a finite thing according to its measure is usually called a mode...[for] the inherence of quantity is called its mode because it is something affecting it [quantity] and ultimately determining its state and manner of existing, without adding a proper new entity, but merely modifying a preexisting one.[44]

In spite of this refinement, one may still question whether the unity of a composed substance is not that of a unity of two principles of being, but only that of a substantial mode, for in Suarez's view, matter and form are not properly and formally one. Rather, they are only composing a unity in which, apparently, matter conserves its proper 'esse.' As his words indicate:

> ...it is one thing to say that something is one absolutely or relatively, and another to say that two things are a unity in the manner that soul and body are said to be one humanity or that various men are one....The second manner of speaking, in order to be true, ought not to be as much formal as causal...because matter and form properly and formally are not one, but rather they compose a unity, and similarly, various men are not so much a people, as much as they compose a people....[45]

The problems with such a unity would seem to be attenuated if one recalls that "form is not the proper cause of matter...[for] this entity of matter, in regard to its proper, partial, 'esse essentiae,' is simple and distinct from "form."[46]

Within the parameters established by Suarez's procedure as virtually dictated in his point of departure, the view of substance and its unity in terms of a mode of being seem to be consistent. He recognized the etymology of 'substance' as deriving from 'subsistere' or 'substare,' and this led him to attribute two 'rationes' or properties to substance:

> ...one is absolute, that is, to exist in and through itself, a property which, due to its simplicity, we express through the negation of existing in a subject, the other is in a manner relative and consists in sustaining accidents.[47]

In contrast, 'subsistere' signifies 'to exist' or 'to be permanent in being' as opposed to that which only exists apparently. Thus 'subsistere' applies as well to accident which is a true real 'esse.'[48] In the instance of 'substance,' 'subsistere' is understood as meaning "to be under other things as fundament, in the manner that one says that the base is under the column...."[49] In this sense, 'subsistere' is practically equivalent to 'substare,' even though 'subsistentia' is derived from the first and means "the proper reason of being in itself and through itself, by which we explain the proper notion of substance."[50]

Suarez's approach to substance does not lead him to deny the division of substance into first and second, as he clearly affirms that first substance is "substance in a primary and eminent manner, not only by reason of standing under, but also by reason of subsisting, speaking formally of actual subsistence...."[51] In his own mind, then, he is not confused about the logical and metaphysical treatments of substance. His expressed understanding manifests this. However, the sharpness of this recognition is hazed by his efforts to chart a course through terrain disputed by Ockhamist, Scotist, and derivational Thomistic conflicts.[52]

Nurtured intellectually in the environment which fostered the 'tres viae' of

Nominalists, Scotists, and Thomistis, as institutionalised in Spain by Cardinal Cisneros in 1508, Suarez was intensely concerned with finding a 'via media.'[53] Both the form and the content of his literary creation, the *Disputationes,* reflect this. His pattern of exposition evidences in a refracted manner Scotus' view that substance is known by parting from the most general genus, 'ens univocum.'[54] An Ockhamist sensitivity for the singular is perhaps mirrored in Suarez's doctrine of 'entity,' in which even matter, relatively considered, partakes of this status.[55]

In point of fact, the point of departure and overall procedure are practically the inverse of what is implied in the doctrine of Aquinas. This is manifested even in a different definition of substance. As Aquinas affirms:

> To be through itself is not the definition of substance, as Avicenna says. For indeed, being cannot be the genus of a thing, as Aristotle proves, because nothing can be added to being that does not participate in it, while the difference must not participate in the genus. But if substance is susceptible of definition, despite its being the 'genus generalissimum,' that definition should run as follows: Substance is a thing to the quiddity of which it is due to be not in something. And thus the definition of substance will not befit God, who has no quiddity besides his 'esse.' God, therefore, is not in the genus of substance, but is above all substance.[56]

It must be so for Aquinas, since his plenary ordination of the noetic to the ontological complements what he judges to be the radical point of departure for metaphysical knowledge in things. His definition of substance bonds with his elucidation of reality. As Gilson realized after many years of reading Aquinas, yet continuing to spontaneously think of substance in terms approximating Suarez's definition:

> 'To subsist through itself is not the definition of substance.' We know the reason: that alleged definition does not point out the quiddity of the thing, but its 'esse' which, in finite beings, is not their quiddity. Now, where there is not quiddity, there is no thing that subsists, no substance.[57]

For Suarez, however, substance need not be defined as a 'thing.' This seems to be due to his manner of interpreting the data in terms of various interrelated focusses: form/matter; act/potency; and 'esse'/essence. Regarding the first, Suarez's distinction between 'complete' and 'incomplete' substance may be taken as suggesting that substance exists in degrees. When he states that matter and form, each possessing their perfections, are joined in a composite having the combined perfections of both plus the perfection of being a perfect substance, one is reinforced in understanding Suarez as comparing both principles to substance as parts to a whole.[58]

This tendency to permit being to be interpreted in terms of an 'addition' of 'parts' and 'degrees' is extended into the elucidation of limited act. Because of this, and perhaps due to the overall structure of metaphysical procedure sanctioned, matter may be legitimately referred to as 'entity' and declared to possess its own essence or specification, "perhaps even without formal cause."[59] The 'addition' of the entities of matter and form to constitute wholes, viewed from outside the Suarezian 'viae' and 'rationes,' must be understood as implying that potency and act, as well, are mutually complementary 'parts' ordered to each other in a relation. Such readily justifies the accusation that Suarez was not primarily concerned with explaining "how a limited act can be created but rather in that of building up an essence out of its parts—an actual essence if the parts have existence, a merely conceptual essence if they do not."[60] The suspicion raised must be that principles are treated as acts, and that act is identified with perfection, such that anything distinguishable in terms of matter and form is attributed both act and perfection.[61]

Finally, within the procedure advanced by Suarez one may apparently consider act in its diverse functions or manners of existing, and yet speak of the 'ratio actus' without notable concern about equivocation.[62] In contrast, in the procedure advocated by Aquinas, the notion of 'ratio actus' seems to have been avoided in dealing with being as such, and relegated to treatments of acts as operations or to action and passion.[63] Such is necessary to maintain the non-quidditative nature of act and avoid any conversion of act into a 'quod.' However, in Aquinas we are faced with a procedure that departs inductively from the being of things in order to consider the evidence for the non-identity of things and their actual being.[64]

Retrospectively, the contrast between the respective definitions emphasized by both Suarez and Aquinas' words reflects the muted tension discernible in different definitions found in the Aristotelian 'corpus' of writings. As noted many years ago by Suzanne Mansion, there is a tension between the description of substance found in the *Categories* and those found in the *Metaphysics* and other contexts. As she observed, the *Categories,* leaving aside the question of authenticity, offers an alteration of the central Aristotelian notion of substance by substituting "not to be within a subject" for "not to be said of a subject," the former opening the door to imprecisions, not the least of which are: a tendency to grant the universal a sort of subsistence in the mind; and, to permit an imaginative fissure in reality between substance and accident, so that "one can hardly see any more how the subsisting subject and its accidents form a true unity."[65] The coincidence of doctrinal implications described by Mlle Mansion and those discernible in the teaching of Suarez is remarkable. Nor should we overlook the fact that it was this description and focus upon substance which was to preoccupy subsequent thinkers.[66]

As Gilson once observed, the doctrinal equilibrium that any particular great speculator attains is precisely the subject of one of the focusses of any historian of philosophy. However, the internal partial limitation of any one principle by any other in that doctrine does not suppress the inherent demand of each principle to be freely developed subsequently by other thinkers to reveal the totality of its consequences.[67] And none can deny that although Suarez's doctrines appear to be manifestly consistent in terms of conceptual elaboration, his resolution of crucial issues remains in a state of ambiguity.[68] Among these must be included that of substance, which merits more attention than it has to date received, since it is Suarez's doctrine which would have conditioned immediately subsequent treatments of correlative notions such as quantity, quality, relation, and subsistence.

Residencia del C.S.I.C.
Madrid, Spain

NOTES

1. *DM,* prooemium; (I:204). Citations will be to the edition prepared by S. Rábade, S. Caballero, and A. Puigcerver (Madrid: Biblioteca Hispánica de Filosofía, 1960-66), 7 vols., which includes minor corrections of the Paris Vives edition of 1856-78, prepared by C. Berton. Citation order is: Disputation; Section; Number; (Volume: page).

2. The assertion that Suarez was the first scholastic theologian to offer a systematic metaphysics in Europe should be qualified since such was previously executed by the Franciscan Nicolás Bonet, a magister in Theology at Paris in the 1330's and later designated by Pope Clement VI as Bishop of Malta in 1342. Cf. José Riesco Terrero, "Nicolás Bonet escribe una metafísica sistemática dos siglos y medio antes que Suárez," *Salmanticensis* 9(1962), 1-21.

3. E. Lewalter's *Spanische-jesuitische und deutscholtherische Metaphysik des 17 Jahrhunderts* (Hamburg: 1935) suggested an historical thread linking Suarez's notion of 'being' as a noun, through Christian Wolff and others, to establish a basis for Kant's conception of the 'Ding an sich.' Cf. p. 51, n. 1; Gustav Siewerth, in his *Das Schicksal der Metaphysik vom Thomas zu Heidegger* (Einsiedeln: Johannes Verlag, 1959), goes so far as to conclude that there "...ist nicht eine einzige Position der modernen Philosophie von Descartes bis Hegel verständlich ohne das Werk des Suarez..." p. 121. Further documentation may be found in: José Ferrater Mora, "Suarez and Modern Philosophy," *Journal of the History of Ideas* 4(1953), 528-47; and the studies by John P. Doyle, "Suarez on the Analogy of Being," *The Modern Schoolman* 46(1969), 219-49 & 323-41, esp. 221, n. 14; 224, n. 29; 225, n. 30; 244, n. 108; 248, n. 114; 328, n. 157; 332, n. 180; *Idem,* "Prolegomena to a Study of Extrinsic Denomination in the Work of Francis Suarez, S.J." *Vivarium* 22(1984), 121-60, esp. 144, n. 131 & 157-60; *Idem,* "Heidegger and Scholastic Metaphysics," *The Modern Schoolman* 49(1972), 201-20.

4. In 1927, Heidegger charged Suarez with the blame for the division ('Einteilung') of metaphysics into 'general' and 'special' ontology. Cf. *Grundprobleme der Phänomenologie*

(Frankfort am Main: Klostermann, 1975), 112. The assertion was ratified by H. D. Simonin, in his review of Eberhard Conze's *Der Begriff der Metaphysik bei Franciscus Suarez* (Leipzig: Meiner, 1928), in countering the latter's effort to credit Christian Wolff with the deed. Cf. *Bulletin thomiste* 2(1929), 523-28, esp. 527. However, as remarked by Pierre Aubenque, Petrus Fonseca had contrasted 'metaphysica generalis' and that which pertains to theology, by noting that the first treats 'ens quatenus est commune Deo et creaturis.' Fonseca's statements appeared six years earlier than the printing of Suarez's *Disputationes Metaphysicae*. Cf. Fonseca, *In Metaph.*, (Lyon, 1591), 490-504; Pierre Aubenque, *Le Problème de l'être chez Aristote* (Paris: Presses Universitaires de France, ²1966), 279, n. 5. For a defense of Suarez against the charge of 'Seinsvergessenheit,' see Carlos G. Noreña, "Heidegger on Suárez: the 1927 Marburg Lectures," *International Philosophical Quarterly* 23(1983), 407-24.

5. *DM*,32,1,16; (V: 232); & 5;(V:224).

6. Cf. *DM*,32,1 & 2; (V:266-7), where Suarez relies on the authority of Saints Isidore and Augustine to corroborate what is found in Aristotle's *Categories*.

7. For example: see *S.C.G.*, II,95, # 1807; *In I Eth. Nic.*,6, # 80; *In VI Phys.*, 11, # 92; *In Meta.*, VI,9, # 2290; VII,1, # 1248; IX,1, # 1768; 3, # 2197; XI,1, # 2419; 3, # 2199; 12, # 2381; XII,1, # 2417. Duns Scotus, as well, finds no difficulty in assimilating the description in its broad outlines. "Modus enim substantiae est per se esse naturaliter..." *Op. ox.*,III, dist. 1, q. 1, # 15; also, *Ibid.*,II,3,1, # 10.

8. *DM*, (I:20-178).

9. Cf. Norman Wells, "Objective Being: Descartes and His Sources," *The Modern Schoolman* 45(1967), 49-61, esp. 58-9, for cautions regarding the reading of Suarez.

10. Cf. *DM*,2,4,3; (I:416-7).

11. *DM*,1,3,1; (I:256-7).

12. For a comparison by Suarez of this concept with that of 'man,' see *DM*,2,1,1; (I:360-1). For examples of the distinction between formal and objective concept in the writings of Cajetan and Fonseca, see Doyle, "Suarez on the Analogy of Being," 224, n. 29.

13. *DM*,2,2,8; (I:377-8). Concerning the intramental aspect of Suarez's doctrine of 'objective concept,' see E. Elorduy, "El concepto objetivo en Suárez," *Pensamiento* 4(1949), 335-423; and Norman Wells, "Old Bottles and New Wine: A Rejoinder to J. C. Doig," *The New Scholasticism* 53(1979), 515-23.

14. Cf. *DM*,1,1,16; (I: 221) & 1,1,17; (I:222). Here, Suarez differs from Scotus, in that the latter insists that different acts of comprehension must be coordinated with different moments in things, not only in regard to the concept of being, but also to genus-species relationships used in explaining the differences in concepts. As Walter Hoeres states, Suarez seems to base his 'univocatio entis' less immediately in things as independent of cognition than Scotus. Cf. "Francis Suarez and the Teaching of John Duns Scotus on 'Univocatio Entis,'" in *John Duns Scotus: 1265-1965,* ed. by J. K. Ryan and B. M. Bonansea (Washington: Catholic University Press, 1965), 263-90, esp. 272-3 & 288-90. Regarding the Scotistic concept of being, consult Stephen Brown, "Avicenna and the Unity of the Concept of Being: The Interpretations of Henry of Ghent, Duns Scotus, Gerard of Bologna and Peter Aureoli," *Franciscan Studies* 25(1965), 116-50, esp. 123-31. For a critical analysis of Suarez's procedure, consult John Doyle's "The Suarezian Proof for God's Existence," in *History of Philosophy in the Making,* ed. by Linus Thro (Washington: University Press of America, 1982), 105-17.

15. *DM*,2,prooemium; (I:359); & 14; (I:383).

16. *DM*,2,4,12; (I:423); & 3; (I:416).

17. As Suarez notes, when being is said of being as a noun or participle, it is said with analogy of proportionality, which amounts to equivocity that involves an extrinsic denomination, in that the designation is proper in only one instance and improper in the others. Cf. *DM*,2,4,9 (I:421-2) & 28,3,11 (V:228-9).

18. While Suarez does not carry his explication this far, he does insist on the intrinsic character of real existence to the thing as though intentional existence were extrinsic. Such arises, in part, from his concern to invalidate any notion of an eternal essence of the creature prior to the divine act of creation. Cf. *DM*,31,1,1 & 2; (V:11-31).

19. *DM*,2,4,7; (I:419); 5; (I:418). Cf. Doyle, "Suarez on the Analogy of Being," 330-1 & 228-9.

20. Suarez concludes that the nature or 'ratio' of being 'per se' consists in a thing's possessing intrinsically what is required for its essence, and thus it is one entity. Cf. *DM*,4,3,6; (I:517).

21. *DM*,4,8,9; (I:546-7); Regarding Scotus and Soncinas, cf. 4,8,2; (I:540-2).

22. *DM*,4,8,9; (I:547).

23. *DM*,4,prooemium; (I:487); & 4,9,14; (I:560). Note also the following concerning the object of metaphysics taken amply: "...si latius sumatur, nullam habet unitatem, etiam formalem..." *Ibid.*

24. *DM*,4,1,6; (I:491); & 12; (I:495).

25. *DM*,32,2,15; (V:248).

26. *Ibid.*, 14; (V:247).

27. Cf. *DM*,28,3,18; (IV:236-7).

28. *DM*,2,6,7; (I:446). Regarding the ambiguity of Suarez's application of 'precision' to the expression 'being insofar as it is being' and how it may lead to an inversion of the reference of the phrase to the concrete so that it becomes understood as referring to the abstract, consult Joseph Owens, *An Elementary Christian Metaphysics* (Houston: Center for Thomistic Studies, 1985), 66, n. 17. For a listing of other texts in which Suarez treats of 'abstractio' or 'praecisio,' as well as similar usages in Descartes, cf. Norman J. Wells, "Descartes and the Modal Distinction," *The Modern Schoolman* 43 (1965), 1-22, esp. 4, n. 11.

29. *DM*,32,1,7;(V:226).

30. Cf. *DM*,32,1,16; (V:232) & 2,30; (V:257-8), the latter text extending this notion to the rational soul. Also, cf. Aristotle, *Meta.*, VII,3,1028b32ff.

31. *DM*,15,5,1 & 2; (II:682-3).

32. *Ibid.*, 11,1-4; (II:777-81).

33. *DM*,5,4,1; (I:633). Regarding this, see the observations of Jorge J. E. Gracia, *Suarez on Individuation* (Milwaukee: Marquette University Press, 1982), 27, n. 34, & 110-1, nn. 15-22.

34. *DM*,5,4,2; (I:633). Suarez does not seem to advert to Aquinas' view that matter, while 'principium diversitatis secundum numerum' (De trin.,IV,2, ad 3), is 'principium individuationis' only as a foundation or fundament in the order of being. "Dicitur ergo primo modo principium illa pars rei, quae primo generatur, et ex qua generatio rei incipit;...primo in domo fit, est fundamentum." *In V Meta.*,1, # 755. Regarding this, see M. D. Philippe, *L'Etre,* vol. 1 (Paris: Téqui, 1972), 440, n. 14.

35. "Simpliciter vero dicendum est formam solam non esse plenum et adaequatum individuationis principium rerum materialium..." *DM*,5,4,7; (I:637-8) & 5,6; (I:636).

36. "...individuum addere supra naturam communem aliquid ratione distinctum ab illa..." *DM*,5,2,16; (I:582). Cf. Jorge J. E. Gracia, "What the Individual Adds to the Common Nature According to Suarez," *The New Scholasticism* 53 (1979), 221-33, esp. 231-2. Also, note the following: "Since for Suarez, the individuation is intrinsic to the form, such separation [of the form by abstraction] will not result in universalization; the form will remain the form of a particular, and it is only by the comparison and further abstraction of the possible intellect that the form is rendered universal." James F. Ross, *Francis Suarez on Formal and Universal Unity* (Milwaukee: Marquette University Press, 1964), 24.

37. *DM*,6,1; (I:645). 'Entitas' is designated "the real essence of a thing as it exists outside its causes," and is applicable to not only complete substances, but also to incomplete ones. Cf. *DM*,7,1,12 & 19; (II:18 & 26-7).

38. *DM*,5,6,1; (I:644-5).

39. *Ibid.*; (I:645).

40. "...materia non est ita pura potentia quin sit aliquis actus entitativus secundum quid." *DM*,13,5,10; (II:433); also, 11; (II:433-4).

41. *DM*,13,5,12; (II:434-5).

42. *DM*,32,1,16; (V:232); 13,5,7; (II:430).

43. *DM*,32,1,16; (V:232).

44. *DM*,7,1,17; (II:23-5).

45. *DM*,4,3,16; (I:525).

46. "...forma non est propria causa materiae, dans illi formaliter proprium esse quo materia existit...illa entitas materiae, quod proprium esse essentiae partiale, est simplex et condistincta a forma..." *DM*,15,8,7; (II:705).

47. *DM*,32,1,1; (V:267).

48. *Ibid.* "...inde vero derivatum est hoc verbum ad significandum idem quod existere seu permanere in esse..." *Ibid.*,3; (V:268). Regarding diverse usages of 'esse,' consult *DM*,31,1,2; (V:12-3) & 2,11; (V:30-1), where Suarez makes the following equivalences: 'esse veritatis propositionis' = only 'obiectivum quid in intellectu componente' and nothing real; 'esse essentiae' = only 'essentia quatenus praescindit ab existentia' and which, 'si vere condistinguitur ab existentia, nihil rei addit ipsi essentiae, sed solum differt ab illa in modo quo concipitur vel significatur'; 'esse existentiae' = the nature 'in ratione actualis entitatis'; 'esse subsistentiae' = 'contractius quam esse existentiae' and constitutes a thing 'in ratione essendi in se,' thus complementing 'esse inhaerentiae' whereby accident as such is constituted; 'esse existentiae substantiae' = constitution of a nature 'in ratione actualis entitatis.'

49. "...sub aliis esse tamquam eorum fundamentum..." *DM*,32,1,3; (V:269).

50. *Ibid.*

51. "...est primam substantiam esse maxime et per prius substantiam, non tantum in ratione substandi, sed etiam in ratione subsistendi, loquendi formaliter de actuali subsistentia..." *DM*,33,2,18; (V:301).

52. Regarding Suarez's accomplishment in refuting the lingering Avicennan essentialism in the 'Thomistae,' consult: Norman J. Wells, "Existence: History and Problematic," *The Monist* 50(1966), 34-43; *Idem*, "Suarez on the Eternal Truths," *The Modern Schoolman* 58(1981), 73-104 & 259-74, esp. 160-4. For background on the 'Thomistae,' consult Leonard Kennedy, "La Doctrina de la Existencia en la Universidad de Salamanca durante el Siglo XVI," *Archivo Teológico Granadino* 35(1972), 5-71; and Norman J. Wells, "Capreolus on Essence and Existence," *The Modern Schoolman* 38 (1960), 1-24.

53. For an analysis of events preceding this act and its subsequent impact, see Melquiades Andrés, *La teología española en el siglo XVI,* 2 vols. (Madrid: Biblioteca de Autores Cristianos, 1976), esp. I:49-51; 224; & 278-95.

54. Cf. Hoeres, *art. cit.*, esp. 274-7, for similarities between Suarez's treatment and that of Scotus, although Hoeres examines several significant divergences throughout his study.

55. Consult *Summulae Physicorum*,I, ch. 17, pp. 21-2. Note, however, that Ockham here means matter considered amply as referring to whatever has its own proper nature and existence, for in itself, it is pure potency. Cf. Allan B. Wolter, "The Okhamist Critique," in *The Concept of Matter,* ed. by Ernan McMullin (Notre Dame: University of Notre Dame Press, 1963), 14-66, esp. 153-4.

56. *De Pot.*,7,3, ad 4; also: "...haec non est vera definitio substantiae...sed est circumlocutio verae descriptionis..." *Quodlibet*,9, a. un., ad 2. Also, cf. *In I Sent.*, 8,4,2, ad 2, Note, however, that God's substance can be referred to 'largo modo' through analogy. Cf. *Ibid.*, ad primum; also see, for example, *S.T.*, I,8,3; 13,1, ad 3; 7, ad 1; 11, ad 1.

57. Etienne Gilson, "Quasi Definitio Substantiae," in *St. Thomas Aquinas 1274-1974: Commemorative Studies* (Toronto: Pontifical Institute of Medieval Studies, 1974), 2 vols., I:111-29,

esp. 122. Regarding the difficulty of locating the precise words attributed by Aquinas to Avicenna as given in the text cited above in note 56, see Gilson's remarks on 111-14.

58. *DM,*15,7,9; (II:700), & 10; (II:700).

59. *DM,*15,8,7; (II:705).

60. David M. Knight, "Suarez's Approach to Substantial Form," *The Modern Schoolman* 39(1962), 219-39, esp. 237.

61. "...ratio actus ex se perfectionem dicit..." *DM,*15,1,16; (II:647). Form is "praecipuus actus et maxima perfectio rei substantialis." *Ibid.*, 5;(II:636).

62. Suarez's analysis of the significations of 'act' and its modalities, including 'actus simpliciter,' which includes formal perfection, may be found in *DM,*13,5,8; (II:431).

63. For example: *In I Sent.,*4,1,1; *S.T.,*I,50,2; I-II,12,2 & 5; II-II,23,4; 24,1; *In IX Meta.,*7, # 1876. Also, consult Joseph Owens, "The Conclusion of the 'Prima Via,'" in *St. Thomas Aquinas on the Existence of God: Collected Papers of Joseph Owens,* ed. by J. R. Catan (Albany: State University of New York, 1980), 142-68 & 262-74, esp. 159 & accompanying notes.

64. Consult Joseph Owens' monograph "Aquinas on Being and Thing," (Buffalo: Niagara University Press, 1981), esp. 13-15.

65. Cf. Suzanne Mansion, "La première doctrine de la substance: la substance selon Aristote," *Revue Philosophique de Louvain* 44 (1946), 349-69, esp. 366-9; and *Idem,* "La doctrine aristotelicienne de la substance et le traite des Categories," *Proceedings of the Xth International Congress of Philosophy* (Amsterdam: North Holland Publishers, 1949), vol. 1, fasc. 2, 1097-1100, esp. 1098. For references to examinations of this issue prior to those of Mansion, see Michael Frede, *Essays in Ancient Philosophy* (Minneapolis: University of Minnesota Press, 1987), p. 25. Frede's interpretation of the contrasting views of substance may be found synopsized on 26-7; 52-3; 56-7; 64-5; & 79-80.

66. That this description took on the aura of a "definitio complete recepta" is evidenced by its durable service. It is encountered in Descartes' *Quatrièmes réponses, Oeuvres,* 12 vols. (Paris: Adam & Tannery, 1897-1913), IX,39. An echo is discernible in Spinoza's affirmation that substance is "id quod in se est, et per se concipitur...." *Ethica,*I, def. 32, in *Spinoza Opera,* ed. by C. Gebhardt, 4 vols (Heidelberg: C. Winter, 1923-4), II,45. And it is precisely this definition that is easily disposed of by Hume in his *A Treatise of Human Nature,* I,iv,5.

67. Etienne Gilson, "Remarques sur l'expérience en métaphysique," *Proceedings of the Xth International Congress of Philosophy* (Amsterdam: North Holland Publishers, 1953), vol. 4, 5-10, esp. 5-6.

68. For example, textual evidence indicates that in spite of Suarez's effort to purge his doctrine of any specter of a genuinely actual essence, the impact of Scotus' doctrines of 'potentia objective' and 'potentia logica' imprinted on Suarez's own developments the ambiguities of Scotus' 'esse intelligibile' of creatures prior to their creation. This is carefully documented in the introductory study of Norman J. Wells to his translation of *Francis Suarez: On the Essence of Finite Being as Such, On the Existence of That Essence and Their Distinction* (Milwaukee: Marquette University Press, 1983), 3-43, esp. 21-7. For parallel tensions which plague the solutions proposed by Suarez, consult John P. Doyle, "Suarez on the Analogy of Being," esp. 329-41; and *Idem,* "Proelegomena to a Study of Extrinsic Denomination in the Works of Francis Suarez, S.J.,"123-4, nn. 12-13; 126, n. 29; 152, n. 173; and 157-60, for implications that might be derived from ambiguities in Suarez's doctrines, but which he did not hold.

SECTION III — MODERN PHILOSOPHY

Thomas McTighe, Chairman
Georgetown University

The Role of Necessity in Descartes' Metaphysics

by Frederick P. Van De Pitte

In recent years there have been several studies which help us to see that there are interesting dimensions to Descartes' work that have not yet been fully appreciated. In particular, there have been works which attempt to show that Descartes is offering an early (and doubtless incomplete) form of transcendental philosophy.[1] This is, of course, too large a topic to deal with in the present context. But there is an aspect of this perspective which can be expressed briefly, and which is extremely important for our understanding of the essential nature of metaphysics — both old and new.

Without going into great detail, the important point for present purposes is that Descartes is a pivotal figure, permitting us to see very clearly the change in metaphysics from its ancient to its modern form. The traditional aspect of Descartes' metaphysics is most often emphasized by commentators, and his debt to Scholastic philosophy has been clearly established by scholars such as Gilson. But in the *Regulae* we find a new perspective; it is simply stated, yet decisive. In speaking of how we are to attain knowledge, Descartes says:

> ...It is a different matter to consider an individual thing relative to our knowledge, than if it were spoken of according to its actual existence.... Here we are considering things only insofar as they are perceived by the intellect....[2]

We need only recall that Descartes had rejected substantial forms to realize that he is saying we are cut off from the actually existing entity, and must therefore focus on what we are able to perceive concerning it.[3] This places Descartes in a position very much like that of the transcendental philosopher, or perhaps that of the contemporary phenomenologist. Like both of

112

these philosophers, Descartes lacks direct access to any ontological order which his ideas may be supposed to represent. He thus requires an immanent criterion of truth, in virtue of which he can distinguish ideas which represent accurately from those which do not. In most of his works Descartes speaks of clarity and distinctness as his criteria for evaluating ideas; but in the *Regulae* his criterion is definitely necessity.[4] A careful reading of Rule XII reveals that deduction is the process by which we isolate individual simple natures, and then combine them into a conception of a unified, whole entity. And in Rule III, deduction had already been defined as "that which is necessarily concluded from other certain cognitions."[5] Our question, therefore, is: What are the precise role and implications of necessity in Descartes' metaphysics?

There is a very strong tendency to conceive of necessity in the context of metaphysics in terms of the necessity of Being itself. This tendency manifests itself clearly in the history of philosophy: as early as Parmenides, and as late as Spinoza. But if we change our perspective to a consideration of metaphysics as the study of substantial reality insofar as it is possible to attain such knowledge on the basis of commonly accepted (and verifiable) human capacities alone, then necessity must take on a different role. For the necessity of Being itself is not directly accessible to us, and it can be established in speculative arguments only by adopting certain controversial premises, e.g., Spinoza's definition of substance.

When, therefore, Descartes begins his investigation from an epistemological standpoint, and attempts to come to know reality in terms of perception and its implications, we may very well wonder how necessity can enter into his scheme at all. But the answer he gives is both simple and direct: We recognize necessity in the operation of the mind itself. The issue first arises in the early stages of the *Regulae,* when Descartes asserts forcefully that deduction ("the pure illation of one thing from another") cannot be badly performed by an intellect even minimally rational.[6] His point is that if 'deduction' is to mean something other than a wild guess, then it must be the case that particular premises (to whatever extent they may be well or badly understood) *determine* the conclusion which the mind draws from them. More aptly stated, there is an inherent ability in the mind to recognize necessity in conceptual relationships. This is an epistemological statement on the face of it. But, of course, it serves very well to satisfy the need fulfilled by the Scholastic doctrine of the will, which Descartes converts to his own needs. Rather than simply an appetite for the good, he sees the will as an appetite for both the good and the true.[7] We see the correspondence of these two doctrines in Descartes' later statements that the will *cannot fail to assent* to an idea clearly and distinctly conceived,[8] or to a good so conceived.[9] Thus, it is the ontological structure of the will which is really at issue; and

Descartes is at a single stroke asserting the determinate nature of the will, and its capacity to recognize conceptual necessity in virtue of this nature. There is an ambiguity here, of course. But this is precisely the nature of "modern" metaphysics. Its claim is that it is impossible to sever metaphysics from epistemology: the two disciplines (or former disciplines) constitute a single, reciprocal relationship. Our task is to see precisely how the details of this relationship are worked out in Descartes' philosophy.

The first point is that Descartes begins with data empirically given. In the *Regulae* he speaks of such data as "occurring spontaneously";[10] there is no procedure by which we can seek them out. Therefore, we must simply employ our intellectual ability to establish clearly what the significance of the data is.[11] The actual procedure Descartes recommends is well-known. He advises us to break down the given into primary components, which he calls simple natures. But these "natures" are not simple in the ordinary structural sense; nor are they ontologically simple (like a Leibnizian monad). Rather, they are simple in the sense that they cannot be more clearly conceived, and thus they are integral wholes which *must not* be further broken down:

> Here we are concerned with things only insofar as they are perceived by the intellect, and we call simple only those of which the cognition is so clear and distinct that it is not possible for the mind to divide them into other, more distinct cognitions: such are figure, extension, motion, etc....[12]

Figure is the example he discusses, and he points out that, while we could break the conception down into further elements (such as "the limits of an extended thing"), this would not make the original notion more clear; in fact it would obscure the conception by bringing in the abstract element "limits." Clearly it is the *meaning* of these natures which is simple or unitary; and it is out of these elements that Descartes goes on to build the concept or the "essential form" of each entity.[13]

As already mentioned, the process of building such concepts is the first task assigned to deduction. When the simple natures isolated in a particular perception are examined closely, a certain hierarchy can be observed among them: both in terms of their essential or contingent role in the conception of the entity, and (among the essential aspects) in terms of their relative or absolute status. Descartes explains in his commentary on Rule VI what he means by 'relative' and 'absolute,' but essentially his point is that the relationships thus established provide a certain kind of cognitive accessibility. His procedure, therefore, is not to consider particular natures in isolation, or to arrange them in accordance with categories, but rather to make comparisons among them in order to come to know one thing by means of others.[14] Finally, we are to combine elements in our conception of an entity only insofar as we can recognize clearly that the union of one with the other is entirely *necessary*.[15] The resulting conceptual configuration is therefore an interconnection of necessary relationships which constitute the concept (or essential form) of the entity in question.[16]

This very important process of forming universal concepts on the basis of contingent, empirical data is too briefly dealt with, of course. It is worthy of a great deal more attention. But if, for the moment, we acknowledge the possibility that such a process could be made to work, then some very interesting implications can be considered. The first point would be that, given such well-defined units as these concepts, judgments could be formulated which would also be necessary. That is, if the concepts with which we begin are well-defined, then all of the relations among them should be clear, and judgments which express these relationships would be able to provide a necessary network worthy of the title "*scientia.*" Thus the ultimate result of such a project would be a conception of reality which would hang together exclusively in terms of necessary relationships. That is, the conception of each individual substance, as well as the total system of substances, would be characterized by this necessity. Once again, this is to say a great deal in very abbreviated form, but it permits us to observe the precise nature of Descartes' new metaphysics and how it is related to the old.

Descartes begins with the contingent and particular data available to anyone as a normal human being. His claim is that the mind is able to manipulate these data so as to permit the recognition of necessary relationships—both actual and potential—among them. If he is correct, then it would be possible for us, simply on the basis of experience (and the mind's capacity to evaluate it, of course), to deduce a conception of reality which is necessary in the strong sense. That is, because the relationships in terms of which the conception of reality was structured were entirely necessary, it would be impossible for us to consider our conception to be simply one optional version among others, or merely a close approximation to reality. Because it was based not on speculative principles, or mere definitions, but rather on the firm evidence of experience, we would have no alternative but to accept this conception of reality as necessarily true.[17] Nonetheless, this conception would have been formulated entirely without any privileged access to "reality as such" (except, of course, in the form of perceptions).

The second point of interest is that Descartes definitely intended his conceptual scheme to be a reflection of "actually existing reality." He took careful pains to provide a theory of objective and formal reality to ensure that what is present in an idea (as mental content, i.e., objectively) is entirely dependant upon an actually existing (i.e., formal) reality, which it represents. His point here is once again very simple. There must be at least as much reality in the cause as in the effect. More specifically, in epistemological terms, there must be at least as much in the actual entity as is displayed in the representation (the idea).[18] Once again this is a mixture of ontological and epistemological elements. But Descartes holds, quite reasonably, that everything must have a sufficient cause. And since the mind is not able to generate its own data (that which "occurs spontaneously"), then whatever comes to us must have a sufficient cause—which cannot be of less reality than what is represented in our carefully deduced concept. The result of all this is that Descartes very definitely has a correspondence theory of truth, which nonetheless employs an immanent criterion. Necessity is seen as a sufficient criterion for the determination of the adequacy of an idea, and for the truth of judgments based on such an idea. Therefore, Descartes will maintain that his "essential form" is the true form of the object, in spite of the fact that there is no transmission of form or intelligible species from the object to the mind. The result is the same, but Descartes thinks it more efficient to do away with "occult entities" such as substantial forms and intelligible species.

To phrase this in another manner, it is reasonable to assume that Descartes sees conceptual necessity to be a reflection of ontological necessity. The point of introducing the "objective-formal reality" distinction is precisely to assert that there is nothing in the content of our ideas which is not derived directly from their object-causes. Therefore, if we establish that necessity is the essential structural component, both within our ideas and among them, then it must be because there is an actual necessity underlying these ideas in their source. This relationship between ideas and the order of existence is explicitly mentioned by Descartes in his correspondence. In one context, existence is necessarily linked to clarity of conception in the sense that: "...whatever we conceive clearly is true, and so it exists if we conceive that it could not not exist."[19] In another, the content of ideas is said to be necessarily in things.[20] But we have not yet seen the full significance of this correspondence theory of truth which functions in terms of a criterion immanent to consciousness. To complete the picture we must add one additional Cartesian element: the doctrine of eternal truths.

Descartes does not mention this position often, but his correspondence indicates that he was strongly committed to it.[21] The essential element is that the essence, as well as the existence, of all aspects of reality flows from the will of God. Thus, those truths which we call eternal *are* eternal precisely because God has chosen them to be principles of reality. The suggestion that, since God has freely "chosen" these principles, he could equally choose others—implying that current truths could change—is countered by Descartes quite simply. He points out that God *could have* chosen otherwise; but having chosen, he cannot change since his immutable will cannot change.

What is more interesting here, however, is the notion of truth that Descartes is employing: The eternal truths are *created*. What Descartes is offering, therefore, is not merely an epistemological insight. Rather, it is an ontological foundation for the theory of knowledge and method already discussed. Moreover, the concept "truth" is the perfect equivocation to supply that foundation. Occasionally Descartes mentions the identity of being and truth.[22] This is certainly what his comments about eternal truths would prompt us to expect. But from a more complete statement on truth, we can see the depth of his orthodoxy:

> ...The word 'truth,' in the strict sense, denotes the conformity of thought with object; but when one attributes it to things which are outside thought, it signifies only that these things can serve as objects of true thoughts, whether of ours or those of God.[23]

This presents us with a traditional conception of entities which are "true" insofar as they conform to the ideas in the mind of God; and our own ideas which are true insofar as they conform to these entities. Reality so conceived is necessary because it flows from the mind of God. We do not have direct access to the mind of God, but we have the perceptions which he permits us through the senses.[24] By means of these perceptions, the mind can recognize elements of necessity, and gradually work out a coherent conception of reality. And once again we see the intricate role played by necessity.

Descartes must maintain that necessity belongs to the mind: this is a clear criterion for distinguishing between ideas which come to us contingently through the senses, and those ("innate" ideas) which must be true because they display the necessity which cannot be found in experience merely as apprehended. Yet he must also conclude that the necessity which characterizes such ideas ultimately reveals the necessity inherent in an objective order, since the content of our ideas is necessarily in things. That is, we could not find this necessity in the order of ideas (objective reality) unless it were originally present in the order of actual entities (formal reality). And, of course, we must recognize that the mind itself belongs to the order of actual entities. As Descartes' very careful method is employed to generate concepts, we can see that the inherent necessity which they embody is revealed in virtue of the necessary structure of the mind itself: the will as a fixed appetite, and the reflective intellect as its means of operation.

But now let us draw some general conclusions of interest to those who are not directly interested in the work of Descartes. What he was attempting to show us is that substantial forms are an unnecessary ingredient in a theory of knowledge. He believed that the philosophers of his period accepted the theory of substantial forms because they thought such forms to be the only possible explanation for how we can have knowledge of material substance.[25] Descartes thought that he could explain knowledge better without such "occult entities," and thus substantial forms became for him excess baggage.

There is obviously a great deal of room for discussion as to whether the outline of Descartes' epistemology and method presented above could actually fulfill his intentions. But until his theory is proven to be untenable, it stands as an important argument against earlier forms of metaphysics. And, in addition, it helps us to see certain valid aspects in the work of later philosophers which we often tend to overlook. For example, if we are able to employ necessity as an immanent criterion for the truth of our conceptions, then metaphysics as a distinct discipline (i.e., in the old sense) is obsolete. In other words, the order of conception so understood *is* the order of the real; necessity as a criterion absorbs and obliterates "correspondence," since the very notion makes sense only if there is a question as to whether the "two orders" correspond. Necessity rather demands an identity of the two. Indeed, we are still perfectly capable of rationally distinguishing between a reality as it might be in itself and reality as the object of our awareness. But there is no way for us actually to get at this distinction: That is, in fact, being and truth are one, for us, and necessarily so.

If, therefore, we begin from an epistemological standpoint (and where else can we begin, as individuals?), then there is an obvious sense in which Kant is correct in setting aside as irrelevant the "noumenal" order. And Husserl is quite right in bracketing the existence of entities under consideration, i.e., refusing to acknowledge this as a separate question worthy of its own answer. Instead, metaphysics, or the investigation of substantial reality—in its modern form—must be recognized as inseparably bound up with the investigation of the conditions under which it is possible for us to assert that we have *knowledge* of real entities. And, perhaps most important of all, it should be emphasized that this perspective does not leave the modern metaphysician open to accusations of having surrendered to idealism. Descartes, Kant and Husserl are all firmly committed to experience as the source of data from which our investigation must begin. And for each of these men, the question of idealism—like the question of an independently existing real order with which we must somehow compare our thoughts—is simply a vacuous notion. Descartes is correct. What is it to us if someone cares to imagine that reality is not what *we know* it to be (through necessary deduction). If necessity can replace substantial forms as a basis for true knowledge, then questions concerning an independently existing (Aristotelian) substance, and questions concerning idealism, must be consigned to the history of metaphysics.

University of Alberta
Alberta, Canada

NOTES

1. See, e.g., Franz Bader, *Die Ursprünge der Transzendental-philosophie bei Descartes,* 2 vols. (Bonn: Bouvier Verlag H. Grundman, 1979-83); and F. P. Van De Pitte, "Descartes et Kant: Empirisme et innéité," *Études Philosophiques,* 1985, pp. 175-90.

2. *Oeuvres de Descartes* (hereafter AT), ed. C. Adam & P. Tannery, 2nd ed. (Paris: Vrin, 1966-76), Vol. X, p. 418, lines 1-3 & 13-14. See also Rule VIII *(ibid.,* p. 399, lines 5-6).

3. Descartes states clearly that we know substance not directly, but only through our perceptions. See, e.g., *Reply to Objections II* (AT, VII, p. 161, lines 17-23); and *Reply to Objections IV (ibid.,* p. 222, lines 5-9).

4. "Clarity and distinctness" and "necessity" need not be seen as two separate criteria. See "Descartes' Role in the Faith-Reason Controversy," *Philosophy and Phenomenological Research,* XL (1980), pp. 344-53, esp. 346-48.

5. AT, X, p. 369, lines 20-22.

6. *Ibid.,* p. 365, lines 3-6; and again at 368, lines 20-21: *"...ab homine malè fieri non posse...."*

7. See "Descartes' Conception of Human Nature as the Basis for a Humanistic Science," *Man and Value: Essays in Honor of William H. Werkmeister* (Tallahassee: University Presses of Florida, 1981), pp. 28-30.

8. Meditations IV and V (AT, VII, p. 59, lines 1-4; and p. 69, lines 16-18).

9. *Reply to Objections II* (AT, VII, p. 166, lines 3-6).

10. Rule XII (AT, X, p. 411, lines 10-12; and p. 428, line 27, where such data are called "simple proposals").

11. *Ibid.,* pp. 428-29. Descartes mentions here that he has provided procedures for such clarification in the first twelve rules.

12. AT, X, p. 418, lines 13-18. Descartes conceives the process of isolating simple natures very much as we might think of focusing a microscope. Beyond a certain optimal point, we begin to blur what had become clear.

13. *Letter to Regius,* January 1642 (AT, III, p. 506, lines 15-19).

14. Rule XII (AT, X, p. 381, lines 7-21). Actually, what Descartes says here is that the relations are specifically *not* in terms of the categories of the philosophers. Wolfgang Röd sees this shift of emphasis from categories to conditions of knowledge to be the essential indicator of a transition from "old" to "modern" metaphysics. See "The Method of Descartes' Metaphysics," read by Prof. Röd at a Descartes Symposium, University of Alberta, September 1985.

15. Rule XII (AT, X, p. 421, lines 3-8; and p. 425, lines 1-3).

16. The essential relationships among elements in a perception are disclosed by a process of imaginative variation much like that employed by Husserl and C. S. Peirce in the present century. The concept which results from this process is an "innate idea" because the mind has contributed the necessary conceptual relationships which were not present in the original perception. See "Descartes' Innate Ideas," *Kant-Studien,* LXXVI (1985), pp. 363-84.

17. This is what Descartes means in that curious passage in the *Replies to Objections II:* "What is it to us, then, if someone should imagine that this (of the truth of which we are so firmly persuaded) appears false to God or to an angel, and therefore—absolutely speaking—is false? What care we for this 'absolute falsity' since we in no sense believe in it, nor have even a slight suspicion of it" (AT, VII, p. 145, lines 1-6).

18. Descartes acknowledges that there may very well be many properties in an entity of which

we are not aware, but he denies that there are any which are inconsistent with what we do know. *Letter to Gibieuf,* 19 January 1642 (AT, III, p. 478, lines 6-9).

    19. *Letter to Mersenne,* March 1642 (AT, III, p. 545, lines 1-3).

    20. *Letter to Gibieuf,* 19 January 1642 (AT, III, p. 474, lines 18-20).

    21. See E. Bréhier, "The Creation of Eternal Truths in Descartes's System," *Descartes: A Collection of Critical Essays,* ed. Willis Doney (Garden City, New York: Doubleday Anchor Books, 1967), pp. 192-208.

    22. "Truth consists in being, and falsity only in non-being..." *Letter to Clerselier,* 23 April 1649 (AT, V, p. 354, lines 7-8).

    23. *Letter to Mersenne,* 16 October 1639 (AT, II, p. 597, lines 11-16).

    24. *Letter to* [*Silhon*], March 1648 (AT, V, pp. 133-35).

    25. *Letter to Mersenne,* 26 April 1643 (AT, III, pp. 648-49).

Spinoza's Conception of the Attributes of Substance

by James H. Husted

For Spinoza "Substance," "Existence," "God" and "Nature" are synonymous terms denoting all that is, being itself. Substance or God exists in infinite ways and Spinoza calls these ways of existing "attributes." Of these ways of existing two are given to man's awareness. These Spinoza calls "extension" and "thought." Historically many, and perhaps most, of the attacks on Spinoza's system have come by way of the attribute of thought. The project of this paper is to re-examine the attribute of thought and turn aside the force of these attacks.

Spinoza understands Substance as "…that which is in itself and conceived through itself,"[1] attribute as "…that which the intellect perceives as constituting the essence of Substance."[2] Substance is the fundamental reality, which must be conceived immediately and ostensively,[3] while the experienced variety of the universe must be explained through the attributes of Substance.[4]

Spinoza's description of Substance might well be read, without distortion, as "…that of which a conception [must] be formed, [and] independently of any other conception."[5] For Substance is existence itself[6] and the attributes of Substance must be perceived before any reasoning process can get under way, perceived as most necessary to conception[7] and as fundamental to existence.[8]

But we have no experience whatever of universal consciousness coextensive with, nor even analogous to, our experience of extension. We think and experience our thinking processes.[9] We experience or infer the thoughts of other thinking beings. But we never experience nor have grounds to infer the thinking of trees and stones.[10] Not this side of sanity do we perceive the thought of all of extended nature.[11] Here lies the fundamental problem—the solution of which is the key to the solution of all the apparent problems with Spinoza's concept of Substance. And that problem, quite simply, is this: What is it, precisely, that is perceived when the attributes of Substance are perceived. If we can discover this our experience of the attribute of thought— as such—should become as immediate as our experience of extension.

Spinoza's descriptions of the attributes and of Substance impose a number of rigid strictures upon any objective understanding of the attributes. These strictures arise from and demarcate what can be true of the attributes, compatibly with Spinoza's descriptions, and with our own experience.[12]

According to what we have covered so far one stricture is evident. The first stricture is: The attributes must be immediately impressed on the intellect prior to any reasoning process, and simply by virtue of the intellect being aware.

A most important stricture arises as the result of an apparent clash between Spinoza's definitions and our experience. First he tells us that the attributes are "...that which the intellect perceives..."[13] and then that "Substance consists of infinite attributes..."[14] Each attribute must be perceived by the intellect and be conceivable as infinite. This is the second stricture.

Next, the attributes are that which is perceived "as constituting the essence of Substance"[15] and essence is "that which being given the thing is necessarily given also, and which being removed, the thing is necessarily removed also."[16] The third stricture is: The attributes must be that which the intellect perceives as being the essence of Substance, as being fundamental to existence itself.

In a letter G. H. Schaller, Spinoza's friend and physician, stated that while he agreed that man is acquainted with no modes that involve or express any attribute other than extension or thought he yet requested a proof "...that we cannot know more attributes of God than thought or extension."[17] Spinoza replied that "...the origin of the knowledge of the human mind is the body's experience of modes."[18] He spoke of conceiving "...nature under the attribute of extension, or under the attribute of thought or under any other attribute."[19] He also said, "We feel and perceive no particular things save bodies and modes of thought."[20] In view of this the attributes must constitute their modes and two attributes must exhaust the perceptual and conceptual possibilities of the modes which fall under our experience. The fourth stricture is: Thought and extension must be irreducible elements and exhaustive of the perceptual and conceptual possibilities of the modes which we experience.

If there is a real identity in Substance between the attributes and if the intellect has a true[21] and adequate[22] idea of the attributes then given extension existence is given also and if extension is removed existence is removed. Given thought existence is also given and if thought is removed existence is removed.[23] If existence is given both thought and extension must be given.[24] The attribute of thought must be such that given thought extension must be given also and given extension thought must also be given—without the other neither can be nor be conceived. The fifth stricture is: The nature of the attribute of thought must be such that without extension it can neither be nor be conceived and without the attribute of thought neither extension nor existence can be nor be conceived.

Then: The attributes constituting the essence of Substance belong to only one Substance, consequently there can be no difference in the conception of

Substance whether it is conceived under the attribute of extension or the attribute of thought.[25] This is the sixth stricture.

Again: Substance is absolutely infinite.[26] But that of which we can deny infinite attributes can be infinite only in its own kind—a sense of "infinity" which involves negation.[27] And we can deny infinite attributes of the infinite attributes. Thus the attributes are infinite only in their own kind—with a sense of "infinity" which involves negation. The seventh stricture is: Each attribute must be conceivable as infinite but not as Substance is infinite for this conception of infinity must involve negation.

If the intellect perceives thought as it is not or extension as it is not then we possess neither an adequate nor a true idea of either. If we do not possess an adequate and true idea of the attributes then we do not possess an adequate and true idea of Substance. But Substance is the keystone of Spinoza's philosophy. He claims that Substance can be defined[28] ostensively;[29] the mind is capable of knowing Substance: "...the mind's highest virtue is to know God";[30] that "the human mind possesses an adequate knowledge of the eternal and infinite essence of God."[31] And finally that "...a definition [in contrast with an axiom] explains a thing insofar as it is external to the intellect."[32] It must be the case then that the attributes are open to a perception which can serve as the basis for a true and adequate idea of Substance. The eighth stricture is: The attributes must be objective aspects of Substance, amenable to the formation of a true and adequate idea by the intellect.

If we are to obtain a true and adequate idea of the attribute of thought we must allow for an intimate relationship between the attribute of thought and the possibilities of God's power of action for "God's power of thinking is equal to his realized power of action."[33] The ninth stricture is: The attribute of thought must be the ground of the connection between God's thought and action.

Another, and major, problem is: How the attributes can be perceivable as different attributes,[34] and yet be one in Substance[35] and coextensive.[36] This is the tenth stricture.

In light of the strictures on Spinoza's conception of Substance one thing is abundantly clear. If Spinoza understood by the attribute of thought a universal and infinite state of awareness or discursive process his system is insuperably untenable.

If the attribute of thought is a psychological, discursive state or process:

1. It cannot be given prior to any reasoning process for it would itself be a reasoning process and the first stricture would be violated.[37]

2. It is not conceivable as being the essence of Substance—"...that...which being removed [Substance] is necessarily removed also..."[38]—certainly not at the same time as extension is conceived as being the essence of Substance,

for a 'truncated' universe, a universe devoid of thought, is conceivable. The conception of thought as psychological violates the third stricture.

3. The fourth stricture is violated, for the attributes do not exhaust the perceptual possibilities of the modes we experience. For we experience a diversity among the modes which would not be possible if extension and a psychological state exhausted the list of perceptible attributes. (Nor would a psychological state or process, as such, be possible.)

4. The intelligibility demanded by the first stricture is lost and the attributes are not amenable to the formation of a true and adequate idea by the intellect. In consequence, the eighth stricture is violated.

No reason is given by Spinoza, nor does experience give us any reason to believe that extension and discursive reasoning are identical in Substance. Quite the contrary. When Spinoza compares the relation of the human and the divine intellects to that between the dog which is a barking animal and the "Dog" which is a stellar constellation he is obviously establishing the widest possible gulf between the attribute of Substance and human thought processes. Human thought and the attribute of thought are different in kind.[39]

Whereas extension is the power of God expressed as extensity and dimensionality, I suggest that thought must be understood as the power of God expressed in His production of that which I will call quiddity—the specific nature and consequent intelligibility of all things—that by which they are known to be and known to be what they are and that by which they *are* what they are.

This suggestion is hardly revolutionary, for according to Spinoza's understanding, "...the intellect of God...is, in reality, the cause of things, both of their essence and of their existence."[40] And this is the only understanding of the attribute of thought compatible with the strictures implicitly or explicitly involved in Spinoza's system; the only understanding which can resolve the apparent problems of Spinoza's conception of the attribute of thought.

And these strictures and problems are resolved as follows:

1. The attributes must be immediately impressed on the intellect prior to any reasoning process, and simply by virtue of the intellect being aware. The attributes are impressed on the intellect as passive—for perception requires an external and discriminable object and externality and discrimination require extension and quiddity—which is precisely what the attributes are. Perception is given prior to any reasoning process. The structure of a reasoning process depends on and is determined by the quiddities of the realities that are the objects of that process. The objectivity of a reasoning process depends on the existence of these realities in extension, i.e., as objects.

2. Each attribute must be perceived by the intellect and be conceivable as infinite. The intellect perceives nothing as inextended. The intellect is conscious of nothing as lacking in quiddity. And the nature of Substance (of the attributes) compels the mind to the conclusion that extension is unlimited and quiddity is universal.

3. *The attributes must be that which the intellect perceives as being the essence of Substance, as being fundamental to existence itself.* Every mode must be somewhere in existence and be of some specific nature. A substance whose dynamic activity produces modes, consequently, must be and be perceived as being extended and possessed of the power to produce quiddity.

If the 'quidditativeness' of existence is given then existence is given and if taken away then taken away. If the extensity of existence is given then existence is given and if taken away then taken away. On this radical a level this is true of no other 'category' of existence.

4. *Thought and extension must be irreducible elements and exhaustive of the perceptual and conceptual possibilities of the modes which we experience.* A mode without a spatio/temporal location or lacking a quiddity would not exist. The attainment of a quiddity or a location is not a task given to a mode after it comes into existence.[41] When it arises from an attribute it arises as a mode of that attribute.[42]

As thought and extension are the two attributes given to perception "as constituting the essence of Substance"[43] so the quiddity and the extension of a mode must be given to the intellect in order for the mode to be perceived and to be an intelligible object of the intellect.

5. *The nature of the attribute of thought must be such that without extension it can neither be nor be conceived and without the attribute of thought neither extension nor existence can be nor be conceived.* If we abstract either extension or quiddity from our conception of existence we are left with nothing for our conception to be a conception of.[44] At the same time an existence lacking extension or quiddity is not existence at all. Substance lacking attributes is existence lacking existence.[45] Without extension quiddity would characterize nothing at all and without quiddity there would be nothing to be extended.

6. *The attributes constituting the essence of Substance belong to only one Substance, consequently there can be no difference in the conception of Substance whether it is conceived under the attribute of extension or the attribute of thought.* What a thing is and that it is extended are two ways of regarding that which, in reality, is one. If anything possesses a quiddity it must, in that way, be extended. If anything exists and is extended then it must possess a quiddity. Between thought and extension there is a virtual distinction. They can never be, nor be perceived as, separate. And while they can be conceived separately they can never be conceived as separate.

7. *Each attribute must be conceivable as infinite but not as Substance is*

infinite for this conception of infinity must involve negation. While the attributes are manifested immediately by Substance, the modes of Substance are produced by the attributes in an infinite chain of causes.[46] This production of modes is a determination of the attributes themselves and determination involves a partial negation.[47] Yet determinate modes are necessary to an infinite Substance as infinite, otherwise "God understands an infinite number of creatable things which he will never be able to create."[48]

On the one hand a mode of thought can be the idea of an idea and, thus, related to extension only in a derivative (albeit a real) sense. Thought as "infinite in its own kind"[49] refers to a psychological and quidditative infinity—a universality, a 'centripetal' infinity.[50] On the other hand, as infinite extension, existence, so to speak, requires less of thought, "…the whole of matter considered indefinitely can have no figure and figure can only exist in finite and determinate bodies."[51] Extension as "infinite in its own kind"[52] extends beyond the primary manifestation of the attribute of thought—beyond figure, into a 'centrifugal' infinity.

8. The attributes must be objective aspects of Substance, amenable to the formation of a true and adequate idea by the intellect. The attributes are not only amenable but essential to the formation of a true and adequate idea by the intellect. Extension is the *conditio sine qua non* of the formation of an objective idea as objective while quiddity is the essential precondition of an intelligible idea as intelligible. The intellect can form no idea, let alone objective, true and adequate ideas, without relying on extension and quiddity.

9. The attribute of thought must be the ground of the connection between God's thought and action. Quiddity is the ground of the connection between God's thought and action. The nature of any action is determined by the nature of that which acts.[53] Nothing can act in opposition to its nature, its nature being that which determines its potentialities for action. "For the power of each thing is defined only by its essence."[54]

10. The attributes must be perceivable as different attributes and yet be one in Substance and coextensive. The coextensiveness of the attributes does not mean an identity of extension for thought is not extended simpliciter. Nor an identity of quiddity for extension is not quiddity.[55] Substance consists of extension, which is qualified, made real and given being by thought, and of thought, which is given its expression and reality in extension. The attribute of thought produces the modes of thought including the individual thoughts of thinking beings—thought contracting itself into quiddity's psychological reverberations. The attribute of extension expands into an ultimately formless infinity, qualified, perhaps, only by the quiddity of that which it is to be. At the same time the order and connection of ideas and the order and connection of things are the same order "…constituting the essence of Substance...consequently Substance thinking and Substance extended are one and the same Substance, which is comprehended now through one attribute and now through the other."⁵⁶

The coextensiveness of thought and extension cannot mean a one to one relationship between bodies and ideas. For this would mean that the infinity of thought and extension would be a numerical infinity—an infinite number of bodies and corollary ideas. Which would mean that existence would be exhausted in modes.

But Spinoza regards number as an *ens rationis,* a "...mode of thinking, or rather of imagining....Eternity and Substance, being only conceivable as infinite, cannot be [conceived as greater or less, or divided into parts] without our conception of them being destroyed."⁵⁷ And the infinity of Substance is an infinity of perfection and power.⁵⁸ The coextensiveness of the attributes is not a numerical coextensiveness but one of 'internal relations.' "...each body insofar as it exists as modified in a particular manner, must be considered as a part of the whole universe, as agreeing with the whole and associated with the remaining parts...there exists in nature an infinite power of thinking, which insofar as it is infinite, contains subjectively the whole of nature."⁵⁹

Of this power of thinking Spinoza says "...neither intellect nor will appertain to God's nature."⁶⁰ Intellect and will are entirely inappropriate to God's nature. If discursive reasoning and desire did pertain to God's nature there would be things unknown to Him and things which He lacked and needed. Therefore the attribute of thought is "...as far as the poles from the human intellect."⁶¹

"From God's supreme power or infinite nature...all things have necessarily flowed forth....Wherefore the omnipotence of God has been displayed from all eternity."⁶² If all things flow from God with a 'tautological' necessity⁶³ and if he is omnipotent⁶⁴ then the attribute of thought cannot consist in an impotent "order of ideas" passively contemplating the attribute of extension. If thought and extension are not two things but two aspects of the same one thing, namely Substance, it is not possible that one is creative and the other is merely discursive, i.e., non-creative.

In a letter written in June of 1676 Ehrenfried von Tschirnhausen, a German industrialist and scholar, inquired of Spinoza how, in view of his conception of Substance, the existence of modes is possible, "...how, from the conception of extension...the variety of the universe can be shown *a priori.*⁶⁵ To this inquiry Spinoza made a most remarkable reply. He answered that the variety of the universe cannot be explained through the attribute of extension, but that "...it must necessarily be explained through an attribute which expresses eternal and infinite essence....Hitherto I have not been able to put any of these matters into due order...if my life is prolonged, I may discuss the subject more clearly."⁶⁶

One may wonder if Spinoza has not, in fact, put these matters into sufficient order and discussed them quite clearly.

If the variety of the universe cannot be explained through the attribute of extension,[67] if man knows no attributes other than thought and extension and if the variety of the universe can be explained it must, obviously, be explained through the attribute of thought.[68] Which is precisely how Spinoza does explain it.

Spinoza asserts that "The knowledge of an effect depends on and involves the knowledge of a cause."[69] And then he tells us that:

> ...the omnipotence of God...will for all eternity remain in the same state of activity...otherwise we are compelled to confess that God understands an infinite number of creatable things which He will never be able to create, for, if He created all that he understands, He would, according to this showing exhaust His omnipotence and render Himself imperfect.[70]

I suggest that the only ground for the assertion that God "...will for all eternity remain in the same state [of the same kind] of creative activity" is the conception of this activity as guided by something other than an ultimately formless extension. I also suggest that this is necessary to justify the assertion of an essential connection between God's activity and his understanding.[71] For God's intellect and His essence are identical,[72] and the essence and power of God are identical.[73] Therefore all that is in the power of God[74] and all things which fall within the sphere of infinite intellect[75] are necessarily the case. Not because the divine intellect is "posterior to or simultaneous with the things understood [since] God is prior to all things by reason of his causality."[76] Rather, because "God's intellect, God's will, and God's power are one and the same...[and] therefore, God's intellect is the sole cause of things...both of their essence and existence...."[77]

And I suggest that this is true both of things which exist and things which do not exist. A particular thing which does not exist, e.g., a triangle, has the same essential nature as one which does exist.[78] The idea of a triangle which does not exist must refer to the quiddity of the triangle not to its (non-existent) extensity—to the thing qua being of thought, not qua mode of extension. If the idea of a particular thing which does not exist is the idea of a mode of extension then both that which exists and that which does not exist are extended—and extension is infinite twice over. The attribute of thought has the potential to contain any and every possible body. But thought, of itself, cannot constitute a body. Nor can extension, as such, constitute a quiddity.

Any conception of the attribute of thought other than the one I have proposed rends the intimacy essential to the attributes, which are, *"formaliter,"* one thing conceived in two different ways.[79] Therefore I suggest that, in Spinoza's system, whereas extension is the power of Substance expressed in dimension and extensity, thought is the power of Substance expressed in the production of the quiddity of all things—an attribute from which "the variety of the universe can be deduced...an attribute which expresses eternal and infinite essence"[80] and, therefore, eternal and infinite power.[81]

Finally I would suggest that for this essence and power to "...for all eternity remain in the same state of activity...."[82] Substance must be characterized by eternal and infinite modal change.[83] And motion alone is not sufficient to explain the infinite variation of infinite modes.[84]

All change involves a movement from one quiddity to another.[85] Yet if every quiddity were the product of a change from another quiddity without an initial or permanent quiddity, as would be the case if the structural nature of change were governed, not by the procession of quiddity from the attribute of thought, but by infinite motion alone,[86] there would be no initial or permanent quiddity,[87] therefore no quiddity and no change at all. In addition to infinite motion there must be a principle prior to change and this principle *must* be quiddity. Without quiddity there is no causation.[88] Without causation there is no change.[89]

Acting "...solely by the laws of His own nature..."[90] "...God is the absolutely first cause..."[91] "...of all that can fall within the sphere of an infinite intellect."[92] An intellect which is synonymous with his power[93] and therefore with his essence[94] and which is "...the cause of things, both of their essence and of their existence."[95]

If extension and thought are one in Substance they are synonymous realities with a synonymity appropriate to realities between which there is merely virtual distinction. And they are one in Substance.[96] But unless the attribute of thought is the source of quiddity in the extended world there is no synonymity between the attributes—only two phenomena different in kind—thought cannot exist by the necessity of its own nature as it must if it is an attribute of Substance,[97] nor be prior to its objects as it must be if it belongs to the divine nature[98]—and there can be no experiential basis whatever for Spinoza's system.

But if the attribute of thought is the source of quiddity then Spinoza's system is in perfect harmony with the nature of that which is and with our natural understanding of that which is.

Duquesne University
Pittsburgh, Pennsylvania

NOTES

1. Benedict De Spinoza. *On the Improvement of the Understanding: The Ethics Correspondence,* trans. R. H. Elwes (New York: Dover Publishers Inc., 1955), Part I Def. III.
2. *Ibid.,* Part I Def. IV.
3. *Ibid.,* Part I Def. III & Part I Ax. II.
4. *Ibid.,* Part I Prop. IV & V.
5. *Ibid.,* Part I Prop. VIII.
6. *Ibid.,* Part I Def. VI & VIII, Part I Prop. XIV, XXIX, C. LXII Part I Prop. VII.
7. *Ibid.,* Part I Def. V.
8. *Ibid.,* Part I Def. IV.
9. *Ibid.,* Part II Prop. XI.
10. *Ibid.,* Part I Prop. VIII Note II.
11. *Ibid.,* C. XXIX.
12. *Ibid.,* Part I Def. IV.
13. *Ibid.*
14. *Ibid.,* Part I Def. VI.
15. *Ibid.,* Part I Def. IV.
16. *Ibid.,* Part II Def. II.
17. *Ibid.,* C. LXV.
18. *Ibid.,* C. LXVI.
19. *Ibid.,* Part II Prop. VII.
20. *Ibid.,* Part II Ax. V.
21. *Ibid.,* Part I Ax. VI.
22. *Ibid.,* Part II Def. IV.
23. *Ibid.,* Part II Def. II & Part I Def. IV.
24. *Ibid.,* Part I Prop. X, Part II Prop. VII, C. XXVII.
25. *Ibid.,* Part II Prop. VII.
26. *Ibid.,* Part I Def. VI.
27. *Ibid.,* Part I Def. VI Expl., Part I Prop. VIII, C. XLI.
28. *Ibid.,* Part I Def. III.
29. *Ibid.,* C.L.
30. *Ibid.,* Part IV Prop. XXVIII.
31. *Ibid.,* Part II Prop. XLVII.
32. *Ibid.,* C. XXVII.
33. *Ibid.,* Part II Prop. VII.
34. *Ibid.,* Part II Prop. I & II.
35. *Ibid.,* C. XL.
36. *Ibid.,* C. XV, Part I Prop. X Note.
37. *Ibid.,* Part I Prop. XVII Note.
38. *Ibid.,* Part II Def. II.
39. *Ibid.,* Part II Prop. XI.
40. *Ibid.,* Part I Prop. XVII Note.
41. *Ibid.,* Part I Prop. XXVII.
42. *Ibid.,* Part I Ax. III.
43. *Ibid.,* Part I Def. IV.
44. *Ibid.,* C. XXVII & Part I Ax. IV.
45. *Ibid.,* Part I Prop. IX & X.
46. *Ibid.,* Part I Prop. XXVIII.
47. *Ibid.,* Part I Prop. VIII Note I & C.L.

48. *Ibid.*, Part I Prop. XVII.
49. *Ibid.*, Part I Def. VI.
50. *Ibid.*, Part I Prop. XV & Part II Prop. I, XXI, XLIII, Part I Prop. X.
51. *Ibid.*, C.L.
52. *Ibid.*, Part I Def. VI, Part I Prop. X.
53. *Ibid.*, Part I Ax. III; Part I Prop. XXVI.
54. *Ibid.*, C. LXVI.
55. *Ibid.*, Part I Prop. X.
56. *Ibid.*, Part II Prop. VII, Part I Prop. XXIII & XXVIII.
57. *Ibid.*, C. XXIX.
58. *Ibid.*, Part I Prop. XI.
59. *Ibid.*, C. XV.
60. *Ibid.*, Part I Prop. XVII Note.
61. *Ibid.*, Part I Prop. XVII.
62. *Ibid.*, Part I Prop. XVII Note.
63. *Ibid.*, Part I Prop. XVI, Part V Prop. XL.
64. *Ibid.*, Part I Prop. XVII, Part II Prop. I, VII & XXI.
65. *Ibid.*, C. LXXI.
66. *Ibid.*, C. LXXII.
67. *Ibid.*
68. *Ibid.*, C. LXVI, Part I Prop. XXIII & XXVIII.
69. *Ibid.*, Part I Ax. IV.
70. *Ibid.*, Part I Prop. XVII Note.
71. *Ibid.*, Part II Prop. VII, Part I Prop. XVII Note, C. LXIV.
72. *Ibid.*, Part I Prop. XXXIII.
73. *Ibid.*, Part I Prop. XXXIV.
74. *Ibid.*, Part I Prop. XXV.
75. *Ibid.*, Part I Prop. XVI.
76. *Ibid.*, Part I Prop. XVII.
77. *Ibid.*
78. *Ibid.*, Part II Prop. VIII.
79. *Ibid.*, Part I Prop. X.
80. *Ibid.*, C. LXXII.
81. *Ibid.*, Part I Prop. XXXIV.
82. *Ibid.*, Part I Prop. XVII Note.
83. *Ibid.*, C. LXVI.
84. *Ibid.*, Part II Prop. XIII, Part II Ax. I, Part I Prop. XVII. XXXIV, XXXV.
85. *Ibid.*, Part II Def. II & Part II Prop. XIII.
86. *Ibid.*, C. LXXII & LXVI.
87. *Ibid.*, Part II Prop. XIII, Part I Def. II & VII, Ax. III & IV.
88. *Ibid.*, C. LXIV & LXVI.
89. *Ibid.*, Part II Prop. XIII.
90. *Ibid.*, Part I Prop. XVII.
91. *Ibid.*, Part I Prop. XVI Coro. III.
92. *Ibid.*, Part I Prop. XVI Coro. I.
93. *Ibid.*, Part I Prop. XVII.
94. *Ibid.*, Part I Prop. XXXIV.
95. *Ibid.*, Part I Prop. XVII Note.
96. *Ibid.*, Part II Prop. VII, Part I Prop. X.
97. *Ibid.*, Part I Def. VII.
98. *Ibid.*, Part I Prop. XVII Note.

SECTION IV—MODERN PHILOSOPHY

Mary J. Gregor, Chairman
San Diego State University

Nominalism and the Inscrutability of Substance in Locke's *Essay Concerning Human Understanding*

by Gregory Reichberg

One of the intriguing aspects of the Fourth Book of the *Essay* consists in the surprising juxtaposition of man's knowledge of God on the one hand, which is "such a Knowledge within our reach, which we cannot miss, if we will but apply our minds to that..."[1] and, on the other hand, man's almost complete ignorance of the constitution of corporeal substances: "...our Faculties," writes Locke, "are not fitted to penetrate into the internal Fabrick and real Essences of Bodies; but yet plainly discover to us the Being of a God...."[2]

If one remembers that most of Locke's scholastic predecessors affirmed that the connatural objects of the human mind are corporeal substances which afford to man his most direct certitude, and that God can only be known (without revelation) through an analogical reflection based on a knowledge of those substances, then Locke's position seems all the more puzzling. Why does Locke, a so-called empiricist, so strongly doubt the mind's capacity to penetrate "the internal fabric and real essences of bodies," whereas he does not have the slightest hesitation in affirming "the necessary existence of an eternal Mind"? Should not his main interest be centered on the mind's power to know material things through the empirical methods of natural science? This, however, is not the case. Locke denies that natural science is capable of attaining real certitude and thus he denies that such an inquiry should have the status of *science*.[3]

In this paper I wish to investigate Locke's reasons for positing the inscrutability of corporeal substances. In particular, I wish to defend the thesis that Locke's thought on this matter has much in common with the nominalism of William of Ockham. What I hope to point out is that Locke's skeptical attitude in regard to the knowledge of material substances proceeds from his position on the problem of universals.

From the time of St. Augustine, Christian thought tended to take the reality of universals for granted; most thinkers posited the existence of essences in particular things, essences which remain identical within the boundaries of a given species. From this point of view, the major difficulty to be resolved is not whether universal essences exist, but rather how can a singular individual *derive* from such universal natures or essences. In order to resolve this difficulty, the tendency of Medieval Aristotelians, Aquinas for example, was to affirm the primacy of individuals in the order of existence—only individuals exist as subsisting entities—and to affirm the primacy of the universal in the order of knowledge. Ontologically, such a project implies a *theory of individuation,* which aims to explain how singular beings can possess at the same time identical essences that make them members of the same species and certain incommunicable properties which confer individuality on each entity so that each substance is rendered distinct from every other substance. Epistemologically, this project requires a *theory of abstraction,* which aims to explain how the individuals grasped by the senses give rise, through the intellect's activity, to a knowledge of universal essences. Because of the necessity of abstraction to obtain all universal knowledge, Aquinas denied that the essence of a corporeal substance could be known directly. He did affirm, however, that such essences could be known, indirectly, by a "'radial' knowledge that goes from the outside in, that attains the center only by starting from the circumference,"[4] so that the mind knows the essence of a substance through the outward signs which manifest it, and which are its operations and properties.

William of Ockham had little use for this indirect knowledge of individual substances. One could in fact describe his epistemology as being founded on the primacy of *individual cognition.* He thus affirmed not only that individuals are the only subsisting things, Aquinas and others said as much, but that the direct and immediate object of the *intellect* (and not just the senses) are singular substances. "He thus reversed the direction which Christian thought had for the most part followed from the time of St. Augustine. From attempting to explain the place of individuals in a world of universal natures or essences, the problem was henceforth to account for universals in an exclusively individual world."[5]

Consequently, the existence of individuals presents no problem whatsoever. The mind has a direct, intellectual intuition of singular substances and therefore no longer has any need for a theory of individuation. At the same time, the doctrine of abstraction is emptied of all ontological reference, because there is no reason to assume the reality of universals in order to explain the structure of singular things as somehow participating in a common species. The truly problematic question consequently centers on the justification of universal, abstract concepts. The *Venerabilis Inceptor* admits that such universals form an integral part of human knowledge, but they no longer fulfill an ontological function. "No universal," writes Ockham, "really exists outside the mind in individual substances, nor is any universal a part of the substance or being of individual things."[6] "What had been an ontological question became a psychological or logical question, to be resolved not by an appeal to metaphysical principles, but conceptually."[7]

In a manner similar to Ockham, Locke entered into polemic with those who defended the extramental reality of species or common essences. Like Ockham, Locke does not take the ontological reality of universal kinds for granted. On the contrary, simple ideas put the mind in immediate contact with individuals, and it is the existence of universal, abstract concepts within the intellect which calls for justification.

The necessity of universal or common terms has absolutely nothing to do with the reality signified by these terms, but solely with the conditions of exercise of human intelligence, which without them is incapable of embracing and communicating in language the almost limitless number of individual substances present in everyday human experience. In order to explain the generation of general concepts in the mind, Locke elaborates a theory of abstraction which is wholly conceptual, i.e., it has no ontological reference: "When therefore we quit Particulars, the Generals that rest, are only Creatures of our own making; their general Nature being nothing but the Capacity they are put into, by the Understanding [through the power of abstraction], of signifying or representing many particulars."[8]

The fact of Locke's negation of species, common essence and the like requires little discussion; it is clearly expressed in numerous passages within the *Essay*. However, the reason given by Locke for his denial is not a simple matter, inasmuch as he does admit that the mind's tendency to form universal ideas through abstraction and the fixing of names has a certain foundation in things themselves. It is precisely the similarity observed among corporeal things which is the "occasion," as he says, for the setting up of patterns in the mind. But why does this observed similarity, "especially in the Races of animals, and all Things propagated by Seed,"[9] not give rise to a true universal or real essence in the mind?

For the most part, Locke's denial will be directed against the theory, stated above, according to which the mind can have an indirect, radial knowledge of the substances of things by proceeding from the exterior inward. (The Cartesian idea that the mind can have a direct intuition of the essence of material substances is, as far as I can tell, hardly discussed in the essay.) The multiplicity of arguments which he advances against a radial knowledge of substance can be reduced, I think, to two basic objections.

First of all, in order to know the essence of a substance by its outward properties or operations, we need to gather together several simple ideas of sensation and unite them according to a *visible, necessary* connection. (Remember, the idea of substance is a *complex* idea composed of simple ideas.) But this necessary connection we are unable to perceive. Why? Because most of our simple ideas are of secondary qualities, and since the secondary qualities depend on primary qualities, qualities of which we are almost completely ignorant, it is impossible to discern a "necessary union or consistency [of the secondary qualities] one with another." For in order to discern their necessary connection, we must know their common root in a common primary quality, but unfortunately "there is no discoverable connection between any secondary Quality, and those primary Qualities which it depends on."[10] This leads us to the second objection. Locke seems to identify the essence of corporeal substances with a certain arrangement of "*insensible corpuscles.*" It is precisely our ignorance of the primary qualities of these corpuscles which "keeps us in an incurable Ignorance of what we desire to know about them [their natural operations]."[11]

We are thus confronted with the following dilemma. We can only know the essence of a substance from the outside, through a necessary connection of its operation with the essence. But paradoxically, in order to truly know the operations or properties of a thing, we must first know the constitution of its essence or insensible corpuscles, because the latter renders reason of the former: "But whilst we are destitute of Senses acute enough to discover the minute Particles of Bodies...we must be content to be ignorant of their properties and ways of Operation...."[12] However, as has already been established, we can only know the essence through those very same properties or operations, of which we are ignorant, unless we know the essence whence they proceed, but we don't know the essence. The mind is therefore confronted with an impasse which severely limits our knowledge of corporeal substances. Thus, writes Locke, "how far soever humane Industry may advance useful and *experimental* philosophy in *physical* things, *scientifical* will still be out of our reach: because we want perfect and adequate Ideas of those very Bodies which are nearest to us, and most under our Command...nor shall ever be able to discover general, instructive, unquestionable Truths concerning them."[13]

In Locke's polemic against the positing of genera and species as designating the *real* essence of things, his ultimate target seems to be those of his contemporaries upholding some form of Scholastic Aristotelianism. In particular, Locke is seeking to eliminate any recourse to the Aristotelian notion of a *substantial form* as the foundation of real continuity and distinction of beings into fundamental types.[14] The exact point of this denial of the substantial form is not without ambiguity. His position is outwardly polemical and appears to be a blanket negation of the Aristotelian view of the structure of individual, subsisting entities.

Within Aristotelianism, however, the substantial form exercises an *ontological* function as the act (energia) which constitutes a singular, corporeal being by concretely realizing the potentialities contained in matter. In addition, the substantial form fulfills an *epistemological* function as the fundamental principle of intelligibility which renders a substance knowable to the human mind.

It is the epistemological function of the substantial form that Locke is explicitly rejecting, because as we have seen, he holds the real essences of things to be wholly unknowable to a human intelligence. Obviously, something which remains entirely hidden can in no way operate as a principle of intelligibility. However, Locke does not conclude that the real essence of a thing—what Aristotle would call the substantial form—is a mere fiction of the mind. He often speaks as if the real essence truly exists, but is entirely out of reach of our limited minds.[15] We are not far from the Kantian *Ding an sich.*

The real essence can therefore only be known by the intuition of a super-human intelligence which would penetrate to the very core of a substance, to that internal "Constitution" from which its "Powers flow" and its "regular shape depends."[16] Human understanding, however, can only come to know the *nominal essence* of a thing, a knowledge which is necessarily *abstract* and *universal*. And as we have seen, Locke's nominalism precludes him from affirming that such an abstract, universal knowledge should directly signify what things are *in themselves:* "...*General and Universal,* belong not to the real existence of Things; but *are the Inventions and Creatures of the Understanding....*"[17]

In the preceding remarks I have attempted to show why Locke denies that universals can directly relate to the real existence of things. However, one should not hastily conclude that Locke's aim is simply to deny that universal concepts have any positive function within human knowledge. On the contrary, such a negation merely sets the stage for Locke's affirmation that universal, abstract terms are *productions* of the human understanding which gives rise to an autonomous conceptual order radically distinct from the order of nature.

All that exists is individual. Only *simple* ideas of sensation and reflection place man in *direct* contact with the singular beings which exist externally. Such ideas "enter by the Senses simple and unmixed" and have as their object the uncompounded perception of *"one uniform Appearance."*[18] The knowledge received via the simple ideas is nonetheless severely limited, since each idea only places the mind in contact with *one* singular quality, whereas a multitude of such qualities will exist blended in a given individual.[19] To arrive at knowledge of substances it is required that the mind possess more than a bunch of atomized qualities; some kind of combination will need to be realized whereby the union of the various qualities which constitute a particular substance can come to be reproduced in the mind. However, such a mirroring in the mind of the real constitution of qualities united in any given substance is, according to Locke, impossible (for the reasons given above).

How, then, in the absence of any adequate knowledge of substances, is the mind to proceed in the acquisition of *true* knowledge? The data received through sensation and reflection, although veridical, really does not lead very far. They are the building blocks or the constituent elements of human knowledge, but not, properly speaking, knowledge itself.[20] Passively received and inalterable, the simple ideas are nothing more than the "Materials and Foundations of the rest";[21] the "rest" being those acts wherein the mind exerts its power and *actively combines* the simple ideas according to its own purposes. Far from being the criteria to which all knowledge must need conform, the simple ideas constitute merely the *elements* of a construction, which in itself is largely autonomous and which depends solely on the mind for the essentials of its design. In this autonomous realm, wherein complex ideas are produced as creatures of the understanding, the ideal of truth will no longer consist in conformity of the mind, through observation, to "what offers itself from without," but rather it is the mind itself which becomes, as it were, the *archetype* to which things themselves will be conformable. One should be quick to add, however, that the various types of complex ideas will conform to such an *ideal* in varying degrees. The complex ideas of substances will still require a partial conformity to outside things, whereas the mixed modes will be a combination of ideas "which the Mind, by its free choice, puts together, without considering any connexion they have in Nature."[22]

Before considering the various types of complex ideas and their degrees of autonomy in relation to external things, it will be helpful to step back an instant and reflect on the relevance of Ockham's nominalism in regard to the question at hand.

The *Venerabilis Inceptor* makes a firm distinction between two fundamentally different types of knowledge. On the one hand, all knowledge must begin with the perception of the existence of singular, contingent things or events. Such a knowledge is called "intuitive" because it has for its object the immediate evidence of some actually existing object. This intuitive knowledge of the singular *hic et nunc* is the fruit of intellection and sensation (internal or external) acting in concert and terminating in some evidential judgement.[23] On the other hand, the mind can focus on the *terms* of a proposition and know the representations of things in abstraction from their actual existence. In this case, the intellect knows things mediately through universal notions which it generates by means of its own activity. The abstracted universal in no way exists in things themselves; it is, according to Ockham, a sign *in the mind* of a plurality of individuals subsisting apart in *rerum natura*. Because this knowledge has for its object universal terms which can exist only in the soul as signs of many individuals grouped together, it is necessarily of a different order than intuitive knowledge; it is an *abstractive* knowledge of that which is inevident and of non-existential import: "Abstractive knowledge," writes Ockham, "is taken for what abstracts from existence and non-existence and other contingent circumstances which concern a thing or are predicated of it ...."[24]

There is much that one could say regarding Ockham's distinction of intuitive and abstractive cognition. However, the point which I wish to make is that this division gives rise to a fundamental disjunction between the structure of the real and the structure of knowledge. It is true that the mind has an immediate cognition of individuals. Nevertheless, such a knowledge is limited to what is contingent. In order to obtain a knowledge of *necessary* truths, the mind must have recourse to abstractive cognition. The operation of abstraction terminates in the production of universal concepts which stand in stark contrast to the pure singularity of actually existing things. "When it [the mind] knows universally it does not make any thing real universal: it merely knows what can only exist individually in another way. How it does so belongs to its own nature and must be taken as given; and with it the discrepancy between the mental and the real which is the foundation of Ockham's epistemology." Following this excellent characterization of Ockham's thought, Leff makes the important addition that "far from seeking to deny an independent conceptual order, Ockham is concerned to stress its autonomy and to rescue what really exists from its confusion with what only exists in the mind."[25]

The distinction between intuitive and abstractive cognition thus marks a separation between being and intelligibility. What exists is absolutely singular, but the mind can only grasp this being by transforming it according to the mental laws of the abstractive process. The important rule is therefore to always be aware of this disjunction and not to confuse the order of being with the order of being as *known*. This means, in the last analysis, that one must be willing to recognize the relative autonomy of the abstracting intellect in regard to the being of external things.

It should not be difficult to see the parallel in Locke's thought to what I have described concerning Ockham. To the latter's distinction between intuitive and abstractive cognition corresponds Locke's fundamental division of simple and complex ideas. If anything, Locke tends to amplify the basic discrepancy between the real and the mental, and to grant to abstract knowledge a much greater autonomy than Ockham would have allowed.

Ockham hoped to retain some kind of intrinsic link with being by affirming that universal concepts are *natural* (as opposed to conventional) signs.

Locke, it is true, does not entirely reject a certain foundation in nature for our abstract ideas of substances; he does admit that in forming such ideas the understanding takes occasion of the *similitude* observed among things.[26] However, the classification of things into *types* is itself a special act of the mind, which merely uses the observed similarities as a *material* for effectuating the purely mental process of abstraction. Far from being directly derived from things themselves, it is the abstract idea itself which becomes the *standard to which things must conform* if they are to be considered a member of one essence rather than another.[27]

The point that I wish to stress is that Locke tends to view the domain of complex ideas as an order based fundamentally on human activity and invention. This activity is not purely spontaneous or active, because man must passively receive the materials on which his own unifying, constructive activity will be grounded.[28] However, once in possession of the materials furnished by the simple ideas of sensation and reflection, the understanding "has the Power to repeat, compare, and unite them even to an almost infinite Variety, and so can at Pleasure make new complex *Ideas.*"[29]

The complex ideas of substances will mark the lowest level in the mind's movement towards a greater autonomy in relation to extra-mental things. The ideas of *relations* and *mixed modes* are defined by Locke precisely as *archetypes* not intended to be copies of any existing thing.[30]

The aim of Book IV, chap. 4, of the *Essay* is to manifest the firm *reality* of those types of knowledge in which the mind's own intrinsic spontaneity becomes the measure to which things themselves must conform, if we are to grant them any reality at all. At this point in the Essay we are about as far from the common notion of "empiricism" as is possible for someone who, like Locke, holds that all knowledge comes from the senses.

Locke does not grudgingly admit the existence of a mind-dependent order in which the understanding stands as the archetype of reality, intelligibility, and the criteria of an unwavering certitude.[31] He affirms without qualification that all of mathematics and even the science of morals is based on such an "ideal existence in the mind," for "the Truth and Certainty of *moral* Discourses abstracts from the Lives of men, and the Existence of those Virtues in the World, whereof they treat...."[32] In addition to the above sciences, Locke mentions religion and jurisprudence as areas of knowledge particularly infused with mixed modes.[33] In all such cases, the nominal essence *is* the real essence; the Species of Things...have no other Essences, but those ideas which are in the Minds of Men."[34]

Locke's thought has often been viewed as a poorly articulated compromise between empiricism on the one hand and rationalism on the other. In my opinion, one can obtain a more coherent reading of Locke when placing his thought within the context of *nominalism.* As I have tried to show, the nominalist will seek to valorize our knowledge of individuals, and thus will seek to ground some form of cognition on a direct perception of contingent things and events—a role fulfilled by intuitive cognition for Ockham and simple ideas for Locke.

However, because the nominalist rejects the inherence of universal forms in things, and places universality solely within the mind, he will insist on the autonomy of the conceptual order. Locke, in particular, seems fascinated with the discovery that much of the knowledge which had previously been attributed to the mind's reception of external objects should, in fact, be viewed as the fruit of human invention. Hence, Locke is greatly interested in developing his theory of relations and mixed modes, which serves as the starting point for a theory of human culture, understood as a mind-dependent order of invention and custom.

In conclusion, if I were asked to resume in one brief sentence the focal point of Locke's agnosticism about substance, I could do nothing better than to quote a well-known affirmation of Thomas Aquinas and simply insert an expression of negation. Thus, Locke would say that "a thing's operation [does not] manifest its substance and its being."[35] In this paper I have endeavored to point out the epistemological reasons which account for Locke's denial of an intrinsic, intelligible link between knowing a thing's operation and knowing the substance from which that operation flows.

However, just as there is an ontological foundation for Aristotle's and Aquinas' view that substance is self-expressive through action, there is correspondingly an ontological basis of Locke's denial of such a natural manifestation of substance in its operation. Again, we can quote St. Thomas for a succinct statement of the issue at stake: "The species of a thing is known from its proper operation; for the operation manifests the power, which reveals the essence."[36] The epistemological link between knower and extra-mental substance is based upon an ontological link within substance between its power and the resulting activity. To be a substance is to exist dynamically as the source of action, and action itself is understood most fundamentally as an intrinsic self-communication of the being whence it emanates. Every substance, to the precise degree that it *is*, is capable of some diffusion of its own intrinsic perfection through action.[37] This holds for the most infirm bodies to the supreme agent God. The study of nature will consist especially in a discernment of the ontological diversification of action within the universe of animate and inanimate beings.

A reading of Locke's *Essay* reveals a much different metaphysical picture. Substance is no longer conceived dynamically as a principle of action, but rather as an inert support for accidents. He subscribes to a "pin-cushion theory" of substance, unfortunately inherited from his scholastic predecessors and teachers.[38] Corporeal substance does not *act,* instead it *undergoes* change passively in a manner not unlike Aristotle's prime matter. As pure potentiality, prime matter is an unknowable something, precisely because it has no share in *actuality,* which is the principle of all intelligibility. Since Locke's material substance does not exercise any proper operation, it is therefore not surprising that it should remain entirely unknowable.[39]

Emory University
Atlanta, Georgia

NOTES

1. John Locke, *An Essay Concerning Human Understanding,* edited by Peter Nidditch (Oxford: Clarendon Press, 1975), book IV, chap. 10, § 6, 621.

2. *Essay,* book IV, chap. 12, § 11, 646.

3. *Essay,* book IV, chap. 12, § 10, 645.

4. J. Maritain, *The Degrees of Knowledge,* trans. G. B. Phelan (New York: Charles Scribner's Sons, 1959), 203.

5. G. Leff, *The Dissolution of the Medieval Outlook* (New York: Harper & Row, 1976), 12.

6. William of Ockham, *Expositio in Librum Praedicamentorum Aristotelis,* prooemium. This occurs in Guillelmi de Ockham, *Opera Philosophica et Theologica,* ed. G. Gál and S. Brown (St. Bonaventure, N.Y., 1967 ff.), *Opera Philosophica,* II, 11: "...nullum universale est extra animam existens realiter in substantiis individuis, nec est de substantia vel essentia earum...."

7. G. Leff, *William of Ockham* (Manchester: Manchester Univ. Press, 1975), 2.

8. *Essay,* book III, chap. 3, § 11, 414. The words in brackets were added by me.

9. *Essay,* book III, chap. 3, § 13, 415.

10. *Essay,* book IV, chap. 3, § 11-12, 544-545. The words in brackets were added by me.

11. *Essay,* book IV, chap. III, § 25, 556. The words in brackets were added by me.

12. *Ibid.*

13. *Essay,* book IV, chap. 3, § 26, 556-557.

14. *Essay,* book III, chap. 6, § 10, 445.

15. *Essay,* book III, chap. VI, § 6, 442.

16. *Essay,* book III, chap. 6, § 3, 440.

17. *Essay,* book III, chap. 3, § 11, 414.

18. *Essay,* book II, chap. 2, § 1, 119.

19. *Essay,* book II, chap. 2, § 1, 119.

20. *Essay,* book II, chap. 12, § 2, 164.

21. *Essay,* book II, chap. 12, § 1, 163.

22. *Essay,* book IV, chap. 4, § 5, 564.

23. Willliam of Ockham, *Ordinatio,* prol., q.I. *Opera Theologica,* I, 31-32; "Et universaliter omnis notitia incomplexa termini vel terminorum, seu rei vel rerum, virtute cuius potest evidenter cognosci aliqua veritas contengens maxime de praesenti est notitia intuitiva."

24. "Notitia autem est illa virtute cuius de re contingente non potest scire evidenter utrum sit vel non sit. Et per istum modum notitia abstractiva abstrahit ab existentia et non existentia...." (*Ibid.,* 31).

25. G. Leff, *William of Ockham*, 123.

26. *Essay*, book III, chap. 3, § 13, 415.

27. *Essay*, book III, chap. 3, § 12, 414-415.

28. *Essay*, book II, chap. 2, § 2, 120.

29. *Essay*, book II, chap. 2, § 2, 119.

30. *Essay*, book IV, chap. 4, § 5, 564.

31. *Essay*, book IV, chap. 4, § 5, 564.

32. *Essay*, book IV, chap. 4, § 8, 566.

33. *Essay*, book III, chap. 5, § 5, 430.

34. *Essay*, book IV, chap. 4, § 8, 566.

35. Thomas Aquinas, *Summa contra Gentes*, II, 79: "Operatio enim rei demonstrat substantiam et esse ipsius."

36. Thomas Aquinas, *Summa contra Gentes*, II, 94: "Ex propria operatione rei percipitur species eius: operatio enim demonstrat virtutem, quae indicat essentiam."

37. Thomas Aquinas, *De Potentia*, q. 2, art. 1: "Unumquodque agens agit secundum quod in actu est. Agere vero nihil aliud est quam communicare illud per quod agens est actu, secundum quod est possibile."

38. W. H. Kenney, S.J., *John Locke and the Oxford Training in Logic and Metaphysics*, Ph.D Diss. (Ann Arbor: University Microfilms International, 1959), 219-268.

39. *Essay*, book II, chap. XXI, § 4 and § 72. In this chapter, active power is ascribed solely to the operations of rational substance, whereas corporeal substance is described in terms of passive power.

Kant and Substance

by Vincent M. Cooke, S.J.

Kant's discussion of substance in the *Critique of Pure Reason* has been called by Jonathan Bennett part of "one of the greatest passages in modern philosophy."[1] At the same time Bennett, like many other commentators, is severely critical of Kant. He says Kant's proofs are "abominably organized" and important lines of argumentation have not yet been shown to be intelligible by any of the commentators, including himself.[2]

In this paper I propose to do three things. First I will briefly state, in what Kant would call dogmatic fashion, what I understand Kant's views on substance to be. I am thus beginning in a very non-Kantian fashion. Kant typically strove to give the impression that his order of proof was identical with his order of discovery. We know that as a matter of fact this was not his actual way of proceeding. Like the rest of us, Kant started with hunches as to what he thought was true, and then he searched about for proofs to establish that his conjectures were indeed correct. While it is certainly true that Kant's transcendental style of argumentation and exposition is part of his claim to greatness, it is also responsible for much of that notorious obscurity which frequently creates the impression that, to use Strawson's phrase, we are following the path of a camel across the great Arabian desert. In order to avoid some of that obscurity I will begin by stating as clearly as I can what I take Kant's goal to be. Secondly, I will examine the main argument which Kant offers to support his position. Here my central contention will be that Kant's argument only makes sense if one keeps in mind the central importance to Kant of the doctrine of Transcendental Idealism, i.e., the doctrine that we know things only as they appear to us and not as they are in themselves. Kant's argument is only obscured, in my opinion, by commentators who try to salvage something of Kant's doctrine on substance, while rejecting what they consider the untenable positions of Transcendental Idealism. My own views are thus influenced by the work of recent commentators, such as Henry Allison, who have tried to rehabilitate the centrality of Transcendental Idealism in their interpretations of Kant's philosophy.[3] Finally, I will offer a few ideas on where and why Kant's doctrine on substance is defective.

Kant's official doctrine on substance is as follows. Experience reveals that we are immediately aware of a world of appearances to which the category of substance necessarily has application. The proof of this claim I will examine in the next section of this paper. What the claim means is, first of all, that whenever I have an experience I make a judgment about something which can exist only as a subject, and never as a predicate (B149, B288). Thus, to say something is a substance is to say I can predicate attributes or determinations of that something, but I can never predicate that something of anything else. For example, if I call the pencil with which I am writing a substance, I can say of the substance that it is yellow, writes well, and is made of wood, but I cannot say of anything else that it is this pencil. Substance is that which can exist only as subject and never as predicate. So much was already said by Aristotle. Kant, like Aristotle, was of course concerned with making an ontological point and not a purely linguistic point about what can function as a predicate in language.

Kant's claim, however, goes further. That which is substance is permanent, unchanging, and sempiternal (A143/B185). Clearly, my pencil is not a substance, given this further specification of the sense of 'substance.' My pencil did not always exist, underwent many changes in the course of its existence, and one day will cease to exist. What we call a pencil is not strictly speaking a substance, but upon analysis it is seen to be a logical construction dependent on modifications, determinations, accidents, or predicates (Kant uses all of this language) of something else which is substance.[4] This substance is matter, i.e., the simple, unchanging, permanent, sempiternal subject or subjects of whatever can be predicated of the world of appearances.

Thus substance, for Kant, has two main characteristics: (1) it is that which is always subject and never predicate; (2) it is permanent, unchanging, and sempiternal. How many substances are there in Kant's view? Strictly speaking, this is an empirical question for Kant. Transcendental analysis claims to prove that any world we can experience must be such that the category of substance is applicable to it. However, transcendental analysis does not reveal how many substances there are. Experience reveals to us a multiplicity of substances, but the argument and resolution of the Second Antinomy makes clear that we are unable to decide by a priori reasoning whether there is a finite or infinite number of simple unchanging substances. All that we can say a priori is that there is an indeterminate number of substances in the world of appearances, and the task is set for us in experience to determine precisely what we will count as substances.

What empirical criterion does Kant offer for identifying substances? He says: "Substance appears to manifest itself not through permanence of appearance, but more adequately and easily through action. Wherever there is action—and therefore activity and force—there is also substance" (A204/B249-B250). He goes on, in the same passage, to note that "action signifies the relation of the subject of causality to its effect." An effect, he argues, is something which happens, and therefore belongs to the world of change. That which is the ultimate ground of the change which is the effect must itself be something which does not change. It is, Kant says, the permanent, that is, substance. Kant concludes: "For this reason action is a sufficient empirical criterion to establish the substantiality of a subject, without my requiring to go in quest of its permanence through the comparison of perceptions" (A205/B250-B251).

The above argument deserves much more analysis than I can give it here. I introduce it merely to make clear the way Kant is thinking of the physical world, i.e., the world which appears to us. We must think the world as composed of an indefinite number of unchanging subjects of activity which produce the changing effects which we perceive in the physical world. The world of appearances, according to Kant, is thus remarkably similar to the world of physical monads described by Leibniz.

Having sketched what Kant means by substance and consequently how he views the physical world, I want now to examine the argument he gives to prove that the world of appearances is such as I have described, i.e., that the world is necessarily thought in accord with the concept of substance in the sense indicated.

In the second edition of the *Critique* Kant inserted at the beginning of the First Analogy a new statement of his argument for what he called the Principle of the Permanence of Substance, i.e., the principle that in all changes of appearances substance is permanent; its quantum in nature is neither increased nor decreased (B224). Despite the appearance that the latter clause concerning quantum in nature involves Kant in making some kind of claim concerning the 18th century theory of conservation of matter, I will presuppose that the principle Kant is trying to prove really says nothing more than that the world of appearances is necessarily such that the category of substance in the sense I have explained is truly predicable of it. I am convinced this is all Kant is trying to prove, but the point is complicated and controversial; I will not try to justify in detail this point of my interpretation here.

Kant's argument, even without the worry that he is trying to prove a priori a physical theory which he elsewhere recognized was clearly a posteriori, has been a major source of puzzlement to his commentators. I want to suggest, first, that like much else in Kant the argument is best understood as offering a response to Hume's views on substance, and secondly, that the argument is much less obscure when one consistently adverts to the fact that the argument presupposes the doctrine of Transcendental Idealism, i.e., that what we are directly aware of are appearances which necessarily are formed by the conditions of possibility for our being aware of them.[5]

The proof-structure of Kant's argument is thus as follows. Hume said that we can be aware of impressions (or what Kant calls appearances), and that we never immediately perceive an unchanging substance; it is only subsequent to our immediate awareness of impressions that we utilize the philosophical fiction of substance to unify our impressions. Kant argues that in order to be aware of impressions or appearances at all it is necessary that the appearances be ordered (regularized) in such a way that the category of substance is applicable to them. Hume claimed there are only two factors to consider, impressions and ideas, very roughly corresponding to Kant's appearances and concepts. Kant argues there is a third thing, overlooked by Hume, the transcendental determinations of time, i.e., the regularized status of appearances which constitutes their conformity to the conditions of possibility of human awareness. That in appearances which takes the place of the permanent object of perception, which Hume rightly claimed he could not perceive, is the permanent conformity of appearances in accord with the transcendental determinations of time, and it is the conformity of appearances to this rule which makes possible the objective validity of the concept of substance in Kant's sense.

I have used some heavy Kantian jargon in the above sketch. I think the matter will become clearer if we look at Kant's argument in detail. There are seven steps in the argument which I summarize and comment on as follows (see B224-B225).

1. When I am aware of appearances (or what Hume would call impressions) I am aware of a particular set of appearances as being present now at this particular time. I distinguish this set of appearances from other sets of appearances which I have been aware of at different times in the past. So much seems to be relatively uncontroversial, and is common ground between Hume and Kant.

2. Kant's next remark is somewhat obscure, but need not be. He says that "time in which all change of appearances has to be thought, remains and does not change." Taken as an empirical remark this seems to suggest that time is a candidate for change, but as a matter of fact it does not change. But this surely cannot be Kant's meaning. A more natural interpretation is to take him to be making the obvious grammatical remark that when appearances change from one set of appearances to another, whatever change there is is in the appearances themselves. Whatever time is, it is not an appearance which changes. We judge the succession and coexistence of things and events in terms of their place in time.

3. Kant now remarks that "time cannot by itself be perceived." This sentence has caused much puzzlement to the commentators. Kant is really doing two things here. First, he is for the moment adopting the perspective of the Newtonian empirical realist who presupposes that he can have some kind of perception of absolute time; Kant denies that human beings have such perception. But Kant is also following up on his previous point. The

reason time cannot be perceived is because time (whatever it is) is not an appearance. It is appearances (what Hume called impressions) which are perceived and which change.

4. Kant next argues that there must therefore be in appearances what he calls a "substratum which represents time in general; and all change or coexistence must, in being apprehended, be perceived in this substratum, and through relation of the appearances to it." What are we to make of this? The notion of *substratum* is perplexing, unless we recall that it was already introduced in the first sentence of the proof, where it had the relatively uncontroversial sense of codifying our awareness that all appearances are *in* time. I suggest that that is all Kant means by *substratum* here. If our judgment that appearances are in time is to be objectively valid, then there must be something in the appearances which makes it true to say that this set of appearances is temporally related to another set of appearances. This ground for the objectivity of our judgments of time Kant, somewhat obscurely, refers to as the "substratum which represents time in general." However, it is precisely this ground for the objectivity of judgments of time which Hume both presupposed and yet failed to give any account of.

5. Kant goes on to identify this *substratum* with the notion of substance. We must recall that it is tautological, for Kant, to say that substance is permanent (or perdures) (A184/B227). The crux of the proof is to identify substance with something which is required by our apprehension of appearances in time. That something is the substratum which represents time in general. This ground for the objectivity of our judgments of time is not itself an appearance in time, and consequently cannot change in time.

6. Kant therefore draws the conclusion that it is something which is permanent amidst all change of appearances.

7. Finally, since it is not capable of changing, Kant concludes, "its quantum in nature can be neither increased or diminished." I take this last point as asserting the simple corollary that since substance cannot change, the number of substances cannot change either, since the only way they could would be by substances coming into or going out of existence, which would be for them to change.

Immediately after this seven-step line of argumentation Kant adds the arguments which he had already offered in the first edition of the *Critique*. These arguments rehearse the points which have now already been made. Therefore, I will not consider them in detail here.

What are we to think of the above argument? Does it prove what Kant considered to be the "obviously synthetic" proposition that "throughout all changes in the world *substance* remains, and that only *accidents* change" (A184/B227)? The first step in answering this question seems to me to be the recognition of Kant's unquestioned assumption, relative to this proof, of two doctrines: (1) Kant's own Transcendental Idealism, which he elsewhere (in the Antinomies) tries to prove, but which he here presupposes, and (2) the doctrine of Psychological Atomism which is the common presupposition of both Hume and Kant, and which, to my knowledge, neither ever tried to prove. By Psychological Atomism I mean the picture which is operative in the theorizing of many philosophers that the mind is given data which is simple and discrete and which serves, according to the story, as the building blocks of the edifice of our knowledge. Given both of these presuppositions, Kant's argument is at least understandable. If all that is "given" to the mind is discrete data, and if for that data to be the object of experience it must be possible to assign objective temporal relations to that data, then, given the doctrine of Transcendental Idealism, it seems plausible that there must be something which gives form to the data, thus constituting Kant's third thing, and that this third thing should be both part of the object of experience and yet not something "given" to perception. The third thing is, in Kantian jargon, the data subjected to the condition of a rule, i.e., the rule that whatever we can experience must be experienced at some objectively determinable time. There must therefore be in the object of experience the ground for the objectivity of our judgments of permanence in time, and that ground Kant calls substance.

Kant's best thought typically operates at the very highest levels of abstraction. Understood at the highly abstract level at which I have restated Kant's argument above, it seems to me that Kant has made a major advance beyond Hume. There must indeed be more in the object of experience than Hume was prepared to admit, and Kant was right in noting that this additional element has to do with our judgments of temporal modality, specifically here, perdurance in time. However, having made these advances, Kant, in his analysis of perdurance and change, fell back on several further presuppositions which he shared with Hume and which seem to me to be quite unjustified. Having seen that there must be present in the object of experience the ground for the objectivity of judgments of temporal duration, Kant, like Hume, presupposes, quite erroneously in my opinion, that something cannot both change and remain the same. If in making judgments of temporal duration we must use the concepts of sameness and difference, Kant, like Hume, presupposes there must be, corresponding to these concepts in the object of experience, some thing which remains the same and some other thing which changes. Hume failed to perceive such an unchanging thing, and therefore denied the objective validity of the concept of substance. Kant saw correctly that there must be in the object of experience a criterion for the judgment that something remains the same amidst change, but he erroneously identified that criterion with an unperceived but necessarily presupposed unchanging something.

What I am suggesting is that Kant, after having made a major advance beyond Hume in recognizing that there must be criteria for judgments of temporal duration in the objects of experience, immediately regressed to a Humean analysis of the concept of identity in change. Kant saw that the notion of change involves sameness amidst difference. However, he simply identifies what remains the same with the object (which he calls the permanent) and then identifies what changes with determinations or modifications of the object. But this leads to the following paradoxical line of thought. Our initial reflection on change provides the data that tables, animals, and bodies do not change (if one thinks of them as substances), but only their texture, colour, shape, movements, in short their determinations, change. But further reflection leads us to see that indeed tables, animals, and bodies *do* change. We therefore conclude that they are *not* substances, but modifications or determinations of something else which *is* substance, and that substance Kant simply calls matter.

This conceptual mistake led Kant to the artificial distinction between *Veränderung* (usually translated as *alteration*) and *Wechsel* (usually translated as *change*). Kant recognized that trying to make this distinction led to the "paradoxical expression, that only the permanent (substance) is altered, and that the transitory suffers no alteration but only a change, inasmuch as certain determinations cease to be and others begin to be" (A187/B230-B231). If I am correct, there really is no distinction to be drawn between *Veränderung* and *Wechsel*. Kant feels compelled to make such a distinction because he has misconstrued the concept of identity in change, which is the concept of *one and the same* thing both perduring and being novelly determined. Kant erroneously analyzes that concept into simpler elements, a permanent thing on the one hand, and a thing which comes into and goes out of existence on the other. What he should have done is to argue that there must be criteria within one and the same changing being in terms of which our judgments about sameness and difference can be objectively grounded. If he had done this, I think I have shown that he would have been faithful to his best insights and would have successfully completed his case against Hume.

Fordham University
Bronx, New York

NOTES

1. Jonathan Bennett, *Kant's Analytic* (Cambridge: Cambridge University Press, 1966), p. 181.
2. *Ibid.*, p. 201.

3. See Henry E. Allison, *Kant's Transcendental Idealism* (New Haven: Yale University Press, 1983).

4. I am here following a suggestion of James Van Clive, "Substance, Matter, and Kant's First Analogy," *Kant-Studien* 70 (1979): 154.

5. This formulation of the doctrine of Transcendental Idealism is the equivalent of my earlier formulation of it as the doctrine that we are aware of appearances and not of things in themselves since I take Kant's concept of a thing in itself to be the concept of something not subject to the conditions of possibility of human awareness. See Allison, pp. 10-13.

SECTION V—PHENOMENOLOGY

John Brough, Chairman
Georgetown University

Overcoming the Heideggerian Critique of Metaphysical Οὐσία

by Bernadette O'Connor, CCVI

Our meeting is devoted to the consideration of the metaphysics of substance. It would seem appropriate, therefore, that we also consider Heidegger's critique of metaphysical thinking about οὐσία, which he translates as *Seiendheit* in distinction from the *Sein* which is the *Sache* of his *Denken*. We shall follow our review of the Heideggerian critique of metaphysical οὐσία with a characterization of Heideggerian *Sein*, and then, in the spirit of Gilson, who reminds us that *"philosophy always buries its undertakers,"*[1] with some remarks about the limitations of Heidegger's *Seinsdenken*.

We begin by noting that for Heidegger metaphysics is essentially thinking about οὐσία, *Seiendheit*, beingness. In the "Introduction" to "What Is Metaphysics?" Heidegger asserts that "metaphysics always represents beings as such in their totality; it deals with the beingness of beings (the οὐσία of the ὄν)."[2] In the "Postscript" to the same essay Heidegger explains that metaphysics "tells us what being is by conceptualizing the beingness of being."[3] In *What Is Philosophy?* Heidegger claims that for philosophy "the Being of beings rests in the beingness."[4] Referring to the ὄν ἦ ὄν of metaphysics in "Hegel's Concept of Experience," Heidegger writes that "in virtue of the ἦ (*qua*, as) beings are thought in their beingness."[5] And in "Recollection in Metaphysics" our thinker equates metaphysics with the "having-gone-forth of [Heideggerian] Being into beingness."[6]

Heidegger acknowledges that metaphysics has its own *Seinsfrage* and even its own ontological difference, but he holds that the metaphysical question of Being asks only about the *Seiendheit*, the beingness, of beings and that in the metaphysical ontological difference between Being and beings Being is subordinate to beings. In the "Letter on Humanism" Heidegger writes:

151

Man first clings always and only to beings. But when thought represents beings as beings it no doubt refers to Being. Yet, in fact, it always thinks only of beings as such and never of Being as such. The [metaphysical] "question of Being" always remains the question of beings....[7]

And the protocol for Heidegger's seminar on "Time and Being" speaks of "the metaphysical character of the ontological difference according to which Being is thought and conceived for the sake of beings, so that Being, regardless of being the ground, is subjugated to beings."[8] Thus for Heidegger although metaphysics may seek a *Sein,* a Being, the *Sein* it thematizes is really only *Seiendheit,* the beingness of beings, the *Sein <u>des Seienden</u>,*[9] not Heideggerian *Sein, das Sein selbst,*[10] *das Sein als solches.*[11]

Let us see in more detail how Heidegger describes metaphysical Being, οὐσία, *Seiendheit,* beingness. We have seen that Heidegger views metaphysical Being as being subordinate to beings. By this he means that whenever metaphysics considers Being it is seeking only the explanation of beings, not Being itself, for itself. Its inquiry is always ultimately oriented toward beings, not toward Being itself. In "Der Wille zur Macht als Erkenntnis" in the first volume of *Nietzsche* Heidegger writes:

> Metaphysically thought, Being is that which is thought *in terms of* beings as their most universal determination and *in the direction of* beings as their ground and cause....
>
> Metaphysics thinks being as a whole in accordance with their priority over Being.[12]

Because metaphysics thinks of Being only in terms of the most universal characteristics of beings and for the sake of beings, that is, to account for their existence, metaphysical Being is in Heidegger's view subordinate to these beings.

We can further determine this metaphysical Being from which Heidegger distinguishes the *Sache* of his own thinking. Another characteristic of metaphysical Being is that it is always presumed to be self-evident. In "Metaphysics as History of Being" Heidegger writes that "*both factors, the precedence of beings and the assumed self-evidence of Being characterize metaphysics.*"[13] Heidegger holds that in metaphysics "the 'is' and Being thought in that 'is' are simply taken for granted."[14] The Being of metaphysics reposes, in Heidegger's view, in a certain unexamined and unrecognized taken-for-grantedness.

Heidegger points out further that metaphysics conceptualizes its Being, that is, beingness, in a twofold manner:

in the first place, [as] the totality of beings as such with an eye to their most universal traits ($\overset{'}{o}\nu$ $\kappa\alpha\theta\acute{o}\lambda o\upsilon$, $\kappa o\iota\nu\acute{o}\nu$) but at the same time also as the totality of beings as such in the sense of the highest and therefore divine being ($\overset{'}{o}\nu$ $\kappa\alpha\theta\acute{o}\lambda o\upsilon$, $\overset{,}{\alpha}\kappa\rho\acute{o}\tau\alpha\tau o\nu$, $\theta\hat{\epsilon}\iota o\nu$).[15]

Metaphysics considers its Being or beingness both as those features which characterize every being and as the divine being which accounts for all other beings. This is what Heidegger means when he says that metaphysics is an onto-theo-logic. In "The Onto-Theo-Logical Constitution of Metaphysics" he explains:

> When metaphysics thinks of beings with respect to the ground that is common to all beings as such, then it is logic as onto-logic. When metaphysics thinks of beings as such as a whole, that is, with respect to the highest being which accounts for everything, then it is logic as theo-logic.[16]

Thus for Heidegger metaphysical Being is always beingness: the basic characteristic which is transcendental, that is, which extends to every being inasmuch as it is, and the supreme being which is the cause of all.

The essential thing to grasp in all of this is that Heidegger considers metaphysics to be completely deprived of any explicit theoretical conception of what he means by Being. This means that all metaphysical talk about Being remains on the side of beings in the Heideggerian ontological difference between Being and beings. The Heideggerian ontological difference is between the *Es gibt,* the it-gives-and-there-are, and the beings which it grants. Metaphysics always moves in the realm opened out by this difference, that is, it moves among beings, without any theoretical knowledge of this difference or its issue *qua* what differs.

Heidegger writes that "confined to what is metaphysical man is caught in the difference of beings and Being which he never experiences."[17] So from the perspective of the Heideggerian ontological difference all metaphysics— even that in which *ipsum esse* is the ultimate intrinsic ontological principle of a being—is concerned exclusively with beings and is ignorant of that Being which is the *Sache* of Heidegger's thinking. Thus any distinction in metaphysics between a thing's matter and form, or its substance and its accidents, or its essence and its existential act, or between the whatness and thatness of a thing designated by the terminological pair *"essentia et existentia"* takes place completely on the being side of the Heideggerian ontological difference. Any such distinction is concerned with the being *qua* being, that is, with beingness.

Metaphysics, then, never attains what Heidegger names with the word

"Being." And inasmuch as metaphysics fails to treat of that which Heidegger considers ultimately worthy of questioning, that which he calls "Being," it is forgetful, oblivious, of this Heideggerian Being. Heidegger charges metaphysics with this *Seinsvergessenheit* over and over again. He writes, for example, that "metaphysics, insofar as it always represents only beings does not recall Being itself."[18] In "Sketches for a History of Being as Metaphysics" Heidegger states that "metaphysics leaves and must leave the essence of Being undecided, in that it remains indifferent from the beginning to a regarding of what is worthy of question."[19] So Heidegger's *Seinsdenken* will be a step back out of metaphysics into the unthought essence of metaphysics, that is, into what differs in the ontological difference, that is, into Being in its difference from beings.

If Heideggerian Being is not $ο\dot{υ}σία$, *Seiendheit,* what is it? Before we answer that affirmatively we must tarry a little longer on the *via negationis.* Heidegger's *Sein* is not a being,[20] not a component of beings,[21] and not the totality of beings.[22] Heideggerian *Sein* is not to be explained in terms of beings.[23] But neither is this *Sein* to be conceived as an explanation of beings; this Being is not God,[24] not any ontic ground[25] or cause.[26] Heidegger's *Sein* is not to be conceived objectively[27] and is not a genus, not even the most universal genus.[28] And finally this Being is not something standing in and for itself.[29]

On the *via affirmationis* we see that Heidegger determines Being as *Anwesen,* presencing.[30] Presencing is the unifying determination of Being which Heidegger seeks and which he tells us he reaches by a leap.[31] Presencing means the unconcealing of beings, their being of concern for *Dasein,* for human there-being, their lingering before us.[32] This presencing is that by which, for Heidegger, who never recants his original phenomenological formulation of the *Seinsfrage,* beings are beings.[33] Heidegger also characterizes Being as $\dot{α}λ\dot{η}θεια$, the primordial and transcendental unconcealing or sheltering in presence by means of which beings are beings, that is, for Heidegger, present or of concern to humans.[34]

Heideggerian Being, which is unconcealing or presencing, is also self-concealing. As it unconceals or makes present beings, Being withdraws or withholds its very giving self. The very beings which it grants hide Being itself. The self-withholding of Being is the Heideggerian $\overset{\backprime}{ε}ποχη$ of Being, the source of the errancy in human history.[35]

This unconcealing, presencing, self-concealing *Sein* is also the original "in which." Heidegger characterizes this "in which," which is Being, as a lighting-gathering-sheltering-in-presence[36] and as temporality.[37] Beings do not exist and then enter this region which is Being; Being does not circumscribe pre-existent beings. Rather beings first come to be beings in this primordial dimensionality, this "in which," which is Being itself.

We just mentioned temporality. The presencing in terms of which Heidegger determines Being has a temporal connotation, and temporality seems to be the originary dimension in which beings come to be, that is, are unconcealed for us. At first the unitary meaning of the Being of *Dasein,*[38] temporality becomes for the later Heidegger the epochal character of Being.[39] The self-withholding of Being in its various dispensations of beings is the source of human history and of the *Seinsvergessenheit* therein.[40] The various destinies of Being account for the various philosophical thematizations of Being and their corresponding thematizations of the nature of human being.[41] The fact that any thinker's word about Being is a dispensation of Being, a response to a fate of Being, is what makes it impossible for Heidegger to judge any such word as more or less excellent than any other such word.[42]

There are two basic relationships present throughout all of Heidegger's writings and implicit in each of the themes by means of which he determines *Sein.* These two relationships are those between Being and beings and between Being and *Dasein,* human there-being. Concerning the relationship between Being and beings Heidegger tells us first that Being and beings are the two terms of the ontological difference.[43] Heidegger picks up everything he has to say about the relationship between Being and beings in the concept of *Austrag,* the mutual bearing out or perdurance, the differing, of Being and beings. *Austrag* names the unconcealing of beings and the concealing of Being in Being's overcoming of, and arrival as, beings. *Austrag* is the relationship of Being and beings from which the two can first issue as two.[44]

Every one of the themes by means of which Heidegger determines Being implies the relationship between Being and human there-being. Heidegger finally expresses this all-pervasive belonging together of Being and human there-being, the sameness of these two, in the concept of *Ereignis,* the primordial relationship, belonging together, which first lets Being and human being issue as themselves.[45] This non-causal, finite and abysmal event of appropriation is incommensurate with propositional statements and hence all but inexpressible.[46]

It is difficult to determine the precise nature of the relationship between *Ereignis,* identity, and *Austrag,* difference. It would seem that the relationship which *Ereignis* names is more primordial than the relationship which *Austrag* names inasmuch as the relation of Being to human there-being bears all.[47] While Heidegger hints that the two relationships are the same,[48] he cannot bring them into perfect symmetry because human being is both ontic—and therefore the co-issue with Being of that *Austrag* which stems from *Ereignis*—and ontological—and therefore co-determinative of Being in that *Ereignis* from which its issuing *qua* ontic, *qua* being, in *Austrag* stems.[49] At the point at which this circling or reciprocal relationship between *Austrag* and *Ereignis* becomes evident Heidegger refers us to the poetic and quasi-mystical expressions of *Ereignis* and *Austrag* in which the former becomes the round dance of the world play, in which earth and sky, divinities and mortals are mutually appropriated,[50] and the latter becomes the thinging of the thing which stays the fourfold of the world, from which world the thing e-vents.[51]

And, finally, we note that Heidegger also endows that Being which is nothing in and for itself, which needs human being in order to essence as Being,[52] with certain quasi-numinous qualities. Heideggerian *Sein* resembles the divine numen experienced by mystics in that it is mysterious,[53] of unbound power,[54] inexhaustible,[55] and of primal dignity.[56] In its storminess,[57] danger,[58] and darkness[59] this nameless Being fills human being with *Angst,*[60] with terror, and with awe.[61] This same Being is also, however, the holy,[62] serene,[63] saving,[64] and joyous.[65] Both near and far,[66] this Being both violates human being[67] and appeals to it.[68] It offers grace and favor to which human being responds with sacrifice and thanksgiving.[69] This Heideggerian *Sein* is ultimately inexpressible and must be experienced.[70]

In all of this it seems to us that what is essential in Heidegger's *Seinsdenken* is that Being is not something other than human being which can stand in and for itself. Heideggerian *Sein* needs human being-there in order to essence as Being. Being is essentially involvement in human being. And yet Heidegger tells us at different points along his path that this Being, which is not except as related to human being, which depends upon human being, can overpower it and receive its service, sacrifice, and thanksgiving. And we should note again that Heidegger finally gives up trying to express this Being, this relationship, in philosophical language and offers us instead the poetic image of the round dance of the world.

All the great Heideggerian themes are as so many radii, each leading to the same center point. This central point is the belonging together, the sameness, of Being and human there-being. This relationship is involved reciprocally, that is, circularly, with the differing of Being and beings. What would be a *circulus vitious* for philosophical thinking becomes for Heidegger a *circulus saltatorius* in the poetic image of the round dance of the world. If we persevere on the path of Heidegger's *Seinsdenken* we find that thinking disappearing into poetic and quasi-mystical imagery.

And what have we to say of Heidegger's *Seinsdenken*? First, we note that there are substantive presuppositions inextricably linked to Heidegger's choice of the phenomenological methodology for his *Seinsdenken.* These presuppositions are that beings are those things that appear[71] and that a reduction to the transcendental consciousness which constitutes or discloses being is necessary.[72] Heidegger sets out in, and never departs from, the phenomenological realm of appearance. In the battle of giants for Heidegger's philosophical soul Husserl triumphs over Aristotle. The thinking of the Stagirite ignited in Heidegger the Being question, but the phenomenological thinking of the Venerable Beginner determined for Heidegger that question and the *Sein* that answers to it as completely as form determines matter.

We understand Heidegger's *Sein* to be a conflation of a number of really different principles. The most fundamental conflation which Heidegger effects in his *Sein* is that of *esse reale* and *esse intentionale.* With the *Doctor Communis* we recognize two orders of *esse,* real *ipsum esse,* by which beings are, stand out from nothingness in the order of existence, regardless of their relationship to human being, and *esse intentionale,* by which the being known becomes present in the knower and the knower becomes the thing known.[73] Heideggerian *Seinsdenken,* beginning from the phenomenological sphere of *esse intentionale,* makes the two *esse*'s to coincide in one *Sein.* For Heidegger, the phenomenologist, to be and to be present are the same.

In a certain basic sense *Dasein,* human there-being, takes over in Heidegger's thought a prerogative that God enjoys in St. Thomas' teaching. Whereas for St. Thomas being is being inasmuch as it corresponds to the creative mind of God, for Heidegger being is being inasmuch as it is present for human there-being. The transcendental relationship in terms of which being is established has shifted from that of beings to God to that of beings to *Dasein.*

It is perhaps because Heidegger has collapsed the real and intentional orders into one phenomenological sphere of presencing that he fails to distinguish between the order of causality obtaining among things and the order of our knowing those things. Heidegger appears to be so averse to metaphysical Being as the cause and ground of beings because he thinks that if Being is *conceived* as the ground or cause of beings it will *be* subsequent to them. We may, indeed, know beings first, but the fact that we conceive them first and then later think Being as their cause does not make Being really dependent upon beings. This appears to be a consistent and fundamental confusion in Heidegger and it apparently derives from the collapse of the orders of real and intentional being into one.

In several places in his writings Heidegger speaks about the "essence" of Being or of presencing or about the "what" of Being.[74] He even suggests that "ἀλήθεια might be the word that offers a hitherto unnoticed hint concerning the essence of *esse* which has not yet been recalled."[75] We gather from these statements that Heidegger makes the mistake that is so often made in the history of philosophy of trying to grasp Being as a whatness, of endowing Being with some quidditative content in order to make it graspable by abstractive apprehension. Could we not envision another chapter in Gilson's *Being and Some Philosophers* entitled "Being and *Anwesen*"? But Being is an act, *ipsum esse,* and the only quidditative content that it has is that of what has the act of being.

And we have seen the quidditative content which Heidegger attempts to fasten on Being: presencing. But to be is not to be present. It has been a constant source of wonder to us how Heidegger, who is so attentive to the lessons that language can teach us, misses seeing that when we say "to be present" we have already said "to be" just as when we think the true we have already thought being.

We remark also that inasmuch as the Heideggerian destinies of Being seem to be fundamentally determinative of human history and responsible for a certain relativism of worth among the various human endeavors it would appear that Heideggerian *Sein* would, at least to some degree, abrogate human freedom and responsibility. It is interesting to note, then, that a thinking which begins by exalting the human as the beginning and the end of philosophy[76] and by founding Being in the human, a thinking, that is, which begins by exalting the human above its proper station, ends by stripping the human of its proper dignity as a responsible agent of free choice.

Then, too, Heidegger's endowing of *Sein* with quasi-numinous qualities appears to us to be an effort, unconscious perhaps, to secure the aesthetic satisfactions which are sometimes associated with the mystic's life of union with God without the inconvenience of an absolute and personal Being who would have us learn, in Jacques Maritain's charming phrase, "the manners of God"[77] in a school of painful purifications. If we cannot play music and dance before the *causa sui* of metaphysics[78] neither need we pray to, and give up all for, the hypostatization which is Heideggerian *Sein*.

In his book *The Unity of Philosophical Experience* Gilson outlines a three-stage progression that often repeats itself in the history of philosophy. First there is a failure of philosophical thinking; this is followed by skepticism about the possibility of attaining truth by human reasoning; and this, in turn, is followed by a recourse to some sort of pseudo-mysticism or moralism.[79] In concluding our partial critique of Heidegger's *Seinsdenken* we suggest that it is not too farfetched to find all three of these stages in Heidegger's thinking. First Heidegger fails to attain real Being because his phenomenological formulation of the *Seinsfrage* consigns him to a universe in which to be is to be present. Then we find a certain relativism and skepticism expressing themselves in Heidegger's thinking when he tells us that we do not have the criteria with which to know whether one philosophy is more excellent than another. And, finally, Heidegger's philosophy is reduced to expressing itself in the quasi-mystical imagery of the round dance of the world.

Gilson holds that all failures of philosophical thinking can "*be traced to the fact, that the first principle of human knowledge has been either overlooked or misused*" and that "the most tempting of all the false first principles is: that *thought*, not *being*, is involved in all my representations."[80] The failure of Heidegger's philosophical reason involves a variation on this first false principle. Because Heidegger makes reflection, which is by definition a bending back over that through the medium of which we have already contacted real being, the first moment of his thinking, his philosophy is a philosophy of intentions in which being is encompassed in thought. However, to recognize Heidegger's error as such is to be free from it and thus able to maintain and serve, as Gilson would have us,[81] philosophy in our time.

St. Mary's University
San Antonio, Texas

NOTES

1. Etienne Gilson, *The Unity of Philosophical Experience* (New York: Charles Scribner's Sons, 1937), p. 306.

2. "Einleitung zu 'Was ist Metaphysik?'" in *Wegmarken* (Frankfurt am Main: Klostermann, 1967), S. 207/English translation by Walter Kaufmann: "The Way Back into the Ground of Metaphysics" in *Philosophy in the Twentieth Century*, Volume III, edited by William Barrett and Henry D. Aiken (New York: Harper and Row, 1971), p. 137 (hereafter referred to as "WM:E"). Unless otherwise stated, all texts cited in the notes are those of Martin Heidegger. All abbreviations are followed by the 'Seiten' in the German original and the page numbers in the cited English translation.

3. "'Nachwort' zu 'Was ist Metaphysik?'" in *Wegmarken*, S. 100/English translation by Werner Brock: "'Postscript' to 'What is Metaphysics?'" in *Existence and Being* (Chicago: Regnery, 1970), p. 351 (translation slightly changed; hereafter "WM:N").

4. *What is Philosophy?*, German-English edition, translated by William Kluback and Jean T. Wilde (New Haven: College and University Press, 1958), pp. 54-55 (hereafter "WP").

5. "Hegels Begriff der Erfahrung" in *Holzwege* (Frankfurt am Main: Klostermann, 1957), S. 166/English translation: *Hegel's Concept of Experience* (New York: Harper & Row, 1970), p. 113 (translation slightly changed).

6. "Die Erinnerung in die Metaphysik" in *Nietzsche* II (Pfullingen: Neske, 1961), S. 487/English translation by Joan Stambaugh: "Recollection in Metaphysics" in *The End of Philosophy* (New York: Harper & Row, 1973), p. 81 (translation slightly changed; hereafter "Erin M").

7. "Brief über den 'Humanismus'" in *Wegmarken*, S. 162/English translation by Edgar Lohner: "Letter on Humanism" in *Philosophy in the Twentieth Century*, Volume III, p. 204 (hereafter "HB").

8. "Protokoll zu einem Seminar über den Vortrag 'Zeit und Sein'" in *Zur Sache des Denkens* (Tübingen: Niemeyer, 1969), S. 36/English translation by Joan Stambaugh: "Summary of Seminar on the Lecture 'Time and Being'" in *On Time and Being* (New York: Harper & Row, 1972), p. 33 (hereafter "PSZS").

9. "Über das Zeitverständnis in der Phänomenologie und im Denken der Seinsfrage" in *Phänomenologie lebendig oder tot?*, herausgegeben von Helmut Gehrig (Karlsruhe: Badenia, 1969), S. 47 (hereafter "ZPDS").

10. HB, S. 148/p. 195.

11. "A Letter from Heidegger to William J. Richardson, S.J." in William J. Richardson, S.J., *Heidegger: Through Phenomenology to Thought* (Nijhoff: The Hague, 1967), pp. x-xi (hereafter "BR").

12. "Der Wille zur Macht als Erkenntnis" in *Nietzsche* I (Pfullingen: Neske, 1961), S. 478/ partially translated by Joan Stambaugh: "Nietzsche as Metaphysician" in *Nietzsche: A Collection of Critical Essays,* edited by Robert Solomon (Garden City: Doubleday, 1973), p. 111 (hereafter "WZM").

13. "Die Metaphysik als Geschichte des Seins" in *Nietzsche* II, S. 411/English translation by Joan Stambaugh: "Metaphysics as History of Being" in *The End of Philosophy* (New York: Harper & Row, 1973), p. 11

14. *Ibid.*

15. WM:E, S. 207/p. 137.

16. "Die onto-theo-logische Verfassung der Metaphysik" ("The Onto-Theo-Logical Constitution of Metaphysics") in *Identity and Difference,* translated by Joan Stambaugh (New York: Harper & Row, 1969), p. 139 (English: pp. 70-71) (hereafter "OTL").

17. "Überwindung der Metaphysik" in *Vorträge und Aufsätze* (Pfullingen: Neske, 1959), S. 66/English translation by Joan Stambaugh: "Overcoming Metaphysics" in *The End of Philosophy,* p. 87 (hereafter "UM").

18. WM:E, S. 196/p. 130.

19. "Entwürfe zur Geschichte des Seins als Metaphysik" in *Nietzsche* II, S. 459/English translation by Joan Stambaugh: "Sketches for a History of Being as Metaphysics" in *The End of Philosophy,* p. 56 (hereafter "GSM").

20. *Sein und Zeit,* zwölfte Auflage (Tübingen: Niemeyer, 1972), S. 230/*Being and Time,* translated by John Macquarrie and Edward Robinson (New York: Harper & Row, 1962), p. 272 (hereafter "SZ"); *Grundprobleme der Phänomenologie* (Frankfurt am Main: Klostermann, 1975), S. 109/English translation with introduction and lexicon by Albert Hofstadter: *The Basic Problems of Phenomenology* (Bloomington: Indiana University Press, 1982), p. 78 (hereafter "GP"); "Zeit und Sein" in *Zur Sache des Denkens,* S. 8/English translation by Joan Stambaugh: "Time and Being" in *On Time and Being,* p. 8 (hereafter "ZS"). The description of Heideggerian *Sein* presented in the text is a summary of the third chapter, "Heideggerian *Seinsdenken,*" pp. 153-329, of the author's doctoral dissertation *Martin Heidegger, Saint Thomas Aquinas, and the Forgottenness of Being* (Duquesne University, 1982). This chapter contains an extensive collection of texts, with the German original in Notes, for each of the great themes (the Nothing; Truth; Presencing; Concealing; Clearing, There, and other spatial metaphors; Language; Thinking; Time; *Ereignis* and *Austrag;* and the Numinous) by which Heidegger determines Being. For the purposes of this paper we give references for only a few of these texts.

21. *Einführung in die Metaphysik* (Tübingen: Niemeyer, 1953), S. 67/English translation by Ralph Mannheim: *An Introduction to Metaphysics* (Garden City: Doubleday and Company, 1961), p. 73 (hereafter "EM").

22. WZM, S. 476/p. 110; "Moira: Parmenides VIII, 34-41" in *Vorträge und Aufsätze,* S. 36/ English translation by David Farrell Krell and Frank A. Capuzzi in *Early Greek Thinking* (New York: Harper & Row, 1973), p. 87 (hereafter "M").

23. SZ, S. 207/p. 251; *Was heisst Denken?* (Tübingen: Niemeyer, 1954), S. 64/English translation by J. Glenn Gray and F. Wieck: *What Is Called Thinking?* (New York: Harper & Row, 1968), p. 66 (hereafter "WD"); HB, S. 165/p. 206.

24. HB, S. 162/p. 204.

25. HB, S. 162/p. 204; ZS, S. 5-6/p. 6; PSZS, S. 49/p. 45.

26. "Die Kehre" in *Die Technik und die Kehre* (Pfullingen: Neske, 1962), S. 42-43/English translation by William Lovitt: "The Turning" in *The Question Concerning Technology and Other Essays* (New York: Harper & Row, 1977), p. 44 (hereafter "K").

27. WM:N, S. 101/p. 353.

28. SZ, S. 38/p. 62; EM, S. 31/p. 33; ZS, S. 6/p. 6.

29. *Zur Seinsfrage* (The Question of Being), translated by Jean T. Wilde and William Kluback (New Haven: College and University Press, 1958), pp. 80-83 (hereafter "SF").

30. BR, pp. xii-xiii; WD, S. 142/p. 235; "Der Spruch des Anaximanders" in *Holzwege*, S. 322/English translation by David Farrell Krell and Frank A. Capuzzi: "The Anaximander Fragment" in *Early Greek Thinking*, p. 37 (hereafter "SA"); ZS, S. 5, 10/p. 5, 10.

31. WD, S. 140-141/pp. 232-233.

32. Das Wesen der Sprache" in *Unterwegs zur Sprache* (Pfullingen: Neske, 1959), S. 201/ English translation by Peter D. Hertz: "The Nature of Language" in *On the Way to Language* (New York: Harper & Row, 1971), p. 95 (hereafter "WS"); ZS, S. 12/p. 12; WD, S. 144/p. 257.

33. SZ, S. 27, 35/pp. 49-50, 60; "Mein Weg in die Phänomenologie" in *Zur Sache des Denkens*, S. 90/English translation by Joan Stambaugh: "My Way to Phenomenology" in *On Time and Being*, p. 82 (hereafter "MWP"); William J. Richardson, S.J., *Heidegger: Through Phenomenology to Thought*, with a Preface by Martin Heidegger, 2nd ed. (The Hague: Martinus Nijhoff, 1967), p. 627.

34. SZ, S. 220, 230/pp. 263, 272; "Vom Wesen der Wahrheit" in *Wegmarken*, S. 96/English translation: "On the Essence of Truth" in *Basic Writings*, edited by David Farrell Krell (New York: Harper & Row, 1977), p. 140 (hereafter "WW"); EM, S. 142/p. 155; "Der Ursprung des Kunstwerkes" in *Holzwege*, S. 73/English translation by Albert Hofstadter: "The Origin of the Work of Art" in *Poetry, Language, Thought*, p. 86; MGS, S. 420/p. 19; "Das Ende der Philosophie und die Aufgabe des Denkens" in *Zur Sache des Denkens*, S. 75/English translation by Joan Stambaugh: "The End of Philosophy and the Task of Thinking" in *On Time and Being*, p. 68 (hereafter "EP").

35. SZ, S. 35/p. 59; PSZS, S. 39/p. 36; WM:E, S. 203/p. 134; "Die Sprache im Gedicht" in *Unterwegs zur Sprache*, S. 44/English translation by Peter D. Hertz: "Language in the Poem" in *On the Way to Language*, p. 165 (hereafter "SG"); ZS, S. 9/p. 9.

36. HB, S. 157, 163/pp. 201, 204; WM:N, S. 103/p. 355; "Aletheia: Heraclitus, Fragment 16" in *Vorträge und Aufsätze*, S. 74-76/English translation in *Early Greek Thinking*, pp. 120-21; "Wozu Dichter?" in *Holzwege*, S. 277-78/English translation in *Poetry, Language, Thought*, p. 123; EP, S. 72/p. 65.

37. ZS, S. 16/p. 15.

38. SZ, S. 304, 327/p. 352, 375.

39. ZS, S. 8-9/pp. 8-9; M, S. 84/pp. 97-98.

40. ZS, S. 8-9/pp. 8-9; SA, S. 311/p. 27.

41. WW, S. 77/p. 121; SA, S. 310/p. 37.

42. "Die Zeit des Weltbildes" in *Holzwege*, S. 71/English translation: "The Age of the World Picture" in *The Question of Technology and Other Essays*, p. 117; EP, S. 62/p. 56.

43. GP, S. 109/p. 78; GSM, S. 475-476/p. 70.

44. OTL, S. 132-33/pp. 64-66.

45. "Der Satz der Identität" (The Principle of Identity) in *Identity and Difference*, translated by Joan Stambaugh (New York: Harper & Row, 1969), pp. 100-104 (36-40) (hereafter "SI"); ZS, S. 5/p. 5; "Der Weg zur Sprache" in *Unterwegs zur Sprache*, S. 258/p. 127.

46. "Zur Erörterung der Gelassenheit: Aus einem Feldweggespräch über das Denken" in *Gelassenheit* (Pfullingen: Neske, 1959), S. 70/English translation by John M. Anderson and E. Hans Freund: "Conversation on a Country Path About Thinking" in *Discourse on Thinking* (New York: Harper & Row, 1966), p. 88 (hereafter "EG"); Erin M, S. 485/p. 78; SI, p. 106 (41); PSZS, S. 27-28/pp. 25-26.

47. WD, S. 45/p. 107.

48. ZS, S. 24-25/p. 24; OTL, S. 132/p. 65; see also Heidegger's answers to questions submitted by Professors Joan Stambaugh and J. Glenn Gray, translated and published with Heidegger's permission in the "Introduction" to *The End of Philosophy*, pp. xii-xiii (German text not available).

49. See the dissertation cited above, pp. 301-305, for a more detailed exposition of the circularity obtaining between *Austrag* and *Ereignis*.

50. "Bauen Wohnen Denken" in *Vorträge und Aufsätze*, S. 23-24/English translation "Building Dwelling Thinking" in *Poetry, Language, Thought*, pp. 149-50; "Das Ding" in *Vorträge und Aufsätze*, S. 52-53/English translation: "The Thing" in *Poetry, Language, Thought*, pp. 179-80 (hereafter "D").

51. D, S. 53/pp. 180-81.

52. WD, S. 74/p. 76; SF, S. 74/p. 75.

53. HB, S. 165/p. 205; UM, S. 90/p. 109; WM:N, S. 103/p. 355.

54. EM, S. 125, 134, 136/pp. 137, 147, 149.

55. "Wissenschaft und Besinnung" in *Vorträge und Aufsätze*, S. 62/English translation: "Science and Reflection" in *The Question of Technology and Other Essays*, p. 182.

56. Erin M, S. 485/p. 79.

57. "Logos: Heraklit, Fragment 50" in *Vorträge und Aufsätze*, S. 25/English translation in *Early Greek Thinking*, p. 78.

58. K, S. 41/p. 43.

59. "Grundsätze des Denkens" in *Jahrbuch für Psychologie und Psychotherapie*, Bd. VI (1958), S. 40/English translation by James G. Hart and John C. Maraldo: "Principles of Thinking" in *The Piety of Thinking* (Bloomington: Indiana University Press, 1976), p. 56.

60. SZ, S. 186, 188/p. 231, 233.

61. WM:N, S. 103/p. 355.

62. "Heimkunft/An die Verwandten" in *Erläuterungen zu Hölderlins Dichtung*, vierte Auflage (Frankfurt am Main: Klostermann, 1971), S. 18/English translation: "Remembrance of the Poet" in *Existence and Being*, p. 251 (hereafter "HV").

63. HV, S. 16-17/pp. 247-249.

64. "Das Wort" in *Unterwegs zur Sprache*, S. 236/English translation: "Words" in *On the Way to Language*, p. 154.

65. HV, S. 16/p. 247.

66. HB, S. 162/p. 204.

67. EM, S. 136/p. 149.

68. HB, S. 154/p. 198; WP, S. 72, 74/pp. 73, 75; *Aus der Erfahrung des Denkens* (Pfullingen: Neske, 1954), S. 17/English translation: "The Thinker as Poet" in *Poetry, Language, Thought*, p. 9.

69. WM:N, S. 105-106/pp. 358-359; EG, S. 357/p. 85.

70. WM:N, S. 105/p. 357; WD, S. 165/p. 170; PSZS, S. 28/p. 26.

71. WD, S. 141/p. 233.

72. GP, S. 103, 155, 444/pp. 73, 110, 312; "Die Idee der Phänomenologie und der Rückgang auf das Bewusstsein" in *Husserliana*, Bd. IX: *Phänomenologische Psychologie*, herausgegeben von Walter Biemel (The Hague: Nijhoff, 1962), S. 356-357/English translation by Thomas J. Sheehan: "The Idea of Phenomenology, with a Letter to Edmund Husserl (1927)" in *Listening*, 12 (Fall 1977), pp. 111-12; SZ, S. 35/p. 60.

73. Thomas Aquinas, *Summa contra gentiles*, Leonine manual edition (Rome: Laziale, 1934), IV, 11, (6). The fourth and fifth chapters of the dissertation cited above list certain elements from the metaphysics of St. Thomas Aquinas with which Heideggerian *Sein* can be compared and contrasted: *ipsum esse creatum; ipsum esse subsistens;* the transcendental *verum;* the agent intellect; *esse intentionale; esse* as the verbal copula; and *Verbum.* It is our conclusion that while Heideggerian *Sein* is strictly equivalent with none of these elements it has some characteristics of each of them.

74. GSM, S 459/p. 56; "Aus einem Gespräch von der Sprache" in *Unterwegs zur Sprache*, S. 118/English translation: "A Dialogue on Language" in *On the Way to Language*, p. 26; EM, S. 31, 78/pp. 33, 87; SA, S. 336/p. 50; ZPDS, S. 47; WM:N, S. 106/p. 359.

75. WM:E, S. 199/pp. 131-32.

76. SZ, S. 38/p. 62.

77. Jacques Maritain, *Distinguish to Unite or the Degrees of Knowledge,* translated by Gerald B. Phelan (New York: Charles Scribner's Sons, 1959), p. 357.

78. OTL, S. 140/p. 72.

79. Gilson, *op. cit.*, pp. 304-6.

80. Gilson, *op. cit.,* p. 316.

81. Gilson, *op. cit.,* p. 317.

Phenomenological Analysis of the Individual Thing And the Triumph of the Accidental

by Atherton C. Lowry

Phenomenology's view[1] of the nature of a thing can be summed up in Merleau-Ponty's statement: "What is given is not the thing by itself, but the experience of the thing, a transcendence in a wake of subjectivity..."[2] As he describes it, the individual or concrete thing appears within the field of consciousness in terms of a *Gestalt,* i.e., as a figure against a background.[3] The thing is "experienced" as a project of consciousness and so can never actually be in itself. That is to say, the thing is fundamentally constituted by a spatiality and temporality consciousness intends, by a spatio-temporal structure or dimensionality which continually keeps the thing at a distance from the perceiver or knower. This transcendence, however, of the concrete individual does not, as already indicated, point to a thing-in-itself but to a structure of space-time relations.

In contrast, following Aristotle's description of individual things in his *Categories,* we see their identity as primary substances, as what

> ...are most properly called substances in virtue of the fact that they are the entities which underlie everything else, and that everything else is either predicated of them or present in them.[4]

Hence, since time and space, via place, fall under the list of Aristotle's categories and so under the classification of accidents, substance in its primary sense is something more fundamental in which they inhere. But what is this something which is more fundamental? In his *Metaphysics*[5] Aristotle pursues this issue, a pursuit to which we will return.

What we propose then to do in this essay is disclose in some detail the phenomenological description of the individual thing and the accompanying rejection of "primary substance," taken in the Aristotelian sense, as a way to describe the "reality" of the thing. In this regard, phenomenological "reality" equals the "process" of the thing. We will follow up this portion of the paper with a critique of the phenomenological position, which, by virtue of such rejection, eliminates metaphysics insofar as "substantiality" is considered a requirement for defining metaphysics.

The key to phenomenological investigation of the thing is process and

164

relation. The thing shows itself within the intentional field as a kind of crystallization of a network of relations. This network refers to an open-ended grouping of relations with the thing itself, with other things, and with the perceiver or knower. For example, I view the elephant at the zoo with a certain color, shape, size, etc. Indeed, I don't just experience one color of the elephant but many shades of color within my perceptual field. So too are there many shapes I can perceive within the larger outline of the elephant as a whole; for example, the shape of the trunk or the shape of the eye. The elephant in its total configuration stands out against a background of other things, presenting a profile or figure in conjunction with the horizontal network of interrelated things. The bush, the rocks, the dirt, the zoo build-ing, a squirrel—all these surround and serve as part of the background against which the elephant stands out. The context of relations constitutive of the elephant is, of course, incomplete without reference to the intender or perceiver. For the relations which emerge as forming the elephant's horizon of appearing also make up the intentional field of consciousness. That is to say, the elephant becomes present within the context of the perspectives of consciousness, the perspectives being the relations of intentionality. So it is that the network of relations or perspectives is the inner logic or meaning of the elephant. Concerning this, we should note the phenomenological use of *Logos*[6] as identifiable with the inner logic of the thing.

Now the "meaning" or "inner logic" of the thing is the phenomenological notion of the "essence" of the thing. However, phenomenology wants to avoid describing the thing's essence as a Platonic form or as the Aristotelian universal of a particular thing. For then the essence would possess a "sub-stantial" character in the sense of being permanent and unchanging. But more later on this. As regards the phenomenological "meaning" of the thing, the description of what is truly fundamental or "essential" about the thing experienced centers on space and time. Hence, the network of relations surrounding and constitutive of the elephant is at bottom a spatio-temporal network. To elaborate, the elephant I first experience is at a great distance. However, this spatial perspective continually changes as I draw closer. Further, each *present* spatial perspective in my perceptual experience takes place within a context of *past* spatial perspectives and in anticipation of *future* possible spatial perspectives. So it is that the horizontal relations of the thing are understood as intrinsically spatio-temporal. Indeed, time takes on a priority over space since it is a single flow of time as a temporal project which binds spatial relations together in a unity of the past and the future in the present. It is time that grounds every synthesizing process and the only time of consciousness is a time spatializing itself, i.e., giving birth to space through a process of spatializing itself. In Merleau-Ponty's words: "...every synthesis is all at once distended and remade by time..."[7] Time and meaning are one, therefore, because the cohesion or unity or presence of the thing is its horizon of meaning.

Turning to the notion of process, we find that for phenomenology the thing is a continually changing manifestation of what both Heidegger and Merleau-Ponty characterize as the "world" in process. The "world," understood as the thing's horizon of relations and indeed as the horizon of all things, as the total and open-ended network of relations of the thing, gives to the thing its *Logos* or meaning. Further, since this meaning is identified with time, nothing exists in itself, nothing is necessary or permanent. Rather everything is "contingent" in the phenomenological sense of being continually temporalized. Thus it is that Heidegger from the beginning of his thought speaks of the being (*Sein*)-process in which being continually conceals itself in the very process of revealing itself.[8] Merleau-Ponty in *The Visible and the Invisible* makes explicit a being (*Être*)-process quite similar to Heidegger's as found in *Being and Time*. In Merleau-Ponty's case, being ceaselessly unfolds as visible and invisible, as brute (wild) being and the *Logos*. For both thinkers, each thing then is present within the field of consciousness ((among basic notions for Heidegger in this regard, we can, to name two, apply There-being (*Da-sein*) and thought (*Denken*). For Merleau-Ponty we can identify body (*corps*) or flesh (*chair*) with this field))[9] as the very manifestation or crystallization of the being-process, of the horizontal network which gives the thing its meaning and which simultaneously is intended or seized by consciousness.

At this point we should note the irony and paradox of phenomenology's founder. Husserl had declared the critical importance of returning to the things themselves. He was indeed anxious to avoid contingency and reach the pure essence of the thing. However, willy-nilly, as Merleau-Ponty points out, Husserl cannot escape describing the on-going alteration of the thing through the ceaseless temporalizing of its network of relations.[10] In this connection, Husserl in Ideas II[11] distinguishes between the level of pure things and the primordial layer of intuited, perceived things. The former level is one of constructed things whereas the deeper level shows the things as experienced through the body-subject's (*Subjektleib*) contact with them.[12] Things on this level have to do with what Husserl toward the end of his life clearly stresses as the task of phenomenology, i.e., to describe the experience of the life-world (*Lebenswelt*).[13] And so it is that such a task, as rooted in the body's intentional experience of the lived world, can but find itself describing what always remains temporal and contingent.

From the above description of the individual thing, we should see clearly that a phenomenological description of the individual thing leaves us in what Aristotle would consider the realm of the accidental. In this regard, we should especially note the phenomenological preoccupation with the accident of time. Further, by Aristotle's definition of primary substance, i.e., the individual thing, accidents must inhere in the substance. Hence, they can only exist if they relate to, as being rooted in, the substance. They must exist then *in the substance.* An accident must thus be the *accident of some thing* and that thing, that substance, must underlie all accidents pertaining to it. Phenomenology, by contrast, ends up rooting the thing in time,[14] a radical reversal of the Aristotelian primacy of substance over accident. This does not mean, however, that phenomenology does away with the individual thing. On the contrary, phenomenology is quite anxious to affirm that, in Merleau-Ponty's phrase, "...'there is' something."[15] It is, nonetheless, on the basis of the efforts of Merleau-Ponty and Heidegger to search out the "there is" *of something* that we can bring out another divergence from Aristotle's notion of substance. In this regard, Heidegger's notion of There-being shows well the stress on the "there" of "being," on the field of consciousness within which being or meaning reveals and conceals itself. In this sense the individual thing becomes present within the "there" as the manifestation of "being." Further, in a later work than *Being and Time,* namely "The Thing,"[16] thought as "there" lets things become present through a process of presencing which is the being-process of revealment and concealment. Put more fully, being dominates thought through "...the thinging of things,"[17] i.e., through the bringing to presence of things in thought. Keeping in mind then the focus on the "being" of the thing via phenomenological ontology, let us explore more clearly and precisely what, for Aristotle, being itself is.

Aristotle's designation of substance or being (οὐσία, ousia), in the primary sense, as the individual thing already sets up a difference from phenomenology concerning what being is. In examining here the "being" of the thing, let us turn to his *Metaphysics.* In Book Zeta, Aristotle follows out in detail the issue of what being is or, as he further expresses it, what being *primarily* is.[18] Considering the different ways of being, Aristotle contends that primary being is not simply matter or simply form, but must be something in particular. In short, it is an individual thing, which is a composite of form and matter. At this point, we note in passing that in Book Lambda Aristotle enunciates a particular being which is free of matter, namely, what we can call the Pure Act of Thinking.[19] Let us return, however, to Book Zeta. In focusing on the composite individual, Aristotle presses home the view that even though the composite individual thing is the primary being, there is still the question of what makes the thing what it is. Aristotle's answer is that the form or essence is the immaterial principle or cause which organizes the matter and gives the thing its structure and actuality. In the words of Veatch:

...with reference to and by means of that which is most truly the substance, the very heart, the very "guts" of the thing...[is] its substantial nature, its essence, its form, its "what," its very quiddity.[20]

With Aristotle's recognition of the fundamental role of form in the constituting of an individual thing, we come to what one might well consider the
most decisive distinction between an Aristotelian and a phenomenological
description of a thing. In phenomenology, as we have seen, essence concerns meaning, the network of relations, the *Logos* of the thing. There is no
form in the "classical" sense of the term. Further, Aristotle's emphasis on the
formal principle of the thing includes, of course, the principle's character as
unchanging and permanent. Phenomenology, on the other hand, as we may
recall, insists on the intrinsic "process" character of the thing. In this regard,
as described earlier, the meaning, the being, the *Logos*, of the thing, continually changes in the endless temporalizing of the thing.

Our critique of the phenomenological position regarding the individual
thing will begin with the issue of the "process" of the thing. Put in the form of
a question: "Does the notion of substantial form do justice to the dynamism
of the thing or does such a notion render the thing basically a 'static' reality"?
Phenomenology has been diligent in defending contingency, i.e., the temporal and changing, and equally concerned with rejecting necessity, i.e., the
permanent and unchanging. The view that all things manifest through and
through a temporal flow and dynamic remains a recurring and apparently
unavoidable description from the phenomenological standpoint. Anything
non-contingent, in the sense of non-temporal, it is claimed, removes us from
the lived experience of the process. Aristotle, of course, hardly ignores the
role of process in his description of the thing. The act-potency dynamic
indeed takes us to the very heart of his thought. What Aristotle introduces
and phenomenology leaves out is the "metaphysical" dimension in the sense
of what is beyond the phenomenal, i.e., of what is noumenal and non-
temporal in character. It is our contention that, like Aristotle, we must
embrace the paradox of the thing and so seize not only what touches
perception, but what makes contact "metaphysically" with the intellect.
What emerges in this lived paradox of the thing is the simultaneous presencing
of contingency and permanence, of the accidental and the substantial, of
matter and form.

Even phenomenology is struck by the persistence and constancy of the
thing. However, such actuality, as it were, is classified as "ontical" while the
heart of the thing, its process of meaning, its "fundamental being," gives the
"ontological" level of temporal flow and contingency.[21] It is our view that
such "ontical" constancy is no "real" constancy at all since the "being" of the
thing is a process. Such a focus on the thing's disclosure of constancy hardly
does justice to the lived permanence and continuity of the thing.

We will perhaps recollect earlier mention of what we called the lived
paradox of the thing. One side of the paradox includes the presence of the
contingent, the accidental, and matter. Hence, this side stresses the thing's

dynamism from the standpoint of the thing's potential whereby through a movement or process the potential is actualized. Let us look now at the other side of the paradox, at the "dynamic" character of the substantial form itself of the thing. Aristotle in Book Theta speaks of the act of a thing and identifies this with its form.[22] That Aristotle further connects act with the notion of completion or fulfillment (ἐντελέχεια, entelecheia)[23] might indicate a "static" description. However, Aristotle's teaching on the act of the thing also emphasizes its meaning as *energeia (ἐνέργεια)*.[24] Indeed the distinction between *energeia* and *entelecheia* makes clear Aristotle's wish to stress that the very act of a thing connotes the "life" or "energy" of the thing. Certainly form as act includes in its meaning *entelecheia*, but it also includes the "dynamism" of *energeia* in the very actualizing of the potential of a thing. It will remain for Aquinas to bring out even more strongly the "action" orientation of the act of a thing. This he does by emphasizing the "verb" character of the thing's act, i.e., the *esse* or "to be" of the thing.[25] We can further say, at least in terms of Aquinas' *On the Principles of Nature,* that for him form and *esse* can be identified.[26] The central point then in all of this is that form need not be viewed as something static. On the contrary, we hold, in the light of Aristotle and Aquinas, that the *act* as "energy," as "life," as a *verb,* signifies the form as qualitatively dynamic even though the form also possesses an immutable character.

Now the affirmation of the "act" of the thing requires an intuition, an *intellectual* grasp of the "being" of the thing. So it is, at this point, that we come to the issue of the "intelligibility" of the thing. We maintain that the "metaphysical" dimension of the thing, as revealed through the intellect's contact with the thing's being, shows us the "permanent" and "non-contingent," i.e., non-temporal, character of the thing in terms of its substantial form or act. Hence, this dimension discloses the substantial form as the irreducible intelligibility at the core of each thing. It is on this basis then that the thing provides accidents with a ground of permanency and intelligibility. As relational, accidents belong to and exist in the thing. Since time is relational and accidental, the thing is also where it exists and belongs. However, phenomenology attempts to make time the ground of things and renders impossible the intelligibility of the thing. For without the stress on the substantial form, on the act or core-being of the thing, everything evaporates into an endless becoming where only the potential and the unintelligible reign.

In the phenomenological description then, the accidentals, particularly time, hold sway. What this entails is a process where the being of time can but perpetuate a groundless base in which all things seem to dissipate as the accidentals or relations of a temporal flow. What counts here is nothing "substantial." Phenomenology indeed describes *the triumph of the accidental.*

So it is that the Parmenidean problem refuses to go away. As he teaches, *being is* and cannot become. Hence, if there is only becoming, then *nothing is*. Now while Parmenides' treatment of becoming is, indeed, a rejection of the same, he, at least, recognized that, for something to be, it must have some kind of unchanging character. Nonetheless, for those of us who wish to re-think the "metaphysical" dimension for our age, there need not be a rejection of the accidental and becoming. Rather accidents and change have their intelligible ground in the thing, i.e., in the thing through its substantial form and where potency relates to this substantial form or act.

Let me close by pointing out that phenomenology is a valuable kind of investigation of the thing. However, the limits of such a description must be recognized. Further, as the phenomenologist encourages us, we must enter more and more into the depth of the thing. But, beyond phenomenology, we must enter a radically non-phenomenological or "metaphysical" dimension. In so doing, we can begin to unlock the intelligibility of the thing and seize its inner dynamic which is, first of all, its substantial act or form. And we can thereby discover that time and the other accidentals are not forever destined to the vagabond triumph of becoming and unintelligibility. Rather they have a home where the victory is intelligibility and being. For their home is substance or what we can also call the individual thing.

St. Charles Borromeo Seminary
Philadelphia, Pennsylvania

NOTES

1. The phenomenologists we take up are Husserl, Heidegger, and Merleau-Ponty. Admittedly, our emphasis weighs strongly in the area of phenomenological "ontology" and so in the thought of Heidegger and Merleau-Ponty. However, it is our view, following Merleau-Ponty's contention, that Husserl's thought, as it develops, moves ever closer to a preoccupation with "ontology." Husserl in his last or *Crisis* years (1934-37) shows his interest clearly in an ontology of the life-world (*Lebenswelt*). On the period of the writing of the *Crisis* see *The Crisis of European Sciences and Transcendental Phenomenology*, tr. David Carr (Evanston: Northwestern University Press, 1970), pp. xvi-xviii; hereafter *CR*. To return to Merleau-Ponty and Heidegger, both, as influenced by Husserl, draw out what, we believe, is implicit in his thought.

2. "Ce qui est donné, ce n'est pas le chose seule, mais l'experience de la chose, une transcendance dans un sillage de subjectivité..." Maurice Merleau-Ponty, *Phénoménologie de la perception* (Paris: Gallimard, 1945), p. 376; hereafter *PP*.

3. Concerning Merleau-Ponty's stress on the *Gestalt* of the thing, see the following: Maurice Merleau-Ponty, *La structure du comportment* (Paris: Presses Universitaires de France, 1967), pp. 237-240; *PP*, pp. 20-22, 71-74, 81-85; Maurice Merleau-Ponty, *Le visible et l'invisible, suivi de notes de travail* (Paris: Gallimard, 1964), pp. 242-243, 245-246, 258-259—hereafter *VI*.

4. Aristotle, *Categories,* trans. E. M. Edghill, in *The Basic Works of Aristotle*, ed. Richard McKeon (New York: Random House, 1941), p. 10.

5. Aristotle, *Metaphysics* (Loeb Classical Library—Greek text and English translation), trans. Hugh Tredennick (Cambridge: Harvard University Press, 1936).

6. Among Merleau-Ponty's works emphasizing the *Logos* are *PP* and *VI.* We also draw attention to *Logos* in the role of being (*Sein*) in Martin Heidegger, *An Introduction to Metaphysics,* tr. Ralph Manheim (Garden City: Anchor Books, 1959) and Martin Heidegger, "Logos" in *Vorträge und Aufsätze* (Pfullingen: Neske, 1954); hereafter *VA.*

7. "...toute synthèses est à la fois distendue et refaite par le temps..." *PP,* p. 278.

8. For our purpose in this paper there is no need to enter into a discussion of the change from Heidegger I to Heidegger II and perhaps even to a Heidegger III. One reference which is quite helpful in this regard is William J. Richardson, S. J., *Heidegger: Through Phenomenology to Thought* (The Hague: Martinus Nijhoff, 1963): chap. I of part II, pp. 259-260, pp. 638-639 ((the *Ereignis* (event) issue)).

9. As stated in the previous footnote, we are not really concerned in this paper with the question of Heidegger I, etc. The same is true regarding the issue of Merleau-Ponty I and II. Let us simply say that *Da-sein* is basic to the earlier writings of Heidegger ((for ex: Martin Heidegger, *Sein und Zeit* (Tübingen: Niemeyer, 1953; hereafter *SZ)* and *Denken* becomes more focused on in the later writings (for ex: Martin Heidegger, *Was heisst Denken?* (Tübingen: Niemeyer, 1961)). Merleau-Ponty in *PP* stresses *corps* and in *VI chair.* With Heidegger's increasing emphasis on *Denken,* being is understood to dominate its "there" or thought. In the case of Merleau-Ponty, the use of *chair* carries with it a stronger and more explicit focus on the being-process.

10. See *VI,* pp. 154-157 and Merleau-Ponty, "Le philosophe et son ombre" in *Signes* (Paris: Gallimard, 1960).

11. Edmund Husserl, *Ideen zu einer reinen Phänomenologie und Phänomenologischen Philosophie—Zweites Buch* (Bank IV of *Gesammelte Werke—Husserliana),* ed. Marly Biemel (The Hague: Martinus Nijhoff, 1952); hereafter *ID* II.

12. Regarding Husserl's use of *Subjektleib,* see *ID* II, pp. 55, 158.

13. See *CR,* pp. 103-186.

14. Let us keep in mind that phenomenological time is simultaneously the time of the life of consciousness, i.e., the time which is me as my intentional field of meaning, and the time which is the horizontal process of meaning or being revealing and concealing itself within the field of consciousness.

15. "...'il y a' quelque chose." *VI,* p. 130.

16. Martin Heidegger, "Das Ding" in *VA.*

17. "...das Dingen des Dinges." "Das Ding," *VA,* p. 176.

18. *Metaphysics,* 1028b2-7.

19. *Metaphysics,* 1072b13-31, 1074b15-35.

20. Henry B. Veatch, *Aristotle: A Contemporary Appreciation* (Bloomington: Indiana University Press, 1974), p. 146.

21. In distinguishing "ontical" and "ontological" levels, we have in mind the distinction Heidegger made famous in *SZ* and which Merleau-Ponty clearly parallels in *VI.* The "ontical" stresses the manifestations of the being-process and the "ontological" the process itself.

22. *Metaphysics,* 1050b3.

23. *Metaphysics,* 1045b25-1046a5, 1047a30-31, 1050a23-24.

24. *Metaphysics,* Bk. Theta (IX): 1046a1-5, sect. VI, sect. VIII.

25. Among passages in this regard: St. Thomas Aquinas, *De veritate catholicae fidei contra Gentiles* (*Opera omnia—*v. 5) (Parmae: P. Fiaccadori, 1855), II, 53, 54; *Commentum in quatuor libros Sententiarum magistri Petri Lombardi* (*Opera omnia—*v. 6) (Parmae: P. Fiaccadori, 1856), I, d.8, q.5, a.2; *Quaestiones disputatae cum quodlibetis* (*Opera omnia—*v. 9) (Parmae: P. Fiaccadori, 1859), Quodlibet XII, q.5, a.5.

26. St. Thomas Aquinas, *De principiis naturae ad fratrem Silvestrum* (*Opera omnia—*v. 16) (Parmae: P. Fiaccadori, 1864).

SECTION VI—THE ANALYTICAL TRADITION

Dominic Balestra, Chairman
Fordham University

Davidson on Mind and Substance

by Denis F. Sullivan

In a series of celebrated papers Donald Davidson has argued from the anomalous nature of the mental to a materialistic monism. In this paper I would like to argue that Davidson's own analysis provides us with grounds for rejecting the monism he proposes. Furthermore I shall try to argue that the rejection of this monism does not lead us from a sensible materialism to an absurd dualism but from a rigid ontology of events to a much richer ontology of substances.

I will begin by examining Davidson's analysis of the anomalous nature of the mental. I shall then try to show how this analysis should lead us not to the kind of deterministic monism which he proposes but to a clarified ontology of substances.

Building on the work of Quine, Davidson identifies mental events and mental states not in terms of such traditionally ascribed properties as subjectivity or immateriality, but in terms of a logical peculiarity of the sentences we use to describe such events and states. These sentences are sentences which contain what Davidson calls mental verbs. Typical examples of such verbs would be: believing, hoping, remembering, desiring; less typical but also legitimate would be: looking for, trying. Now sentences containing such verbs often have what Quine calls extensional opacity; the substitution of extensionally identical terms does not necessarily preserve truth value. It is in terms of this extensional opacity that the mental is identified. Any state or event is to be characterized as mental if it can be described by a sentence which contains a mental verb generating extensional opacity.[1]

An example might clarify this position. Let us say that we see someone throwing a package into a roaring fire. When we ask him what he is doing he replies: "I am trying to burn the contents of the package." He believes the package to contain old love letters. But let us suppose that he is mistaken;

the package really contains the deed to his house. Note that "the deed to the house" is extensionally identical with "the contents of the envelope"; both terms refer to the same object. But if we substitute one for the other we get: "I am trying to burn the deed to the house," a sentence which is almost surely false.

Notice the story is different if we describe the same event in what Davidson would call physical language. Suppose the gentleman in question were to have said not "I am trying to..." but rather "I am burning the contents of the package." Notice that here the normal rules of substitution would apply; the substitution of coextensive terms would necessarily preserve truth value. If the first sentence is true, then the sentence "I am burning the deed to the house" must also be true.

Mental events and mental states, then, are those events and states which can be described by sentences which contain mental verbs in such a way as to generate the required extensional opacity. This approach to the mental might seem peculiar but it should be noted that it covers in an obvious way most of what is usually considered to be mental. Thus take the sentence "John thinks the woman in the black dress betrayed him." Now suppose, unbeknownst to John, the woman in the black dress is John's mother. It certainly does not follow that John thinks his mother betrayed him.

Let us now turn to Davidson's account of the anomalous nature of the mental. To say of something that it is anomalous is to say that it is not governed by a law. Now for Davidson there are two kinds of anomaly which affect the mental. The first is that there can be no psychophysical laws, that is, no laws correlating kinds of mental events with kinds of physical events.[2] The second form of anomaly, which is derived from the first, is that there can be no strict deterministic laws whatever on the basis of which mental events can be predicted and explained.[3] Let us begin with the first.

Davidson tells us that the key to the anomalous character of the mental lies in the wholism of the mental realm. "Beliefs and desires issue in behavior only as modified and mediated by further beliefs and desires, attitudes and attendings without limit."[4] In other words we ascribe a belief or desire to an individual not just because of what we see him do but because of what we assume about his other desires and beliefs, what we believe he notices, or happens to think of or immediately expect. By changing our assumptions about this background we can change our interpretation of his action and our ascription of his more proximate beliefs and desires. As in trying to understand a bit of speech, so in interpreting a person's action, we work against a background theory of a person's whole mental life.

It is not just this wholism of the mental which gives the mental its anomalous character for, as Davidson admits, a similar wholism exists in physical theory.[5] Rather it is a question of allegiance. In physical discourse while the background theory obviously imposes constraints, our primary allegiance is to the observational data. In psychological discourse, while we must make sense of the observational data, our primary allegiance is to an overall theory of the mental life of the individual observed. This is why the notions of coherence, rationality and consistency play a role in the psychological realm for which there is "no echo in physical theory."[6]

The significance of this divergence of allegiance becomes more obvious when we reformulate the issue in more explicitly teleological terms.[7] What, we may ask, is the difference between a teleological account of events and a physical account? In giving a physical account what we are usually after is the establishment of correlations between different kinds of change: Whenever you drop sodium in water it explodes. This search for significant correlations usually takes place against the background of some established theory or set of theories and is usually a part of a search for a system of correlations. But still the enterprise is characterized by a certain kind of atomicity. Once a given correlation is established it assumes at least a limited autonomy. Its limits might be pointed out; it might be interpreted as part of a broader correlation; but still it has a certain stubborn independence.

What goes on in constructing a teleological account is quite different. Here there is much less interest in establishing correlations between different kinds of events and much more interest in figuring out how various particular events tell a story, how they are all part of an attempt, although some of them will be mistaken attempts, to realize some purpose or set of purposes.[8] Notice that here the primary allegiance is to the overall tale of how a purpose or set of purposes is pursued. It is this point about the commitment of teleological explanation which underlies Davidson's claim that there is a gulf between what goes on in psychology and what goes on in physics.

In passing it should be noted that we can also see the importance of the teleological in connection with the extensional opacity which Davidson takes to be the mark of the mental. When we are using a teleological sentence such as "He is trying to burn the contents of the package" we are not just picking out events but we are also trying to situate those events in a teleological history. Consequently we treat such sentences as true or false not just in terms of the events picked out but also in terms of whether they are picked out in such a way as to fit into a certain kind of tale. Thus the sentence "He is trying to burn the deed to the house" may be false even though the sentence "He is trying to burn the contents of the package" is true because while both sentences are about the same event the first sentence does not fit this event into the appropriate tale.

Returning now to the main point. The gap between the commitments of the teleological (or psychological) on the one hand and the physical on the other make it impossible to correlate kinds of physical events with kinds of psychological or mental events. This is because the question of whether or not a person has a certain set of beliefs and desires must always remain open in a way in which questions about the existence of physical states need not. A simple example should make this clear. Let us say that through brain observations, behavioral observations and questioning we have established, with regard to a particular experimental subject, on a number of occasions, a correlation between a particular complex neuronal firing and a desire to drink beer. Now could we on the basis of those observations formulate a strict law correlating that kind of neuronal firing with the occurrence of a desire to drink beer? Davidson's answer would be no because if we did, then on future occasions we would be able to ascribe the desire to drink beer on the basis of our observing on those occasions the requisite neuronal firing. But this cannot be because it is of the logical nature of desire that we cannot ascribe a desire to an agent simply on the basis of a particular observation but rather on an overall theory of the character and life of the agent. Thus if we insist that we have established a strict correlation what we have done is abandon our original concept of desire. We have, as Davidson says, changed the subject.[9]

We can also see the influence of the commitment of the teleological (or psychological) to wholism in another way. Let us suppose, contrary to fact, that the presence of psychological states and events could be established in the same way and with the same surety as physical states and events. We could ask whether or not we could correlate psychological explanations with physical explanations. The answer, for Davidson, would again be no. We can see this if we turn for a moment to his theory of action.

In order to correlate a psychological explanation with a physical explanation what we would have to do would be establish a correlation between causal statements using talk about beliefs and desires and purely physicalistic causal statements. Thus we would have to establish a correlation between statements like "whenever the desire to eat is present and there are the required environmental circumstances, the subject eats" and statements of the sort, "whenever the neuronal complex x-14 fires and there are the required environmental circumstances, the subject eats." Now statements of the second sort might be found; it is the object of at least some of the physical sciences to try to find them. But statements of the first sort cannot.

Here again a crucial role is played by the wholism of the mental. The desire to eat, even in the presence of fine food, will not in itself produce the behavior of eating. Thus one would have to notice the food, not believe it to be poisoned, not be on a diet and so on without end.[10] And even aside from this point, just as someone can have all the evidence and still not draw the conclusion, so one can have all the reasons for acting and still not act.[11] Here we can see an unbridgeable gap between any set of beliefs and desires, and the action which they might, *or might not*, cause. Thus again we see the impossibility of psychophysical laws.

Let us now turn to the second sense in which the mental is said to be anomalous: mental events cannot be predicted and explained on the basis of strict deterministic laws. We have just seen that there cannot be any psychophysical laws, so if there are to be any laws which would strictly govern mental events, they would have to be purely mental or psychological laws. But, Davidson tells us, there can be no such purely psychological laws because the mental is not a closed system; the physical world extensively interacts, in perception and action, with the mental world.[12] Hence the possibility of finding any deterministic laws fades and we have our second anomaly.

So far we have been analyzing Davidson's argument for the anomalous character of the mental. We can now turn to briefly consider the surprising conclusion which he derives from this anomalous character, which is that not only can mental events be physical events but that they must be physical events. To put this another way: While our psychological descriptions and explanations cannot be correlated with and reducible to physical descriptions and explanations, all mental events are physical events. Thus there is only one world, the physical world, even though it can be described in irreducibly other ways. This is anomalous monism.

Davidson's argument for anomalous monism is disarmingly simple. Physical events cause psychological events in perception; psychological events cause physical events in action. Now for the key and troubling premise: "...when events are related as cause and effect, then there exists a closed and deterministic system into which these events, when appropriately described, fit."[13] But as we have seen, there cannot be any laws connecting the psychological and the physical. There cannot even be strict causal laws within the psychological. What this means is that the psychological event which is either the cause (in action) or the effect (in perception) must have a physical description so that it can fit into an exceptionless causal law. Thus every psychological event must have some physical description and hence be identical with some physical event.

To avoid confusion it must be emphasized that Davidson is here talking about particular events. My desire on a particular occasion to eat cake must have a physical description and hence be identical with some physical event, let us say the firing of a certain set of neurons. But this does not mean that that kind of desire, the desire to eat cake, must always be correlated with that kind of neuronal firing. On another occasion my desire to eat cake might be identical with some other neuronal kind of firing. Thus while we have an identity on the level of particular events, we have an anomaly on the level of general description.

So far, while I have suggested some modifications, I have been more intent on analyzing than on criticizing Davidson's work. I would like now to get critical. I will first try to argue that Davidson's move from anomaly to monism is not convincing. I will then argue that if one resists this move one is left with a position which has some interesting possibilities.

What troubles me most is not so much Davidson's conclusion as one of the premises on which it is based. In itself I find nothing frightening in Davidson's claim that every mental event has some physical description and thus is identical with some physical event. What makes this position troubling is the premise of causal determinism upon which it is based. Given this premise, psychological (and teleological) events are absorbed not just into a physical universe but into a universe governed by exceptionless causal laws and it is questionable whether they could have any real place in such a universe at all.

Let us start then with Davidson's assumption that every singular causal statement is an instantiation of some exceptionless causal law. As Elizabeth Anscombe has mentioned, certainly one needs to have a reason to believe such a thing.[14] Davidson himself has admitted this fact and claims he has a reason which he hopes eventually to commit to writing.[15] But until he does it seems that we have a right to remain skeptical.

Aside from this general doubt about determinism, there are more specific grounds for doubt taken from Davidson's own work in action theory. As I pointed out, according to Davidson, there is a necessary and unbridgeable gap between any complex of beliefs and desires, no matter in what detail they are specified, and the actions they result in. I may desire to go to work and believe that in order to go to work I must get out of bed. On the basis of this psychological state I either may, *or may not*, get out of bed. Furthermore, and this is Davidson's point, there is no way in which we can amend our description of this psychological state so that we can conclude that I will get out of bed. Thus it seems to be part of the very nature of psychological causality that while psychological causes explain and ground the actions which are their effects, they do not necessitate them.

That this characteristic of being non-necessitating is a part of our very notion of psychological causality can be seen by a consideration of the phrase "could have done otherwise." Many philosophers, and most ordinary people, believe that if an action is performed freely then the agent who performed it "could have done otherwise"; he might have not done the action at all. Now Davidson finds this notion of "could have done otherwise" philosophically confused.[16] His position on this point is, I believe, a peculiar product of his knee-jerk commitment to compatibilism.[17] I say this because he has provided us with the philosophical resources to make good sense of it. The concept of "could have done otherwise" derives from the fact while the only way we can explain why an agent acted is because of his beliefs and desires, these beliefs and desires can never necessitate his action. When a man acts freely he does so because of his beliefs and desires, but he might not have. We believe this because of what we believe about the relationship between psychological causes and the actions they determine.

Note the significance of this point about the nature of psychological causality for the issue of determinism. To say that there must be some physical description which unites a psychological state and the action it causes in an exceptionless causal law is to say that the apparent gap between the psychological cause and its action effect is just that—*an apparent gap.* But this gap seems to be one of the underlying characteristics of psychological language. Thus if this gap is apparent, so, it seems, is the whole psychological domain. It seems, then, that Davidson's determinism commits us to seeing human actions and even man himself as merely phenomenal, as merely an aspect of what Sellars calls the manifest image.

There are some hints that Davidson might accept this conclusion. Thus he writes that "...the nomological slack between the mental and the physical is essential *as long as* we conceive of man as a rational animal" (emphasis added).[18] And again in speaking of the indeterminacy of the social sciences: "...the limits thus placed on the social sciences is set *not by nature* but by us *when we decide* to view men as rational agents with goals and purposes" (emphasis added).[19] These passages give the impression that the psychological domain and hence man himself exist not by nature but by our decision to describe the world in a certain way; man is a mere figment of a particular mode of discourse.

But this will not do and Davidson knows it. To say that the psychological domain is a mere figment of a mode of description is to say that we could formulate a consistent description of the world without any use of psychological concepts. But this is impossible. A description of the world must be constructed in language and that language becomes, of course, part of the world. But, as Davidson points out, we need the concepts of belief and desire to understand the concept of language. Thus there can be no language without belief and desire.[20] It seems, then, that the psychological domain must be part of the real. But it cannot be irreducibly real if all that is accounted for in terms of psychological causation, causation by beliefs and desires, can also be accounted for in terms of exceptionless causal laws. Psychological causation would have no place in a world where every event was determined by exceptionless causal law. So we must conclude that some events are caused by beliefs and desires and these events are *not* determined by such exceptionless laws.

In the end, then, more or less on the basis of Davidson's own analysis we seem led not to an anomalous monism but to more of an anomalous dualism. In addition to physical causality, causality by antecedent event and causal law, there seems to be a second kind of causality, a causality in terms of beliefs and desires or teleological orientation generally. Thus in the end there seem to be two ways in which the world might work.

So far I have been arguing that beliefs and desires, teleological orientations, really make things happen. But what are these beliefs and desires, these teleological orientations? It should be obvious that such beliefs and desires do not just hover about in some mysterious space; rather they are always the beliefs and desires of someone or of some thing capable of having beliefs and desires. Broadly speaking, beliefs and desires, teleological orientations, are attributes of substances or of certain kinds of substances. So let us turn for a moment to the notion of substance.[21]

A substance is a perduring object, an object which survives through time. Since it survives through time it must be able to survive certain kinds of change. But it must also have certain kinds of characteristics which remain and in terms of which we can identify it as the same substance. Now what is the nature of these identifying characteristics?

One possibility is that these identifying characteristics could be described in terms of a set of laws. Thus we might say that whenever the substance in question is placed in the sun it turns red; whenever it is placed in water it floats. But this way of describing the identifying characteristics of a substance would be of no help to us. It would fit substances into the kind of monistic world which Davidson envisions. Everything would be explainable by exceptionless causal laws.

But certain substances, persons especially, and also many animals, don't seem to fit neatly into such a world. This is not to deny that there are features about human beings which can be described in law-like terms. But while these might be necessary to identify a human being, they certainly do not seem sufficient. They are characteristics more apt to identify a corpse than a man.

What makes a human person a human person is the fact that his life tells a certain tale, a tale of the pursuit of a goal or a set of goals. Now the pursuit of these goals, the attempts made, the paths taken, can never be completely anticipated. This is why the defining characteristics of human beings, and of perhaps many other living things, must go beyond anything which can be expressed in any set of causal laws. Teleological histories escape the standard causal nets. And it is in terms of such teleological histories that at least certain substances are identified.

Of course each person (or each animal) is not absolutely unique. He is a member of a species; he is a kind of substance. But what this means is that in addition to sharing with the other members of the species those aspects which could be described in terms of relatively strict causal laws, he also shares some sort of purpose or set of purposes. But once again each individual will pursue these goals in his own way; each life will have its own tale to tell.

It seems, then, that if we persistently press Davidson's analysis of the anomalous nature of the mental we are led not to his deterministic monism but to a particular ontology of substance. In the end it seems that we must conclude that substances such as persons and anything else to which it is reasonable to attribute a teleological history really exist and are not reducible to sets of events linked by exceptionless causal laws. Thus our rejection of Davidson's monism leaves us not with a strange world of minds and bodies but with the old and familiar world of people and animals and things.

St. Vincent's College
St. John's University
Jamaica, New York

NOTES

1. Donald Davidson, *Essays on Actions and Events* (Clarendon Press: Oxford, 1980), pp. 210f.

2. *Ibid.,* p. 214.

3. *Ibid.,* p. 208.

4. *Ibid.,* p. 217.

5. *Ibid.,* p. 222.

6. *Ibid.,* p. 231.

7. While Davidson ordinarily discusses the anomaly of the mental in psychological terms, he shows no aversion to a teleological approach. Cf. *Essays on Actions and Events,* p. XII and *Inquiries into Truth and Interpretation* (Clarendon Press: Oxford, 1984), pp. 156f.

8. Davidson makes a related point. Cf. *Inquiries into Truth and Interpretation,* pp. 15f.

9. Davidson, *Essays on Actions and Events,* p. 216.

10. *Ibid.,* pp. 76ff.

11. *Ibid.,* p. 77.

12. *Ibid.,* pp. 223f.

13. *Ibid.,* p. 231.

14. Elizabeth Anscombe, "Causality and Determination" in *Metaphysics and the Philosophy of Mind* (University of Minnesota Press: Minneapolis, 1981), p. 147.

15. Davidson, "Replies" in *Essays on Davidson* (Clarendon Press: Oxford, 1985), p. 247.

16. Davidson, *Essays on Actions and Events,* pp. 74f.

17. *Ibid.,* p. 63.

18. *Ibid.,* p. 223.

19. *Ibid.,* p. 239.

20. *Ibid.,* p. 238 and pp. 255-59; see also "Belief and the Basis of Meaning" in *Inquiries into Truth and Interpretation,* pp. 141-154.

21. Davidson seems to admit the necessity of an ontology of substances but he does nothing to develop it. Cf. Davidson, *Essays on Action and Events,* p. 175.

On Things That Do Not Now Exist and Never Have Existed

by Charles J. Kelly

If one says that Socrates does not exist, one usually does so with the understanding that though the individual substance Socrates does not now exist, he once did. The claim is that Socrates no longer exists. However, if a knowledgeable speaker were to insist

(1) Pegasus does not exist,

he would do so with the implicit conviction that it is also true that

(2) Pegasus never existed.

Claims such as (1) and (2) have proved notoriously vexing for philosophers to comprehend, even more so than those about defunct substances. We might encapsulate their bewilderment in what have come to be called 'Meinong's Puzzle' and the 'Unqualified Version of Plato's Beard.'

As recently presented Meinong's Puzzle 'has to do with the working of singular terms that denote things that do not exist.'[1] It claims that if (1) is true, there is no such thing as Pegasus. This consequent in turn entails that 'Pegasus' denotes or names or means nothing. But if 'Pegasus' denotes or names or means nothing, it does not mean anything with the result that (1) itself is also meaningless. Furthermore, if 'Pegasus' names nothing and 'Cerberus' also names nothing, how can there be a difference in meaning between (1) and 'Cerberus does not exist'?

Whereas Meinong's Puzzle focuses on the denotation of the subject of the present tensed (1), the concern of the Unqualified Version of Plato's Beard (*UVPB*) is with (2), which 'seems at once to name something and to say that there never has been anything which could bear this name.'[2] (2) seems insignificant in that it could not be true without making 'Pegasus' devoid of reference.[3] Accordingly, the *UVPB* can be *roughly sketched* as a *reductio* with (2) and (5) in contradictory opposition:

(2) Pegasus never existed	[Assump.]
(3) 'Pegasus' named Pegasus	[2]
(4) If 'Pegasus' named Pegasus, Pegasus once existed	[Pr.]
(5) Pegasus once existed	[4,3,M.P.]

Whereas Meinong's Puzzle was based on there being nothing for the 'Pegasus' of the present tensed (1) to name, the *UVPB* is based on the intuition

181

expressed by (4) that if Pegasus has been named there once upon a time must have been a Pegasus to be named.

It is well known that contemporary philosophy has been marked by two rival approaches to these problems. They have been characterized as Inflationist and Deflationist.[4] The Inflationist solution to Meinong's Puzzle, for example, retains the notion that 'Pegasus' functions as a genuine proper name in the subject position of (1). It accordingly denies the claim that 'Pegasus' denotes nothing or that it names no object. In steadfast adherence to Mill's dicta that proper names are attached to the objects themselves and that all names are names not of ideas but of things real or imaginary,[5] it unflinchingly concludes with him that an imaginary object must be distinguished from our idea of it and that Pegasus as well as any hobgoblin or leprechaun is a non-existent object.[6] It has thus been deduced that Mill's heirs can give their anti-Fregean account of (1) only by holding the uncomfortable position that 'Pegasus' denotes a non-existent object with the rest of the sentence predicating non-existence of that object.[7] This objection generates as a reply the Meinongian distinction between *Sosein* and *Sein* with the upshot that the solution for the Inflationist of the *UVPB* is found in the rejection of (4) as necessarily true: an object can *be* or *have been* without existing or having existed.

The Deflationist account of Meinong's Puzzle, on the other hand, denies that 'Pegasus' is a proper name. So (1) would be translated as 'It is not the case that there is one and only one object that pegasizes' with the proper name reduced to a predicative description.[8] In this spirit it can also be paraphrased as a metalinguistic claim about the name 'Pegasus.'[9] For Deflationists 'Pegasus' just cannot denote; it could 'no more be a proper name than is the movement of a clenched fist in a charade a knocking on a door.'[10] Since different descriptions could be given in the denominalizations of 'Pegasus' and of 'Cerberus,' the differences in their meanings can be easily retained. Naturally, Deflationists go on to meet the *UVPB* by rejecting (3).

The strength of Deflationism is its avoidance of the Platonic explosion of paper entities engendered by Inflationism. But the strength of the latter, its continued employment of proper names like 'Pegasus' as logically genuine, is the precise weakness of the former. The way to a robust economy, it seems, lies in devising a structure which allows 'Pegasus' to continue to work as a Millian proper name which denotes an object without devaluing the true worth of real things by needlessly multiplying entities. To this preliminary task we now turn.

I. An Outline of a Neo-Aristotelian Syntactics

To invoke the name of Mill in this context is to harken back to a pre-

Fregean rejection of the definite description theory of the sense of a proper name.[11] But, to ground and appropriate Mill's purely denotative view of proper names, it is best not to rely on his own two name theory of the proposition. Rather, let us capitalize on and modify some recent insights into the traditional formal logic.[12]

A. *The Wild Quantity of Propositions With Proper Name Subjects.* A Fregean analysis would represent a sentence such as 'Socrates is moral' as 'Ms' with 's' as the logical subject serving as the argument for the unsaturated functional 'M_' as the logical predicate. A pre-Fregean logic, however, would usually parse it as of the form 'Every Socrates is moral' with the proper name 'Socrates' understood as a term applicable to a single object. With subscript '[p]' appended to such proper names it can join Leibniz in regarding the universal affirmative 'Every Socrates$_{[p]}$is moral' as logically equivalent to the particular affirmative 'Some Socrates$_{[p]}$is moral.' Singular propositions with proper names as subjects have 'wild' or 'indifferent' quantity. As such they are differentiated from propositions with general terms as subjects; these latter do not generate the logical equivalence of the universal and particular forms.[13] The immediate result of this is that the negative propositions 'No Socrates$_{[p]}$is moral' and 'Some Socrates$_{[p]}$is not moral' (parsings of 'Socrates is not moral') must also be acknowledged as logically equivalent and as each contradictorily opposed to the mentioned affirmatives. 'Wild quantity' thus entails that there is not the contrary opposition between singular propositions that there is for propositions with general terms as subjects.

This indifference to unique quantification justifies the absence of the quantifier in the surface grammar of singular proper name propositions. More significantly, it can readily explain the valid inference to 'Something that is a thing is a planet' from 'Mars is a planet' and 'Mars is a thing' by indifferently categorizing it as a third figure syllogism in either *Darapti, Disamis* or *Datisi.* There is no need in this logic to add a primitive principle of existential generalization.[14]

B. *Complete Triadicity.* Since the pre-Fregean Aristotelian determines both general and singular propositions as syntactically homogeneous, *every* proposition can be parsed as consisting of a subject term, a predicate term, and a syncategorematic quantifier or syntactical device that shows the way that the predicate is latched on to or denied of the subject.[15] With brackets around the term designated as its subject, with parentheses surrounding that stipulated as predicate, and with the unsurrounded italicized '*Q*' representing the syncategorematic term, every Aristotelian proposition is of the triadic form:

(6)Q[S](P).

Thus, 'Socrates is moral' could be parsed either as '*Every*[Socrates$_{[p]}$]]

(is-moral)' or as its logical equivalent '*Some* [Socrates$_{[p]}$](is-moral).' We can think of 'Everybody admires somebody' as having the same form as 'Plato admired Socrates.'[16] The former might be parsed as '*Every*[body] (admires some body)' with the latter translated and parsed as '*Every*[Plato$_{[p]}$] (admired some Socrates$_{[p]}$).'

The main syntactical device or '*Q*' term need not appear as the first item in an analysis of a proposition. Thus '(Every body admires)*some*[body]' and '(Every Plato$_{[p]}$admired)*some*[Socrates$_{[p]}$]' are legitimate alternative parsings of 'Everybody admires somebody' and 'Plato admired Socrates.' This is significant for there are two quite distinct senses in which 'Everybody admires somebody' entails and is entailed by 'Somebody is admired by everybody.' This is shown by constructing four syllogisms: two in *Barbara* which appeal to the suitably interpreted convertibly necessary truism that whoever admires somebody somebody is admired by and two in *Darii* which appeal to the suitably parsed necessarily true major premiss that whomever everybody admires is admired by everybody:

[A]: (7) (Some body is admired by)*whoever*[admires some body]
      (8) *Every*[body](admires some body)
      ———————————————————————————————————
      (9) (Some body is admired by)*every*[body]

[B]: (10) [Some body is admired by]*whoever*(admires some body)
      (9) (Some body is admired by)*every*[body]
      ———————————————————————————————————
      (8) *Every*[body](admires some body)

[C]: (11) [Every body admires]*whomever*(is admired by every body)
      (12) (Every body admires)*some*[body]
      ———————————————————————————————————
      (13) *Some*[body](is admired by every body)

[D]: (14) (Every body admires)*whomever*[is admired by every body]
      (13) *Some*[body](is admired by every body)
      ———————————————————————————————————
      (12) (Every body admires)*some*[body]

Thus, while (8) and (9) are logically equivalent as are (12) and (13), the former pair is not logically equivalent to the latter.

Granting the logical dynamics of wild quantification '*Every*[Plato$_{[p]}$] (admired some Socrates$_{[p]}$)' is logically equivalent to '(Some Socrates$_{[p]}$was admired by)*some* [Plato$_{[p]}$].' However, these are not logically equivalent to

'(Every Plato$_{[p]}$admired)*some*[Socrates$_{[p]}$].' This last is equivalent to '*Some*[Socrates$_{[p]}$](was admired by every Plato$_{[p]}$).'[17] The differences between these two sets are not merely logical. In responding to the question, 'Who admired Socrates?,' one can answer 'Plato.' '*Every* [Plato$_{[p]}$] (admired some Socrates$_{[p]}$)' with 'Plato' as the subject is the appropriate parsing here. The implication is that Plato once existed, since 'Whoever admired Socrates once existed' is a necessary truth. On the other hand, if the question put is, 'Whom did Plato admire?,' the answer 'Socrates' invites a parsing with 'Socrates' as subject: '(Every Plato$_{[p]}$admired) *some*[Socrates$_{[p]}$].' But here there is no entailment of the existence of Socrates as Plato's admiration for Homer indicates that 'Whomever Plato admired once existed' is at best a contingent truth.

Complete triadicity means that not only a proposition itself can be parsed according to the structure exhibited in (6), but also that each such subject and predicate, if it be complex, can be so rendered. Thus '*Every*[Plato$_{[p]}$] (admired some Socrates$_{[p]}$)' is more finely parsed as '*Every* [Plato$_{[p]}$] ((admired)*some*[Socrates$_{[p]}$])' with its logically equivalent passive rendered as '(*Some*[Socrates$_{[p]}$](was admired by))*every*[Plato$_{[p]}$].'[18]

C. *The Atemporality of Proper Names and Natural Kind Terms.* Complete triadicity generates a twofold manner for justifying the paradigmatic enthymeme: 'Socrates is a man' entails 'Socrates is mortal.' The suppressed necessarily true major premiss invoked could be 'Whatever[is a man](is-mortal)' which with the minor parsed as '*Every*[Socrates$_{[p]}$](is a man)' by *Barbara* entails '*Every*[Socrates$_{[p]}$](is-mortal).' It is also possible to appeal to 'Every man is mortal' as the suppressed major with the consequent construction of a third figure syllogism in *Datisi*:

(15) *Every*[man](is-mortal)
(16) (Every Socrates$_{[p]}$is)*a*[man]

---

(17) [Every Socrates$_{[p]}$is]*something that*(is-mortal).

In neither case, however, is the substantive 'man' transmuted into the adjectival 'is-human' as is the custom with the prevailing interpretations of first order predicate logics. In fact, both natural kind terms and proper names can retain their status as substantives said without time. 'Tully is Cicero' can be parsed as '*Every*[Tully$_{[p]}$](is every Cicero$_{[p]}$).' The Fregean view that proper names must function only as subjects and can never constitute the whole predicate (though they can be part of the predicate) is thus respected. In this regard it is important to recognize the converse of '*Every*[Tully$_{[p]}$] (is every Cicero$_{[p]}$)' as '*Someone that*[is every Cicero$_{[p]}$](is every Tully$_{[p]}$).' The appeal here is to the suppressed premiss 'Tully is Tully' parsed as '*Every*[Tully$_{[p]}$](is every Tully$_{[p]}$).' Again 'is Tully' is not an adjectival form that expresses a temporal property of Cicero or one that allows itself in any way to be 'pegasized.' Proper nouns and natural kind terms are said without time and are not reduced to temporally laden verbs or adjectives.

II. The Application to Meinong's Puzzle and the UVPB

These syntactical insights which also, we believe, underpin Aristotelian essentialism can now be applied to our puzzle and our paradox.

A. *Meinong's Puzzle*. The initial move here was to insist that (1) entails that there is no such thing as Pegasus. This latter claim might be paraphrased and rendered as a negative proposition with a timelessly classified predicate:

(18) *Nothing that*[exists](is every Pegasus$_{[p]}$).

(18) follows in *Cesare* from the necessary truth

(19) *Everything that*exists

and from (1) interpreted, paraphrased and parsed as the present tensed

(1.1) *Nothing that*[is every Pegasus$_{[p]}$](exists).

The crucial issue, however, is the soundness of the Puzzle's inference from (18) to

(20) 'Pegasus' denotes nothing.

Validity in *Camestres* requires that (20) be paraphrased and parsed as the universal negative

(20.1) (Every 'Pegasus$_{[p]}$' denotes)*nothing that*[exists].

The suppressed major premiss here is

(21) 'Pegasus' denotes Pegasus

paraphrased and parsed as

(21.1) [Every 'Pegasus$_{[p]}$' denotes]*whatever*(is every Pegasus$_{[p]}$).[19]

Is (21.1) necessarily true?

To understand why it is not it is helpful to reflect upon

(21.2) *Every* ['Pegasus$_{[p]}$'](denotes every Pegasus$_{[p]}$)

as well as upon both

(21.3) (Every 'Pegasus$_{[p]}$' denotes)*every*[Pegasus$_{[p]}$]

and the passive equivalent of (21.3), namely,

(21.31) *Every*[Pegasus$_{[p]}$](is denoted by every 'Pegasus$_{[p]}$').

(21.2) is necessarily true. The very essence of a proper name is to *denote the object* it names. Since 'denotes' is not herein a binary relation between name and thing but part of a monadic predicate,[20] there is no implication that there exists an object which is being named. "'Pegasus' *denotes Pegasus*," "'Socrates' *denotes Socrates*," and "'Cerberus' *denotes Cerberus*" are alike all necessarily true linguistic propositions about proper names. Thus the passive equivalent of (21.2),

(21.21) (Every Pegasus$_{[p]}$ is denoted by)*every*['Pegasus$_{[p]}$'],
is also necessarily true. It is, however, only contingently true that an object like Socrates *be named or be denoted by 'Socrates.'* Socrates by any other name would still be Socrates. Accordingly, (21.3) and (21.31) could be at most only contingent truths. They are in fact not true. (21.31), for example, entails that Pegasus either now exists or once existed, that is, is real, through the necessary truth that
    (22) *Whatever*[is denoted by every 'Pegasus$_{[p]}$'](exists or some time existed).
Furthermore, since existent things, potential bearers of names, could be differently dubbed, one cannot say that it is necessary that whatever *is denoted by 'Pegasus'* is Pegasus. This is the claim of (21.1), which is at most contingently true; since Pegasus does not now exist and never has existed, it is in fact not true. It is thus crucial to distinguish the *de facto* false (21.1) from the necessarily true
    (21.4) *Every*['Pegasus$_{[p]}$'](denotes whatever is every Pegasus$_{[p]}$).
We can now point to a new way out of Meinong's maze. On the assumption that the truth 'Pegasus does not exist' might also be rendered as the simple negative
    (1.2) *No*[Pegasus$_{[p]}$](exists),
it is possible to reject "'Pegasus' denotes nothing" parsed as
    (20.2) *Every*['Pegasus$_{[p]}$'] (denotes no thing).
(20.2) is necessarily false as the necessarily true (21.2) entails that *every*['Pegasus$_{[p]}$'](denotes some thing). But (1.2) is perfectly compatible with the contingent truths (20.1) and
    (20.3) (Every 'Pegasus$_{[p]}$' denotes)*no*[thing].
In fact, in this context we must insist that both "*Every*['Pegasus$_{[p]}$'](denotes every Pegasus$_{[p]}$)" and "*No*[Pegasus$_{[p]}$](is denoted by every 'Pegasus$_{[p]}$')" are true. Proper names herein retain their denotative integrity without engendering needless objects.

The amphibolous structure of these propositions also enables us to classify "'Cerberus' names nothing" parsed as "*Every*['Cerberus$_{[p]}$'](names no thing)" as necessarily false, but to accept "(Every 'Cerberus$_{[p]}$' names) *no*[thing]" as contingently true. The difference in meaning between 'Pegasus does not exist' and 'Cerberus does not exist' is easily preserved. In the former 'Pegasus' *means Pegasus* while in the latter 'Cerberus' *means Cerberus.* Though these names necessarily *denote their bearers,* it is not necessarily the case that their bearers *are denoted by these names.* Recognition of the ambiguity attached to active/passive voice equivalence is the essence of a response to the final query posed by Meinong's Puzzle. Some needed clarifications about this response are best made, however, in the context of applying similar considerations to the *UVPB.* To this we now turn.

B. *The UVPB.* Whereas Meinong's Puzzle focused on the present tensed
(1), the *UVPB* assumes the past tensed (2). We translate (2) as 'Pegasus at no
time existed' and parse this as
   (2.1) *Every*[Pegasus$_{[p]}$](no time existed),
while conceding the theoretical possibility of parsing it with a gapped
predicate as
   (2.2) (Every Pegasus$_{[p]}$|*no*[time]existed).
It is (2.1) which the *UVPB* regards as entailing its implicitly contradictory
opposite (5) translated and parsed as
   (5.1) *Every*[Pegasus$_{[p]}$](some time existed).
By obversion the universal affirmative (5.1) is equivalent to the universal
negative
   (5.2) *No*[Pegasus$_{[p]}$](no time existed),
which by wild quantity generates the particular negative, '*Some*[Pegasus$_{[p]}$]
not(no time existed),' explicitly in contradictory opposition to (2.1).

   The question must arise as to how the past tensed (3) should be parsed.
The choice is between
   (3.1) *Every*['Pegasus$_{[p]}$'](named every Pegasus$_{[p]}$)
and
   (3.2) (Every 'Pegasus$_{[p]}$' named)*every*[Pegasus$_{[p]}$].
(3.2) claims that the object Pegasus *was named by the name 'Pegasus.'* This
contingent proposition could be true only if Pegasus once existed. With (3.2)
accepted as its antecedent
   (4) If 'Pegasus' named Pegasus, Pegasus once existed
must be recognized as necessarily true. But this does not render the *UVPB* a
successful *argument* as (3.2) is not entailed by (2.1). On the other hand, the
necessarily true (3.1) is entailed by (2.1). (3.1) is true even if Pegasus never
existed. This means, of course, that with (3.1) as its antecedent (4) cannot be
considered to be necessarily true. The *UVPB* is again undermined. There is
thus no contradiction in embracing both (2.1) and (3.1) either as independent propositions or by deriving the latter from the role that 'Pegasus' plays as
the subject of the former. By accepting (3) as (3.1) one can retain for
'Pegasus' its status as a genuine proper name, while recognizing a distinct
sense in which (4) can be rejected as a necessary truth. Contradiction only
arises with the joint independent *assertion* of (2.1) and (3.2). In short, if (2)
entails (3), (4) is not necessarily true; if (4) is necessarily true, then (2) does
not entail (3).

III. Conclusion

   It should be observed that the crux of this response to both Meinong's
Puzzle and the *UVPB* is based on viewing all propositions in a medieval

manner as structured according to the triadic form '$Q[S](P)$' with the 'Q' term as a syntactical device which quantifies the subject as it shows the way the predicate term and the subject term are attached or detached. From this perspective it can be said that a proper name subject *denotes or names an object or thing*. This is not to endorse, however, the commonly held position that views a proper name subject as a device used by a speaker to pick out what he wants to talk about while the rest of the sentence expresses what property he wishes to attribute to that individual.[21] This position in effect claims that an object which is the bearer of the name *is denoted by the proper name* serving as the subject of the proposition.[22] It is this contemporary view which engenders Meinong's Puzzle and Plato's Beard. To reject it, however, in favor of a tripartite syntactics is not to accept the position of those traditional distributionist logicians who endorse the Noun Phrase/ Verb Phrase constituent analysis of a proposition in which the quantifier is seen as part of the subject.[23] By disambiguating the distinct senses in which active and passive voice statements are equivalent, our triadic syntactic proposal for understanding speech about things which do not now exist and never have existed is neither Inflationist nor Deflationist. Admittedly, it is heavily speculative and seemingly Procrustean. Its capacity for dealing with other puzzles and paradoxes, however, will be the ultimate test of its viability.

Le Moyne College
Syracuse, New York

NOTES

1. Leonard Linsky, *Oblique Contexts* (Chicago: University of Chicago Press, 1983), p. xxvii.

2. C. J. F. Williams, *What Is Existence?* (Oxford: Clarendon Press, 1981), p. 110; see also p. 260.

3. Williams, p. 117.

4. Richard Cartwright, "Negative Existentials," in *Philosophy and Ordinary Language*, ed. Charles E. Caton (Urbana: University of Illinois Press, 1963), pp. 55-66. Cartwright acknowledges Isaiah Berlin as the source for this terminology.

5. John Stuart Mill, *A System of Logic*, eighth ed. (London: Longmans, 1965), I,ii,1-3 (pp. 14-17).

6. Mill, I,iii,3 (p. 33).

7. Alvin Plantinga, "The Boethian Compromise," *American Philosophical Quarterly*, 15 (1978), p. 130.

8. W. V. O. Quine, *From a Logical Point of View* (New York: Harper, 1963), pp. 7-8; Alvin Plantinga, *The Nature of Necessity* (Oxford: Clarendon Press, 1974), pp. 159-163.

9. Williams, pp. 258-61.

10. Barry Miller, "Strawson on Existence as a Predicate," *Philosophical Papers*, 10 (1981), p. 97.

11. Peter Geach has argued that this theory was ultimately disavowed by Frege himself. See

"Problems About the Sense and Reference of Proper Names," *Canadian Journal of Philosophy,* Supplementary Vol. VI (1980), pp. 87-88.

12. As presented by Fred Sommers, *The Logic of Natural Language* (Oxford: Clarendon Press, 1984); hereafter, *LNL.*

13. *LNL,* pp. 12-40.

14. Cf. *LNL,* p. 39.

15. We depart at this point from the neo-Leibnizian view expounded in *LNL* in favor of an older medieval Aristotelian view mentioned and described, though not endorsed, by Peter Geach in *Reference and Generality,* third ed. (Ithaca: Cornell University Press, 1980), pp. 201-02, 209. See Thomas Aquinas, *Summa Theologiae,* I,31,aa. 3 and 4.

16. *LNL,* pp. 18-19.

17. Cf. *LNL,* pp. viii, 9-15, 37-47.

18. Henceforth, however, parsings will be only as complete as the context demands.

19. We again respect the Fregean insistence that proper names themselves, though they can be parts of predicates, can never serve as full blown predicates. Cf. *LNL,* pp. 125-27, 135-36. In this connection it is helpful to note that opposition to 'Socrates is moral' can be expressed by either the *privative* affirmation 'Socrates is amoral,' the *contrary* affirmation 'Socrates is immoral,' or what might be called the *indefinite* affirmation 'Socrates is not-moral.' This last is equivalent to the claim 'Socrates is either amoral or immoral.' Each of these three entails but is not entailed by the *contradictory* affirmative 'Socrates is not moral' parsed as '*Every*[Socrates$_{[p]}$](is not moral).' The latter is equivalent by obversion to the *simple negative* 'Socrates is not moral' parsed as '*No*[Socrates$_{[p]}$](is-moral).' Verbs and adjectives can thus have privative, contrary, and indefinite predicates as well as contradictory ones. Names, however, admit only of contradictory ones. 'Pegasus is not Cerberus' can be correctly unpacked as '*Every*[Pegasus$_{[p]}$]((is)*not every*[Cerberus$_{[p]}$]).' 'Not-Cerberus' is not well formed. It is interesting to observe that this is in accordance with Aquinas' view. He notes that if 'non-man' were imposed from a *privation* it would require an existing subject. He thus concludes that it is imposed from a *negation* as it can be predicated of both being and nonbeing:one can say 'A horse is non-man' and 'A chimera is non-man.' (See Thomas Aquinas, *Aristotle: On Interpretation,* trans. Jean T. Oesterle (Milwaukee: Marquette University Press, 1962), I, 1.4 n. 13.) We construe him as meaning that it is permissible to say, in our mode of parsing, '*A*[horse]((is)*not a*[man])' and '*A*[chimera]((is)*not a*[man]).' But one cannot say '*A*[horse](is not-man)' or '*A*[chimera](is not-man).' Names can have negations, that is, they can be regarded as contradictory predicates, but not as privative, contrary, or indefinite ones. As Aquinas perspicaciously indicates, contradictory predicates unlike the other three are not existence entailing.

20. Cf. Alonzo Church, *Introduction to Mathematical Logic,* I (Princeton: Princeton University Press, 1956), pp. 4-5; nn. 8-9.

21. Keith Donnellan, "Speaking of Nothing," *Philosophical Review,* 83 (1974), pp. 11-12.

22. Williams, p. 110.

23. This is the position of *LNL,* pp. 9-10, and of George Englebretsen, *Three Logicians* (Assen: Van Gorcum, 1981), pp. 85-94.

SECTION VII—APPROACHES TO GOOD AND EVIL

Francis R. Hittinger, Chairman
Christendom College

Practical Solipsism and "Thin" Theories of Human Goods

by Olaf Tollefsen

Thomas Nagel has argued that to deny the objectivity of one's reasons for acting, or to lack such objective reasons, is to fall into practical (rather than theoretical) solipsism, i.e., it is to fall into the position of having to carry on one's practical deliberations as if one were the only full-fledged moral agent in existence.[1] And Nagel contends—correctly, I believe, although I shall not argue the point here—that practical solipsism is untenable.[2] If so, then it is philosophically important to be clear about what sorts of metaethical claims, or claims about practical reasoning, are implicitly solipsistic. One such claim is the subject of the present essay.

Many contemporary thinkers have adopted what John Rawls christened a "thin" theory of human goods—a theory which, as John Finnis aptly puts it, "...offers to identify as the basic human goods those goods which *any* human being would need *whatever his objectives.*"[3] Such theories identify as the basic human goods the fulfillment of whatever conditions must obtain if an agent, any agent, is to have some real opportunity to pursue his subjective purposes, *whatever* those purposes may be. Theories of this sort are often attempts to escape the controversies surrounding claims that one or another set of human ends are the goods that are truly constitutive of human flourishing or well-being. Failure to resolve those difficulties in a generally acceptable way would seem to block the articulation of any kind of public or communal morality, i.e., any kind of moral standard to which all could rationally adhere, and which, in consequence, could be employed as a guide to construct truly just social institutions. And considered in this way, thin theories of the good seem to be attempts to avoid practical solipsism, for they seem to aim at a conception of justice that requires equal respect for all agents and their values and projects in the creation of the social structure in which they must live and act. However, I shall contend here that if Nagel is right that one's reasons for acting must be objective if one is to avoid practical solipsism, then thin theories of basic human goods fail, for an agent who carried on his practical deliberations on the basis of such a theory could not avoid practical solipsism. I shall argue for this thesis by first remaking the case for the claim that one's reasons for acting must be objective if one is to avoid practical solipsism, and then, second, by arguing that no actual agent could deliberate on the basis of a thin theory of the good without in effect reducing his reasons for acting to purely subjective principles.

Nagel's thesis is, in essence, that in order to avoid practical solipsism, one must be able to ascribe objective value to one's ends, or be able to associate one's subjective purposes with an objectively valuable end in the appropriate way.[4] I shall take this to be equivalent to saying, first, that it is an agent's ends that give the agent reasons for acting, and, second, that those ends must be such as to give any agent just the same sorts of reasons for acting. (I am here assuming, of course, that having a reason to act is not equivalent to having a moral justification for acting in that way, and I am also assuming that two agents who have the same basic sorts of reasons for acting in a certain way, i.e., who have the same objective value as their end, may, because of differences in circumstances [both moral and non-moral] have different secondary reasons for acting, or even reasonably draw different practical conclusions about whether they are justified in acting.)

The first of these two points—that it is one's ends that give one reason to act—may seem so obvious as to be trite, but in the subsequent discussion here it plays an important role, for it marks the difference between the theoretical and the practical uses of reason. One's practical use of reason is aimed at ultimately reaching judgments about what one is to do or refrain from doing, and reasoning in that way is possible only if one has some end or ends in view, i.e., only if one is reasoning about possibilities one finds worth pursuing—possibilities that are worthy, in some way, of action on one's own part. When one has no ends in view in that sense, one's reasoning is not truly practical, for it cannot terminate in a judgment about how one is to act, but only in a judgment about what someone should do if they did think some possibility had value, i.e., actually gave them reason to act. But the hypothetical by itself gives no one reason to act.[5]

The second point, that one's ends must be such as to give any agent reason for acting, is what Nagel argues marks the difference between solipsistic and non-solipsistic doctrines of practical reasoning. In the analysis which follows here—which owes much to Nagel's—I shall argue that it is the very practicality of other agents' deliberations about how they are to act that is excluded from my deliberations about how to act if none of the ends for which we can act have objective value.

Now, I take it that to recognize, *in one's theoretical reasoning,* that others are full-fledged moral agents is to ascribe to them the same essential proper-ties one ascribes to oneself as a moral agent.[6] But to recognize others as full-fledged moral agents *in one's practical deliberations* is different: it is to deliberate according to some conception of practical reasoning that requires that the essential properties of moral agency, in any case in which they are instantiated, be relevant *as such* to the outcome of one's practical delibera-tions. Practical solipsism is thus the result of deliberating on the basis of a conception of practical reasoning that precludes this. It is practical in the full sense, rather than theoretical, precisely because its results are actions done and a life lived in a way incompatible with the recognition of others as full-fledged moral agents. Of course there are many properties that have been alleged to be essential to moral agency, all of which are matters of philosophical controversy. But those debates can be set aside here, for in the present context only one alleged property of moral agency is crucial, and that is the very practicality of practical reason itself. That it is essential to moral agency seems inescapable, for without it the conception of having reasons for acting is empty. What is at issue is whether that property, instantiated in other agents, can as such be relevant to the outcome of one's own practical deliberations if it is also the case that no human ends have objective value. That it cannot is clear from the following considerations.

First, any identification of an agent's purpose(s) must include in it some specification of some state of affairs that the agent thinks worth bringing into being or maintaining in being. (This is to say no more than that without such a specification, no potential course of action is under consideration by an agent. An agent may allege that he values some thing, say, theoretical knowledge, but if this does not at some point resolve itself into the possibility of action, of really doing something in pursuit of that value, the agent's claim to value knowledge seems empty from the point of view of practical reason.) Now, on the assumption that no human ends have objective value, i.e., that none are such as to give any agent reason for acting, it follows that the description of any state of affairs is by itself never enough to identify the bringing into being or preservation in being of that state of affairs as someone's purpose, for there could be nothing in the state of affairs itself, and hence nothing specified in its description, that could give anyone reason to act. In order for the bringing into being or preservation in being of some state of affairs to be someone's purpose, certain subjective conditions in an agent must obtain. Typically, we express the obtaining of such conditions in an agent in terms of an agent wanting, needing, inclining toward, being interested in, or being disposed to act for something. If such subjective conditions do not obtain in an agent with respect to some state of affairs, then the bringing into being or preservation in being of that state of affairs cannot be a purpose for that agent. In short, and on the assumption that no human ends have objective value, the obtaining of the relevant subjective conditions in an agent are necessary conditions for anything having value at all.

Second, and still working on the assumption that no human ends have objective value, the previous observations imply that even if two agents want, need, are inclined toward, are interested in, or disposed to act for the bringing into being or preservation in being of the same state of affairs, they cannot be strictly said to have the same end. The state of affairs—call it S—which each agent wishes to bring into being or preserve in being is, of course, the same, but S is not by itself an end for either agent: S is an end for either agent only in virtue of the obtaining in either agent of the subjective conditions for value-conferral. Thus, to say that S is an end for some agent, A, is to say that S gives A reasons for acting because A wants, needs, is inclined toward, is interested in, or is disposed to act for S. Hence any other agent's wanting, needing, being inclined toward, being interested in, or being disposed to act for S is in no way constitutive of S's role as an end for A. *S, considered precisely in its role as an end for any agent other than A, cannot give A reasons for acting as an end gives an agent reasons for acting.* Of course S's role as an end for agents other than A may be practically significant for A in ways other than the way in which ends are practically significant, for other agents having S as an end may be circumstances in view of which A must shape his own plans for pursuing S. But S, insofar as it is an end for agents other than A, cannot enter into A's practical deliberations as an end in the strict sense.

It follows, then, that if no human ends have objective value, then no agent can consider other agents ends as ends in the strict sense within his own practical deliberations. Hence no agent, in his own practical deliberations, can consider other agents as full-fledged moral agents, for the essential practicality of others' deliberations about how they are to act are excluded from his own deliberations. I conclude, then, that Nagel's thesis is essentially sound: practical solipsism is unavoidable unless some human ends have objective value.

Nagel cautions us that the distinction he draws between objective and subjective reasons is purely formal; any reason for acting can be stated as if it were objective, but that does not actually make it so. The distinction between the two kinds of reason obviously requires a supplementary theory of value if the distinction is to have any practical consequences.[6] That problem, the problem of constructing a cognitively adequate theory of value is, as I suggested earlier in this paper, the impetus behind many thin theories of the good, for attempts to construct a theory of value, like philosophical enterprises generally, do not result in easy and enduring agreements among philosophers. Various philosophical problems are clustered around that fact, but the core practical issue can be stated quite simply: How can there be any common set of rational principles of action for individuals with conflicting conceptions of objective value? Of course, each such conception will generate precepts about how one is to treat other agents who act on mistaken conceptions of objective value, just as each will generate precepts about how to treat other agents who deliberately do evil. Indeed, the power of a conception of what is objectively good to generate a consistent and complete set of such precepts is one of the criteria likely to be used to judge its plausibility. Nonetheless, each system of precepts will conflict, to one degree or another, with other systems of precepts drawn from other, conflicting conceptions of objective value. And there appears to be no position from which to adjudicate among such conflicting conceptions of objective value and the systems of precepts they generate, and hence no position from which it would be possible to articulate a theory of justice both rich enough in content to regulate the communal life of moral agents and rationally compelling to all.

It is just this problem that thin theories of the good are often aimed at resolving. Some certainly are not, but are merely subjectivist theories of value, and the principles of action they propose are simply the results of prudential calculations about what will best satisfy an agent's own interests. However, other thin theories—Rawls' is certainly a notable example—rest on a fundamental recognition of each individual as a full-fledged moral agent, and are intended, as Rawls puts it, "...to be fair between individuals conceived as moral persons with a right to equal respect and consideration in the design of their common institutions."[7] But how to achieve that equality of respect and consideration is the problem for the proponent of a thin theory of the good.

As already indicated, thin theories of the good prescind from attempting to resolve the claims of conflicting conceptions of objective value, and in so doing create a fundamental methodological problem. Setting aside the question of which human ends really do have objective value requires that one's method of arriving at rational principles of action treat every claim to objective value as having equal weight, and this is, in effect, to treat all human purposes as if they were merely subjective purposes. And this easily leads to solipsism, for the principles of action reason requires an agent to adopt *vis a vis* his subjective purposes are just those that offer the greatest likelihood of bringing those purposes to fruition—a thoroughly solipsistic conception of value and practical reason. To avoid this consequence, the proponent of a thin theory aimed at escaping solipsism must identify principles of action by hypothetically altering the conditions under which agents deliberate about their purposes and how they will pursue them so that the principles of action which will then emerge cannot be solipsistic. And by far the most plausible attack on this problem is to consider which principles of action reason would require that an agent adopt if the agent were ignorant of his natural endowments, social resources and specific purposes—just that information that makes solipsistic practical reasoning really possible.[8] With the conditions of deliberation, choice and action altered in that way, reason then requires that an agent adopt just those principles of action which would hold good whatever his actual purposes, natural endowments and social resources. Out of this emerges a thin theory of the good.

It must be emphasized that the justification for this methodology just mentioned is the thin theory's proponent's prior rejection of practical solipsism. The practical solipsist has no reason to consider what principles of action reason would require him to adopt if the conditions under which he deliberates, chooses and acts were hypothetically altered, for he is concerned only with his success at satisfying his actual interests in the actual world—with the most effective way of pursuing his interests with the natural endowments and social resources he actually has. But the proponent of a thin theory of the good of the sort under discussion here does have some conception of objective value, one which excludes practical solipsism. Thus his methodology of hypothetically altering the conditions under which an agent deliberates, chooses and acts is both generated and justified by his more fundamental understanding of the nature of moral agency itself, together with whatever reasons he believes justify rejecting any attempt to settle the question about which human ends really do have objective value. Thin theory methodology is aimed at making ethical principles consistent with non-solipsistic conceptions of value and practical reason. Whether it achieves that consistency is the question that must now be addressed.

Consider, then, the position in which an agent attempting to act on a thin theory of the good is placed. Since the proponent of a thin theory rejects any attempts to adjudicate conflicting claims about the objective value of human ends, the only such claims that he can exclude from his derivation of thin theory precepts are those that are formally solipsistic—claims by an agent that his ends are objectively valuable simply because they are his. This will otherwise leave the proponent of a thin theory with a very large array of claims about the objective value of human ends which he must treat, as a matter of methodological principle, as having equal claims to validity. Many of these claims will be mutually exclusive, but they must somehow all be recognized; to reject any would be to fail to give one or another agent the respect due to him as a moral person: the proponent of the thin theory construes respect just as a refusal to reason practically on the basis of any evaluative judgment about what any agent considers objectively worthwhile. Thus the action-guiding principles derived by thin theory methodology must hold good for any agent, no matter what conception of objective value he otherwise holds, and work in such a way as not to deprive any agent of a reasonable opportunity to actually pursue his ends. And this, I submit, is a requirement no thin theory can meet without being trivialized.

On the one hand, if the theory really is "thin" enough that its action-guiding principles are both consistent with every conception of what is objectively good and such as to allow every agent a reasonable opportunity to pursue his ends, the theory can generate no significant action-guiding rules, for such rules must, at the very least, resolve conflicting claims to objective goods fairly, and this those rules by their very nature cannot do. How, for example, could a thin theory resolve a conflict—i.e., construct a social institution that really was both impartial and enabling—between a serious pacifist and someone who thought that retributive justice required that serious violations of his family's honor required the death of the guilty individual(s)? On the other hand, if a thin theory is restrictive enough to avoid such difficulties, it is no longer such as to enable agents to really act for what they take to be objectively worthwhile; the agent himself "thins" out, as he can act on no conception of what is objectively good rich enough to make his own action and life significant. A life lived solely for the sake of not violating any and every possible conception of the good, if it could be lived at all, would be one empty of any significant human enterprise.

What, then, could an agent in such a dilemma actually do? Deprived of either any effective action-guiding principles or any conception of the objective good rich enough to give some point to his action, he would have no recourse but to fall back upon purely subjective, i.e., solipsistic, principles of action. From those principles the agent could no doubt derive some type of contractarian moral theory that would guide him in the construction of his social institutions, but that enterprise would of course be entirely contrary to the spirit of the kind of thin theory of the good under discussion here. It would require of him that he consider other agents and their ends not as agents *per se,* i.e., not as moral *persons,* but as circumstances in view of which his own pursuit of his ends would have to be modified and restrained in various ways. Hence I conclude that if practical solipsism is untenable, so too are thin theories of the good; they compel an agent to deliberate solipsistically, regardless of their intent.

I do not know that any agent who reasons on the basis of a thin theory of the good actually finds himself in the dilemma I have just articulated, for I suspect that no thin theory of the good is as thin or as limiting as consistency demands, but instead actually embodies a conception of objective value which is fairly rich in content. If so, thin theories of the good are, in the end, just additional examples of theories of value, to be considered and evaluated like any other such theory. And that activity is, after all, a central feature of non-solipsistic moral agency. A lack of concern about which human ends really do have objective value, an unwillingness to plunge into the messy business of coming to grips with that problem, is the mark of someone who, whatever his beliefs about the objectivity of value, is willing to deliberate, choose and act as a solipsist. And to such an individual there is little to say; as Nagel says in reference to the solipsist, "[w]hat further objections can be raised if someone remains unabashed about coming apart in this way?"⁹

Saint Anselm College
  Manchester, New Hampshire

NOTES

1. Thomas Nagel, *The Possibility of Altruism* (Oxford, 1970). The central arguments are in part three of the book.

2. Nagel, XIV, esp. 144-145.

3. John Finnis, *Fundamentals of Ethics* (Washington, D.C., 1983), II.6.

4. Nagel, 90.

5. Nagel, 117-118. Darwall has argued that Nagel's line of reasoning here fails [Stephen L. Darwall, *Impartial Reason* (Ithaca, 1983), 125-129]. What is at issue here appears to be the nature of practical reason itself. Darwall, as against Nagel, denies that the motivational content of a practical judgment is part of what one judges in making such a judgment. But, as I have argued here, that cannot be so; in judging what one is to do, one must judge that there is reason to do it, i.e., that there is an end worthy of one's efforts which can be accomplished by the course of action one is considering. See also Finnis, I.1, for a further discussion of this strong distinction between the theoretical and practical uses of reason.

6. Nagel, 126.

7. John Rawls, "Fairness to Goodness," *Philosophical Review*, 84 (1975), 359.

8. Rawls makes this same point from a Kantian perspective in his *A Theory of Justice* (Cambridge, Massachusetts, 1971), 251-253.

9. Nagel, 145.

The Privation Account of Evil: H. J. McCloskey and Francisco Suarez

by Douglas P. Davis

According to a recent survey of the literature on the problem of evil, contemporary work on this problem has for the most part been narrowly focussed upon the technical details of the problem.[1] One of the larger issues that seems to have been missed in the current debate is the impact one's understanding of the nature of evil might have upon the problem of evil. Indeed, the distinction between the problem of evil and the understanding of the nature of evil is rarely mentioned. This approach contrasts with that of Augustine or Thomas, who clearly explain what they take to be the nature of evil and indicate how a proper understanding of its nature helps to answer the problem of evil. The bifurcation between the problem of evil and its nature did not arise for the medievals largely because their treatment of the problem of evil rested upon a number of common assumptions which are no longer shared.[2] One of the chief of these is the belief in the co-extension between being and value. For many philosophers today the claim that something is good to the degree that it has being is barely intelligible. This may be due to the perceived vagueness of the concept of being or to a sharp dichotomy maintained between fact and value.[3] In any case, it is the rejection of the characteristically scholastic view of evil as consisting in privation that I wish to probe. In particular, I wish to focus upon one evaluation of the scholastic perspective on the relation between the nature and problem of evil found in H. J. McCloskey's *God and Evil.*[4] This book is unusual in the contemporary literature for the emphasis placed upon the question of how one's view of the nature of evil conditions one's response to the problem of evil. In this paper I shall limit my attention to McCloskey's criticism of the privation theory of evil, the metaphysical rather than the theological problem of evil; a problem concerning the nature of evil rather than its incompatibility with God's existence. McCloskey directs his criticism at representative authors of the view that evil consists in privation, authors such as Augustine, Thomas, Gilson and Journet among others.[5] I wish to argue that regardless of his success or failure with the preceding authors, most of his points fall short of impugning another writer squarely within the same tradition, Francisco Suarez.[6]

McCloskey's attack upon the privation account of evil can be divided into two parts. In the first part he sets aside the question of the truth or falsity of this view and argues that if it were true the very problem of evil would disappear. In the second part he argues that the privation account of evil is false. He employs four arguments: First, he argues that not all privation is evil; second, that not all evil is privation; third, that the privation account cannot explain the causal power of evil; and fourth, that the account is too vague. I will argue that Suarez's position avoids most of McCloskey's criticisms. More specifically, I argue that McCloskey has little ground for the first part of his attack which largely depends upon the second, and that in the second part Suarez's view avoids the first and third arguments and could be interpreted in a way which would avoid the second and fourth arguments.

McCloskey initially sets aside the question of the truth or falsity of the privation account of evil, arguing that even if it were true the problem of evil would not arise. In its stead, there would be two other problems, namely, the worship-worthiness of the deity and the justification for the creation of a world that is less good than it could be. First, if God is good only in a non-moral sense of 'good,' then there appears to be no reason to worship him, and second, since God could possibly have avoided creating a world in which privation is so pervasive, why did he not create a less defective world? The disappearance of the problem of evil is due to the lack of any specifically moral sense of the word 'evil' in which privation is evil. According to McCloskey, if evil is understood as privation, this being interpreted as the lack of what a thing ought to have, there does not appear to be any specifically moral sense in which evil is bad.

> I suggest that for exponents of the theory there is no problem of evil, but only an illusion of a continuing problem due to "proper good," "entitled to be there," "naturally there," "ought to be there," being given a moral interpretation which is incompatible with the theory. If good equals being, and privation, the absence of appropriate, natural being, there is no sense of evil according to which this absence of proper good can be said to be evil. The problem disappears. In fact, the writers concerned show that they hanker after another sense of evil according to which it is evil that an avoidable privation should occur. However, if evil is wholly explicable as privation, then it may well be asked 'What does it matter if beings capable of privations, develop or occur with privations?'[7]

There are three points that can be made against this argument. The first is that McCloskey argues under the mistaken assumption that metaphysical and moral categories are exclusive of one another when applied to evil. McCloskey is arguing that if evil is defined as privation then one cannot say that privation is evil in a moral sense, for privation is not a moral concept. The sense of 'ought' employed in the definition of privation is not a moral sense, but rather a metaphysical sense.[8] He goes on to say that the writers in this tradition hanker after this impossible concept, namely, a moral understanding of privation.

McCloskey here assumes that if evil is given a non-moral definition in terms of privation, then there is no possibility of evil being given a moral sense. But this is simply false. While McCloskey is correct in pointing to the non-moral character of privation as a metaphysical category, this does not prevent the application of moral distinctions. It is as if in pointing out that goodness is a property, one had thereby ruled out the possibility of a moral sense of good. Suarez is very clear on this point. After characterizing evil as privation, he then distinguishes between moral and natural evil as privations which apply to beings insofar as they are either free or not free.[9] Hence, evil can be constituted by privation and yet retain its moral significance.

The second point has to do with the claim that if the privation account is true then the problem of evil is transmuted into the problem of God's power to create a world better than one in which privation occurs. McCloskey's reasoning, which is not fully expressed, seems to go like this. Since privation is not morally evil (according to McCloskey's view) then there is no problem of evil, but rather a problem of privation. The existence of privation still needs to be justified since it may have been possible for God to create a world without privation. "This," he says, "is not the problem of evil so much as the problem of the less good world."[10] The question presupposed here is what is to count as the problem of evil. I would suggest that the problem of the less good world can be viewed as the problem of the more evil world. McCloskey does not wish to label it in this manner because he does not believe the analysis of evil as privation is correct. But even if McCloskey were right about privation, the problem of the less good world is unavoidable in a full-blown theodicy and, consequently, could be said to be part of the problem of evil.

Thirdly, McCloskey points to the problem of the worship-worthiness of God, asserting that being *qua* being, even if it is pure and unlimited, is not a proper object of worship. The unstated argument appears to be that if evil is taken to be a lack of being, then the highest degree of being will also be the highest degree of good; but since being *qua* being is not a proper object of worship, neither is God, understood as the highest degree of being. Suarez, however, believes that God's goodness is not exhausted by saying that he is the most perfect being. Good and being are co-extensive, according to Suarez, but they do not have the same meaning.[11] God may be said to be good in more than one sense. There may be a non-moral, metaphysical sense of good which applies to God with respect to his being, as well as a moral sense which applies to him with respect to his action and character, and the two senses need not exclude each other. Thus the problem of the worship-worthiness of God does not arise simply because a non-moral, metaphysical sense of the word 'good' is used.

In the second part of his critical evaluation, McCloskey aims to show that the privation account is false. He begins by claiming that not all privations are evil. He points to examples such as baldness and the lack of two toes when the other toes adequately compensate for the loss. There is no loss of function in these cases although there is privation. The privation in such cases would still be the lack of what ought to be present, namely, the hair or toes. Yet, according to McCloskey, even when there may be a loss of function, in some cases this would not be considered evil, as when sterility occurs in a mother who has many children and would be killed by yet another pregnancy.

For Suarez, however, if such losses are in fact privations, then they must be evil regardless of compensating mechanisms or fortuitous circumstances. If they can be characterized as lacks of what their natures require, then they are privations, and hence, evils. McCloskey again manifests his resistance to the possibility of a conception of evil which is metaphysical in character. He belies his belief that evil should matter to those afflicted by it, but under Suarez's view the harm or lack of it that may occur does not define evil. Evil is privation, the lack of what is proper to a nature.

Such an understanding of evil sounds foreign to the contemporary ear, particularly when Suarez says that heat is evil for water. Yet the quarrel between McCloskey and Suarez is not merely semantic, each devoted to mutually exclusive definitions of the term 'evil,' for in the first place Suarez does maintain a place for moral evil, and secondly, he does take seriously the claim that some evils are positive in nature rather than privative. And this is McCloskey's second reason for rejecting the privation account of evil.

This objection is not a new one. There were stock scholastic counter-examples to the privation account. Among the positive evils mentioned were included moral evils such as intemperance, avarice and lying, and non-moral evils such as pain, the natural incompatibilities as between heat and cold, and monstrosities, i.e., physical defects such as a sixth finger on one hand. Suarez's strategy for dealing with these positive evils was to distinguish between evil in itself and evil for another, and characterize positive evil as a kind of evil for another.

Evil in itself, according to Suarez, is simply a privation inhering in a subject and evil for another is a kind of disagreeability (*disconvenientia*) or incompatibility (*repugnantia*) between a form and a subject. The chief difference between these two kinds of evil is that evil in itself does not involve a relation to a form in the same way that evil for another does. Evil for another is considered positive because the form involved in the privation has being. Considered by itself, the form is not evil, but good; yet in relation to some subject, a privation arises. The privation that comes about in the relation between the form and subject Suarez describes in various ways but he focusses on the lack in the form or subject of what is necessary for each to be agreeable to or compatible with the other. For example, the heat in fire is a form which introduces privation in relation to water by lacking the coldness which would make it agreeable to or compatible with the coldness of water. Suarez, then, tries to account for the existence of positive evils by pointing to a form which is involved in all such evils, but nevertheless he maintains that the evilness is ultimately due to the privation which must be present.

In this second argument McCloskey cites pain, suffering and moral evil as examples of evils that are not privations, pointing out that all these evils are positive in nature. But Suarez would agree that these are positive evils, since he classifies each of these evils as evil for another. In fact, in the following passage McCloskey echoes Suarez's own words on pain: pain cannot be the mere deprivation of pleasure.

> Perhaps, as others have suggested, it will be argued that pain is not itself a privation, but that its evilness consists in its involving a privation. Its evilness, it might be claimed, consists in pain depriving us of a state of contentment. This is how Journet argues. I suggest that such a move is a desperate one, and as implausible as attempts to explain a colour, for example green, as consisting in the absence of red, yellow, blue, orange, etc.[12]

Suarez mentions the fact that pain deprives one of a state of contentment, but he refuses to claim that this is why pain is evil. Pain is a positive form which is disagreeable to the subject. Of course, Suarez works the notion of privation into his account of pain, but in the following passage he does not go as far as McCloskey suggests in identifying the evilness of pain with the privation of pleasure.

> It must be granted that not only is [pain] evil causally, that is, because it excludes the opposite pleasure, but also because it is itself disagreeable and inappropriate for the animal...Yet it is not disagreeable by reason only of a positive entity taken with precision, but because, on account of that, it includes a lack of a perfection necessary for it to be a form agreeable and proper to man.[13]

Suarez comes very close to the position McCloskey rejects, but he makes the distinction between the causal consequences of the form found in pain and the relation between the form and its subject. The evilness of pain is found in the relation between the form of pain and the subject of it. Suarez does not specify what this form is but this is likely to be an empirical question. He says that the disagreeable character of pain is a lack in the relation between the form and subject of what would make the two agreeable in this context, adding that this lack is not the lack of pleasure. Immediately we wish to know what it is which we could add to pain to make it agreeable to a subject of it. Suarez, of course, does not supply an answer to this question and consequently, his account has the appearance of circularity. Positive evil is a kind of disagreeability or incompatibility which is simply the lack of agreeability or compatibility. The circularity, however, is merely apparent since pain as a general phenomenon requires a general explanation. In each particular instance of pain, Suarez might instruct us to look and see what is the cause of the disharmony. At this point of the analysis an empirical investigation must take over.

In the case of the positive evil of fault, Suarez is a little more specific than in the case of pain. He makes the same point about the causal effects of the positive form but goes on this time to specify what is missing in the relation between the form and subject.

> The evil of fault is an evil [which] properly [pertains] to man [insofar] as he is rational and uses free will, and therefore, it is not always said of privation alone but also of positive act, not however by reason of [something] positive alone but to the degree it lacks the rectitude it ought to have...Hence, not only is it evil because it excludes from the subject a contrary act or a good habit...but because it itself is disagreeable to the rational nature. It is disagreeable, however, not on account of a determinate (*praecisam*) entity, but [insofar] as it underlies the lack of rectitude it ought to have as has been said.[14]

The evil of fault, which is a general label for moral evil, sometimes consists in an act which is positive as an act but which lacks the "rectitude" it ought to have in order to be agreeable to the rational nature. This lack of rectitude is the lack of a conformity to rational principles which order the moral life of human beings. Here we have the specification of what is lacking, the privation which constitutes this kind of evil whereas in Suarez's explanation of pain it is just this specification which is missing.

Thus, although Suarez considers evil to consist in privation, he recognizes the difficulty of maintaining this claim in the face of examples such as those which McCloskey raises, and hence, employs the category of evil for another to explain these cases.

McCloskey's third argument is that evil has causal power, a feature which is incompatible with evil considered as privation, since no privation can be a cause. He cites a number of examples to show that the proponents of the privation theory believe that evil can be a cause. He goes on to say that even though our ordinary speech about causes is imprecise so that we sometimes speak of absences as being causes as when we say, for example, that a lack of food causes death or illness, nevertheless, if a completely specified causal explanation were to be given in scientific terms, no absences could figure in it.

> Positive presences are what enter into carefully stated scientific causal explanations. This fact means that an important, positive element is absent from the privative analysis of evil. It cannot adequately explain the roles of evil as causes.[15]

McCloskey's argument can succinctly be stated in the following way:

1. Exponents of the privation theory attribute causal power to evil (e.g., pain, suffering) and evil beings (e.g., evil persons and spirits).
2. Only positive presences have causal power.
3. Evil is not a positive presence according to the privation theory.
   Therefore, the privation theory cannot explain the causal power of evil.

The argument rests upon the notion of "causal power." McCloskey claims that only positive presences really have causal power even though we often speak as though absences may have causal power. His argument for this (premise two above) is that a precise scientific explanation of phenomena cannot include mention of absences or lacks. Thus, we might distinguish between two senses of 'causal power' in this argument. The first might be called '*prima facie* causal power.' This is the causal power attributed to something at the level of ordinary discourse, an imprecise designation according to McCloskey. Then there is 'real causal power.' This is the causal power attributed to something at the level of precise, scientific analysis. There are good reasons to suspect that in the above argument the first premise employs the notion of *prima facie* causal power, and the second premise and conclusion rely upon the notion of real causal power. Firstly, if the exponents of the privation theory are medieval authors such as Aquinas and Suarez, they cannot be supposed to have had in mind a contemporary notion of scientific analysis which is reductionist in character. Their understanding of causal power was within the framework of the Aristotelian four causes. Secondly, even if the exponents of the privation theory are recent authors such as Gilson and Journet, it is unlikely that in their philosophical arguments they would be relying on a peculiarly narrow sense of 'causal power' rather than the ordinary sense. Indeed, it is hard to imagine either of these authors couching their arguments about evil in precise, scientific language simply because such language is not suited to their purposes. In order for the argument to work, McCloskey would have to argue that the exponents of the privation theory are committed to the scientific sense when attributing causal power to evil and evil beings. Furthermore, Suarez's view permits positive evils to have causal power, since they involve positive forms which are real entities having the power of efficient causation.

McCloskey's fourth argument is that the view that evil is privation renders the concept of evil vague. If a privation is a lack of that which by nature is proper to an individual, then unless it is clear exactly what features are proper to the individual, the concept of evil will be vague. This is, of course, not so much a difficulty with the concept of evil as a difficulty with the concept of a nature. If the notion of a determinate nature could be clarified sufficiently, then the boundaries of evil could be more precisely indicated. To put the problem in Suarez's terminology, it will be unclear whether a particular lack is a negation or a privation. A negation is a lack of that which is not implied by the nature of the individual, as, for example, the lack of wings in human beings. A privation, however, is conceived as a lack of a feature which is implied by the nature of the individual. For Suarez and many other medieval writers the nature of human beings was given by the genus and specific difference, namely, animality and rationality. Thus, whatever features are implied by 'rational animal' are candidates for privation. This belief in sharply demarcated natural kinds McCloskey challenges, citing the existence of mutants as counter-examples. It is not clear what would count as a privation in the case of animals which are "between" species. He asks if an emu suffers privation in lacking wings that would enable it to fly.

One way to understand Suarez's view would be to characterize the nature in terms of its final cause rather than its determinate properties. The nature of an individual determines what is its end, i.e., its final cause. Some of the capacities of the individual contribute to the attainment of that end, and some are incidental to it. Anything which thwarts the attainment of the final cause, then, is contrary to the nature and could be considered a privation since it would prevent a nature from being fully realized. That is, it would be a lack of what ought to be present as determined by the efficient realization of the subject's final cause. If, for example, the final cause of human beings is taken to be the development of the rational capacities, then the lack of hair would simply be a negation whereas the lack of sight would impede the development of one's rational capacities, and hence be a privation. The advantage of this understanding is that the question of what is and is not a privation can be decided in terms of the efficient fulfillment of the end which is determined by the nature, a procedure which may afford more precise results than determining what characteristics are implied by the genus and specific difference. The difficulty in this, of course, lies in specifying the final causes of things.

Another possible solution to the problem of vagueness would be to bring Suarez into the contemporary scene by furnishing him with the current arguments for a theory of natural kinds. I will not attempt this task. It is not clear to me that the current theories of paradigmatic particulars are very close to scholastic views on genus and species since the former but not the latter make kind terms function as proper names. Nevertheless, Suarez's account might be made more precise by recasting it in some contemporary theory of natural (and nominal) kinds.

We have seen how Suarez might have responded to McCloskey's arguments against the privation account of evil. The first part of McCloskey's argument depends upon his four arguments for the untenability of the privation account. Against the first and second arguments concerning the co-extension of privation and evil, it was shown that Suarez's concept of evil is quite different than McCloskey's, appealing to a different set of intuitions, but one which nonetheless accounts for McCloskey's counter-examples. In short, it is a broader understanding of evil. Against McCloskey's third argument, the ambiguity in McCloskey's use of 'causal power' was pointed out, and it was argued that Suarez could maintain that positive evils have causal power. Finally, against the fourth argument it was noted that the real problem lay in the concept of a nature rather than evil, and several suggestions were offered to make this notion more precise.

McCloskey's book is remarkable in its thoroughness. Rarely does recent work treat the relation between the problem and the nature of evil. Although I have tried to show that his arguments fail to demonstrate that at least Suarez's theory of evil is false, the main thrust of his book against the possibility of a theodicy has been left unchallenged.

St. Bonaventure University
  St. Bonaventure, New York

NOTES

1. This is one of the points made by Michael Peterson in "Recent Work on the Problem of Evil," *American Philosophical Quarterly* 20 (1983) pp. 321-340.

2. Of course, within the Catholic tradition the nature of evil has always been a topic of philosophical discussion.

3. Current thought is actually divided on the fact/value dichotomy. See Robert Holmes "Frankena on 'Ought' and 'Is,'" in *The Monist* 64 (1981) pp. 394-405 for the possible interpretations of the dichotomy.

4. The Hague: Nijhoff, 1974.

5. He cites Augustine's *Enchiridion*, Thomas' *Summa theologiae* I. q. 48,9, and *Summa contra gentiles* Bk. 3, chs. 7-13, Gilson on Thomas in *The Christian Philosophy of St. Thomas Aquinas* (N.Y.: Random House, 1956), Charles Journet's *The Meaning of Evil* (N.Y.: P. J. Kennedy, 1963).

6. Suarez was a prominent Spanish philosopher and theologian who lived from 1548 to 1617. For a translation and introduction to his views on good and evil see Jorge J. E. Gracia and

Douglas Davis, *The Metaphysics of Good and Evil of Francisco Suarez* (Munich: Analytica Series Philosophia Verlag, forthcoming).

7. McCloskey, pp. 30, 1.

8. The non-moral sense of 'evil' belongs properly to the philosophy of nature rather than to the metaphysics proper (as defined by Aristotle and understood by most medieval authors), but for ease of expression I shall continue to describe it in the same way as McCloskey which is a broader use of the term 'metaphysics.' For the distinction between the philosophy of nature and metaphysics see James A. Weisheipl, "Medieval Natural Philosophy and Modern Science" in *Nature and Motion in the Middle Ages,* ed., William E. Carroll (Washington, D.C.: Catholic University Press, 1985).

9. *De malo* in *Disputationes metaphysicae,* Disp. XI, Sect. II, para. 2 in vol. 25 of *Opera omnia,* ed., M. André (Paris: Vives, 1856) p. 362a.

10. *Ibid.*

11. *De bonitate* Disp. X, Sect. III; in Vives, pp. 346b-355a.

12. McCloskey, p. 36.

13. *De malo* Sect. I, para. 18; in Vives vol. 25, p. 361a.

14. *De malo* Sect. I, para. 17; in Vives vol. 25, p. 360b.

15. McCloskey, p. 41.

SECTION VIII—THOMAS AQUINAS

Francis Kelley, Chairman
St. Bonaventure University

Ad Mentem Thomae: **Does Natural Philosophy Prove God?***

by John F. X. Knasas

In his *Cosmological Argument from Plato to Leibniz,*[1] William Lane Craig fans the coals of a neo-scholastic debate that once flamed in the journals. The debate's topic was whether the *prima via* is an argument of natural philosophy or of metaphysics.[2] The *prima via* is Aquinas' first of five philosophical *demonstrationes* for God given at *S.T.* I, 2, 3c. Characteristic of Aquinas' reasoning are the following points. Aquinas begins from some instance of obvious motion. Provided examples are wood becoming hot and a stick going to another place. Then using notions of potency and act to delineate the respective natures of something in motion and a mover, Aquinas argues that what is in motion is moved by another. Finally, Aquinas concludes that the "another" must be an unmoved mover. It is fair to say that implicit here is a disjunctive procedure. The *via* can immediately conclude to an unmoved mover or mediately reach it through a necessarily finite series of moved movers. The disjunction is explicit in the *Contra Gentiles* version of the *prima via.* The last line of the *prima via* is written in quite *blasé* fashion. Aquinas remarks, "and this [unmoved mover] everyone understands to be God." "Everyone" presumably includes the Christian believer who is Aquinas himself.

Characteristic of what I will call the natural philosophy, or physical, interpretation is that the starting point is understood hylomorphically, i.e., in terms of matter and form. Hence, motion is a process to actuality in the sense of form. This physical interpretation has two variations. What distinguishes the two is how the remainder of the argument is understood.

---

* The more extensive version of this article is forthcoming in *Divus Thomas.*

On the one hand, the argument can be completed without involving principles of any other philosophical science — viz., metaphysics. Such seems to be the position of Vincent Smith and Craig.[3] On the other hand, the completion of the argument demands metaphysical principles, but something natural philosophy accomplishes is responsible for the apprehension of those principles. That accomplishment is a proof of the immaterial. Such seems to be the position of Thomas C. O'Brien, James Weisheipl, and James Doig.[4]

Characteristic of the metaphysical interpretation is that the starting point of the argument is understood metaphysically, i.e., in terms of essence and existence. The *prima via* is a metaphysical argument straight away. Hence, motion is a process to actuality in the sense of *esse*. Such is the position of Etienne Gilson, Frederick Copleston, Gerard Smith and Joseph Owens.[5]

Craig's remarks show that the correct interpretation of the *prima via* is still a live issue. And well it should be. The debate involves not only the cogency of Aquinas' reasoning for God. It also impinges on the status and nature of Thomistic metaphysics. No student of Aquinas can afford to turn a deaf ear to it. One avenue in the debate that I have found relatively unexplored is the accurateness of the natural philosophy interpretation. Since the metaphysical interpretation is a recent development, the debate has whirled around attacking or defending it. In the bustle of this activity, the natural philosophy interpretation has largely escaped an in-depth analysis. My intention is to contribute to the metaphysical interpretation. My procedure will be a process of elimination. The *via* is either physical in one of the above senses or metaphysical. I will analyze the reasons that the physical interpretation proposes for being *ad mentem Thomae* and will find them lacking. This should swing attention to the metaphysical approach.

As mentioned, the first variant of the physical interpretation understands the *prima via* as reaching God in and through physical principles alone. The principles of no other speculative science intrude upon the reasoning. This interpretation faces insurmountable textual problems.

First, Aquinas expressly regards matter/form reasoning as attaining only a more universal cause that is less than divine. The reasoning does not attain the most universal cause, God. The text is 44, 2, of the *prima pars*. The *corpus* of the article presents a three-stage breakdown of the history of Western Philosophy. Of the second stage Aquinas says:

> An advance [in the knowledge of truth] was made when [philosophers] understood that there was a distinction between the substantial form and matter, which latter they held to be uncreated, and when they perceived transmutation to take place in bodies in regard to essential forms. These transmutations they attributed to certain more universal causes, such as the oblique circle, according to Aristotle, or the Ideas, according to Plato.[6]

Aquinas says that philosophers advanced further by attaining the considera-tion of *ens inquantum ens.* Such an object permits a reasoning for the most universal cause, God.

By way of comment, four points should be especially noted. First, the second stage mentioned is that of natural philosophy. The notions of matter and substantial form hammered out at this stage are the intrinsic principles of the subject matter of natural philosophy.[7] Using them Aristotle rose only to a more universal cause than was attained at the first stage. It is a body. In particular it is the sun. The "oblique circle" refers to the sun's perceived orbit around the earth.[8] This orbit is also called the ecliptic.

Second, the more universal cause of the second stage is not identifiable in any respect with the God of Aquinas' religious belief. It is clearly a less than divine being. Aquinas is not regarding matter/form principles as attaining God in some respect less than the universal cause. Rather, he regards these principles as attaining God not at all.

Third, philosophy advances further in its knowledge of truth not by further implications of natural philosophy principles. Rather, one must change to a new viewpoint. It is the viewpoint of being as being (*ens inquantum ens*). This expression designates the subject of metaphysics. In sum, the second stage exhausts the principles of natural philosophy.

Fourth, in the above text, Aristotle is used only as an example of someone who did natural philosophy. Aquinas' mention of Aristotle here does not mean that Aquinas holds that Aristotle fails to demonstrate God. The text ascribes this failure only to reasoning based on matter/form principles. Earlier in the *De Potentia* III, 5c, Aquinas appears to give to Aristotle, as well as to others, a knowledge of the creator God. Yet, the ascription is done on the basis of Aquinas' claim that Aristotle attains a view of universal *esse.*[9] For Aquinas this is the viewpoint of metaphysics.

Prima pars 44, 2c, then, is Aquinas' unabashed admission that to his mind natural philosophy principles alone do not produce reasoning reaching God.

Secondly, if anything, what we find the Thomistic texts expressly and repeatedly asserting is that the philosophical knowledge of God is the privilege of metaphysics. The only other knowledge of God mentioned is not philosophical but theological. These texts are found at *In de Trin.* V, 4c, and in the proem to *In Meta*[10] and so, temporally speaking, bracket the *quinque viae.* These texts make perfectly clear that for Aquinas God is philosophically reached in metaphysics. There is no admission that any other philosophical science does the same.

Against these two main points, some apparently contradictory texts are not withstanding. Texts thought to say that natural philosophy proves God do not do so expressly. For instance,

> Natural science does not treat of the First Mover as its subject or as part of its subject, but as the end to which natural science leads....the First Mover is of a different nature from natural things, but it is related to them because it moves them. So it falls under the consideration of natural science, not in itself, but insofar as it is a mover.[11]

First, the text does not identify the first mover (*primus motor*) as God. At *C.G.* I, 13, Aquinas does use a similar phrase, *"primum movens,"* to refer to the outer-most celestial sphere.[12] Second, in his reply, Aquinas does not say that the first mover is immaterial. He merely says that it is "of a different nature from natural things." The objection had described the first mover as "free from all matter." Aquinas' reply, then, is couched in a terminology that makes no commitment to the immateriality of the first mover. It is terminology that could well apply to the ungenerable and incorruptible heavens. In conclusion, the text offers nothing that necessarily goes beyond *prima pars* 44, 2c. On matter/form principles, the natural philosopher only goes to the heavens, *causae universaliores*.

Nor is Aquinas' famous remark at the end of his commentary on the *Physics* an admission that natural philosophy demonstrates God. The famous remark is:

> And thus the Philosopher ends his general discussion of natural things with the first principle (*primo principio*) of the whole of nature, who is over all things, God, blessed forever, Amen.

But by its reference to God as "first principle," this remark seems just to take up earlier thoughts from the commentary on Book VIII. These earlier thoughts never spoke of the first principle as a cause merely of substantial forms. Rather, the first principle is a universal cause that as such accounts for the very being (*esse*) of things. Aquinas says,

> [Averroes' opinion that the first universal agent presupposes some uncaused matter] does not agree with Aristotle's intention. For he proves in *Metaphysics*, II, that that which is most true and most being is the cause of being for all existing things. Hence it follows that the very being in potency which primary matter has is derived from the first principle of being, which is the most being. Therefore, it is not necessary to presuppose something for its action which has not been produced by it.[13]

While God's universal production of being is not strictly speaking a motion, a little later in this same context of creation Aquinas has no difficulty referring to God as the First Mover.[14] Also, Aquinas presents both Plato and Aristotle as arguing for an eternal universal production.[15] Aquinas' only disagreement with this conclusion is that the effect from which it starts, viz., motion, is not demonstrably eternal. As emanating from the first principle, motion could come to be without a preceding motion. Aristotle seems to miss this. Nevertheless, a creation in time does not deny a first principle. So Aristotle's conclusion is secure.

In conclusion, in all of this commentary no discussion of the first principle as less than a creator is found. Aristotle's and Plato's first principle is never presented as a cause only of substantial forms. In a passage reminiscent of *prima pars* 44, 2c, a cause of substantial forms is relegated to a lower level of previous thinking. Plato and Aristotle went beyond to "the principle of the whole of being" (*principium totius esse*).[16] I find no basis for restricting a reading of the commentary on Book VIII to a merely physical level. Everything seems to indicate a metaphysical understanding of the talked about first principle and first mover.[17] It might be mentioned that this metaphysical interpretation would place the commentary in line with *prima pars* 44, 2c and *De Potentia* III, 5c. In these texts God is reached only from a metaphysical principle, *esse*. The physical principle of substantial form falls short of proving God.

To conclude, because of textual incompatibilities, the first physical interpretation cannot claim to be *ad mentem Thomae*.

The inadequacy of the first variant is implicitly acknowledged by the recentness of the second variant. Though it is acknowledged that metaphysics, not natural philosophy, proves God, it is held that natural philosophy is crucial for metaphysics. Through its demonstration of immaterial being less than God, natural philosophy affords us the basis to hammer out the subject of metaphysics with its intrinsic principles of essence and existence. Without a previous demonstration of the immaterial, there can be no science of metaphysics. Hence, no proof of God. Natural philosophy, then, is an indispensable stage in any Thomistic argument for God and so for the *prima via,* too.

Both textual and philosophical arguments are offered for the above being *ad mentem Thomae*. The most forceful textual argument is expressed by Weisheipl this way:

> ...it is natural philosophy that discovers the existence of separate substances, i.e., some non-material being, and thus establishes the subject matter of a new science, namely the science of being as such. In Book VI of the *Metaphysics* Aristotle says: 'If there were no substance other than those which are formed by nature, natural science would be the first science; but if there is an immovable substance, the science of

this must be prior and be first philosophy.' Thomas not only comments on this clear statement but he repeats it twice more in his commentary.[18]

Aquinas' comment referred to by Weisheipl is as follows:

> ...if there is no substance other than those which exist in the way that natural substances do, with which the philosophy of nature deals, the philosophy of nature will be the first science. But if there is some immobile substance,[19] this will be prior to natural substance; and therefore the philosophy, which considers this kind of substance, will be first philosophy.[20]

Again, this text and others are taken as indicating that according to Aquinas' own intention natural philosophy both proves immobile substance and in doing that establishes the subject matter of metaphysics. God can be argued from this point.[21]

Philosophically speaking the second variant is explained in two ways. First, with a knowledge of immaterial beings provided by natural philosophy, existence (*esse*) stands out as a distinct commonality shared both by bodies and spirits. Elders succinctly says,

> However, once this insight [that being is not necessarily material] is reached, our attention shifts from the *quidditas materialis* to the *esse* which gives reality to both material and immaterial things. This shifting of attention is furthered by the fact that the *essence* of immaterial being is unknown to us, so that the *esse* of things is now understood as that which is most intimate, most formal and most perfect.[22]

Second, Smith argues that the metaphysical composition of essence and existence is necessary to deal with the problem of the one and the many on the spiritual level.[23] Since we are dealing with spirits, the matter/form composition cannot be applied. On the level of bodies, the composition explains many individuals within one species. The individuals are one by communicating in the same specific form; they are many by their respective matters. Supposedly on the immaterial level substances would be multiplied by having their respective existences.

What is to be thought of the second physical interpretation? Neither the textual nor philosophical bases are solid. The interpretation is questionable at best.

Taken by themselves the texts cited by Weisheipl say neither that natural philosophy proves immobile substance nor that such a fact establishes the subject of another science. All the texts say is that without immobile substance natural philosophy is first philosophy. Insofar as natural philosophy proponents focus on these texts alone, they leave themselves open to the charge of committing a *non sequitur.*

Yet my remark may be myopic. In his commentary on Boethius' *De Trinitate,* Aquinas appears to say that natural science proves separate substances. Aquinas remarks,

> Moreover, the sensible effects on which the demonstrations of natural philosophy are based are more evident to us in the beginning. But when we come to know the first causes through them, these causes will reveal to us the reason for the effects, from which they were proved by a demonstration *quia.* In this way natural science also contributes something to divine science,...[24]

Taken in a wider context, do not Weisheipl's texts bear out the second variant?

No, I do not think so. The *De Trinitate* comment is not decisive because it is ambiguous. As the Latin makes clear, the first causes are not reached from the demonstrations of natural philosophy. They are reached from the sensible effects from which those demonstrations proceed. Also, the text does not say that the demonstrations of natural philosophy reach separate substances. Rather, Aquinas uses the neutral phrase "first causes."[25]

In light of this indecisiveness, earlier cited texts become that much more important. At *prima pars* 44, 2, Aquinas gave matter/form reasoning the ability to go only to a more universal cause identified with a celestial body. Also, at *In de Trinitate* V, 4c, and in the proem to the commentary on the *Metaphysics,* not only is knowledge of God reserved to metaphysics but as well knowledge of the separate substances, or intelligences. *Both* God and the angels are reached in metaphysics. No other philosophical science is mentioned.

Here especially it cannot be said that natural philosophy reaches separate substances under one aspect, e.g., as movers, while metaphysics reaches them under another, e.g., as creators. For Aquinas only God is a creator; all other beings cause *esse* secondarily, through motion.[26] If Aquinas says separate substances are reached in one science, then they are reached in no other.

In conclusion, if "first causes" refers to termini of physical arguments, in all probability the reference is to the celestial bodies, the *"causae universaliores"* of 44, 2. I find no textual evidence that Aquinas gave natural philosophy an ability to prove separate substance. Hence at best, Weisheipl's textual argument is elliptical.[27]

The textual basis for the second physical interpretation is non-existent.

Perhaps it is just as well, for the philosophical basis of the second variant is also in trouble. Without a textual basis, the philosophical basis must recognize its conjectural character. In that respect, it must come to terms with Aquinas' explicit words that the human intellect grasps the thing's *esse* through its second operation — not through a demonstration of separate substances.[28] These words occur only early on in Aquinas' theological career. Yet one finds no subsequent indication that they were ever taken back.

Also is the philosophical basis even cogent? Problems exist for both its reasonings.

To the argument of Elders and O'Brien, it can be said that it is not clear that existence (*esse*) distinctly stands out as the commonality in bodies and spirits. Rather, does not the demonstration of spirits only show that our concept of substance is not identical with body? It seems so. Nothing is said about existence. Once existence is already distinctly appreciated before the demonstration of the immaterial will such a demonstration say something about it. Namely, existence is an act that can actuate more than bodies.

To the second point it can be remarked that no appeal to the essence/existence distinction seems necessary to deal with the one and the many on the immaterial level. This level would consist of beings that are form alone. Since form is finite, then by their finitude immaterial beings would distinguish themselves from one another.[29]

In conclusion, neither variant of the physical interpretation of the *prima via* withstands the test of wider textual comparison. As presently formulated, neither can claim to speak for Aquinas. Hence, a strong disposition in favor of the metaphysical interpretation emerges.[30]

It is rather surprising that the physical interpretation has persisted for so long. The above contrary texts have long been in the public domain of Thomistic scholarship. Yet the physical interpretation has largely remained unperturbed. Development, though, has occurred. As mentioned, among natural philosophy proponents a discernible shift from the first variant to the second exists. Aquinas' metaphysics is now recognized to be involved in the *prima via*. This recognition is an interpretive gain. What is crucial is that the development continue. An examination of the textual considerations mentioned above is an untried avenue for resolving Thomistic discussion of the correct interpretation of the *prima via*.

University of Saint Thomas
Houston, Texas

NOTES

1. William Lane Craig, *The Cosmological Argument from Plato to Leibniz* (New York: Barnes and Noble, 1980), pp. 162-172.

2. The debate began with Joseph Owens' metaphysical interpretation in "The Conclusion of the *Prima Via*," *The Modern Schoolman,* 30 (1952/53), 33-53; 109-121; 203-215. Vincent Smith's "The Prime Mover: Physical and Metaphysical Considerations," *Proceedings of the American Catholic Philosophical Association,* 28 (1954), 78-94, reaffirmed the physical interpretation and provoked Owens' response, "A Note on the Approach to Thomistic Metaphysics," *The New Scholasticism,* 28 (1954), 454-476. The discussion quieted down until the publication of Thomas C. O'Brien's *Metaphysics and the Existence of God,* Washington: The Thomist Press, 1960. O'Brien presented a more nuanced physical interpretation. Owens reviewed the book in *The New Scholasticism,* 36 (1962), 250-3. William Wallace, *op. cit.,* pp. 529-31, critiqued the review, and Owens, *ibid.,* 37 (1963), pp. 359-63, replied to the critique. Throughout the 60's and 70's, Owens continued to defend his position but without reaction in the journals. For these articles, see the Owens bibliography in John Catan, *Aristotle: The Collected Papers of Joseph Owens* (Albany: State University of New York Press, 1981), pp. 229-40.

3. For Smith, see *op. cit.,* pp. 79-80: "If the premises of the ensuing discussion can support their conclusion, then, far from reserving to metaphysics the proof for a Prime Mover, the philosophy of St. Thomas requires such a proof as the necessary approach to metaphysics — without which metaphysics, as a science, cannot come into existence." For Craig, see *op. cit.,* pp. 172-5.

4. For the elements of O'Brien's position, see *op. cit.:* pp. 158-64 for natural philosophy's proof of the immaterial as productive of a grasp of *ens — habens esse;* p. 217 for the demonstration of *esse subsistens* from *ens;* pp. 238-9 for the application of the previous to the *quinque viae.* For Weisheipl, see "The Relationship of Medieval Natural Philosophy to Modern Science: The Contribution of Thomas Aquinas to its Understanding," *Manuscripta,* 20 (1976), pp. 193-6. For Doig, see *Aquinas on Metaphysics* (The Hague: Martinus Nijhoff, 1972), pp. 241-7.

5. For Gilson, see *The Spirit of Mediaeval Philosophy* (New York: Charles Scribner's Sons, 1940), pp. 73-6. Copleston, *A History of Philosophy,* 2, 2 (New York: Image Books, 1962), says: "The 'third way' of proving the existence of God appears to presuppose the real distinction between essence and existence in finite things." (p. 53) "...The fundamental proof [in the *quinque viae*] is really the third proof or 'way,' that from contingency. In the first proof the argument from contingency is applied to the special fact of motion or change." (p. 65) For Gerard Smith, see *Natural Theology* (New York: The Macmillan Company, 1951), pp. 108-13. For Owens' references, see *supra* n. 2. Unlike other metaphysical proponents, Owens understands the *prima via* to focus on the *esse* of the motion itself.

6. As edited by Anton Pegis, *The Basic Writings of St. Thomas Aquinas* (New York: Random House, 1945), pp. 428-9.

7. "The natural philosopher ought to consider nature. But nature is both form and matter. Therefore he ought to consider both matter and form." *In II Phys.,* lect. 4, n. 167; trans. by Richard J. Blackwell, *Commentary on Aristotle's Physics* (New Haven: Yale University Press, 1963), p. 82.

8. *De Gen.,* II, 10, 336a 32.

9. *"Posteriores* vero philosophi, ut Plato, Aristoteles et eorum sequaces, pervenerunt ad considerationem ipsius esse universalis." *De Pot.* III, 5c; Marietti ed., p. 49. Etienne Gilson, *op. cit.,* p. 438, n. 4, fails to find a Thomistic attribution of the notion of creation to Aristotle. Gilson's reason is that at *S. T.* I, 44, 2c, Aquinas seems to contrast Plato and Aristotle with others who rose to a consideration of being as being. Anton Pegis, *St. Thomas and the Greeks* (Milwaukee: Marquette University Press, 1939), pp. 101-4, n. 64, concurs with Gilson. Pegis also cites Aquinas' *opusculum, De Articulis Fidei:* "Tertius est error Aristotelis, qui posuit mundam

a Deo factum non esse." Gilson, however, appears to be confused on the reference of "utrique" in "Utrique igitur consideraverunt ens particulari quadam consideratione..." The reference is not to Plato and Aristotle but to the two preceding stages that Aquinas finds in Western philosophy. Pegis' text need only refer to Aquinas' opinion that Aristotle taught an eternal creation. On this point, see my text n. 14.

10. "Philosophers, then, study these divine beings [God and angels] only insofar as [*nisi prout*] they are the principles of all things. Consequently, they are the objects of the science that investigates what is common to all beings, which has for its subject being as being. The philosophers call this divine science....Accordingly, there are two kinds of theology. There is one that treats of divine things, not as the subject of the science but as the principles of the subject. This is the kind of theology pursued by the philosophers and that is also called metaphysics. There is another theology, however, that investigates divine things for their own sakes as the subject of the science. This is the theology taught in Sacred Scripture." *In de Trin* V, 4c; trans. by Armand Maurer, *On the Division and Methods of the Sciences* (Toronto: Pontifical Institute of Mediaeval Studies, 1963), p. 44. "Now this threefold consideration [one fold of which is a consideration of God and the angelic intelligences] is not to be attributed to different sciences but to one. For the above-mentioned separated substances [God and the angels] are the universal and primary causes of being. What is more, it belongs to the same science to investigate the proper causes of any genus and the genus itself, as for example natural philosophy investigates the principles of natural body. So it must belong to the same science to investigate the separated substances and being-in-general, which is the genus of which the above-mentioned substances are the common and universal causes." *Proem In Meta;* in Maurer, *op. cit.,* pp. 88-9.

11. *In de Trin.* V, 2, ad 3m; Maurer, *op. cit.,* p. 23. Vincent Smith, *op. cit.,* p. 85, n. 28, rests his position on this text.

12. *C.G.* I, 13, *Quia vero.*

13. *In VIII Phys.,* lect. 2, no. 974; Blackwell, *op. cit.,* p. 476. My point is borrowed from Joseph Owens, "Aquinas and the Proof from the *Physics," Mediaeval Studies,* 28 (1966), pp. 143-4. Also, especially see *ibid.,* p. 141, on which Owens notes that Aquinas *(In VIII Phys.,* lect. 1, no. 970) distinguishes between natural science and the science of the first principle.

14. "For when one asks whether or not movers and mobile objects have always existed if there has not always been motion, one must answer that the first mover *(primum movens)* has always existed. All other things, whether they be movers or mobile objects, have not always existed but began to be from the universal cause of the whole of being *(a causa universali totius esse)." In VIII Phys.,* lect. 2, no. 987; Blackwell, *op. cit.,* p. 484.

15. "Therefore, if we were to think that the production of things by God is from eternity, as Aristotle and many Platonists held, it is not necessary, in fact it is impossible, that some non-produced subject be understood for this universal production." *In VIII Phys.,* lect. 2, no. 974; Blackwell, *op. cit.,* p. 476.

16. "For the ancient natural philosophers were unable to arrive at the first cause of the whole of being. Rather they considered the causes of particular mutations. The first of them considered the causes only of accidental mutation, holding that everything which comes to be is altered. The next ones arrived at an understanding of substantial changes. The last ones, as Plato and Aristotle, came to a knowledge of the principle of the whole of being." *In VIII Phys.,* lect. 2, no. 975; Blackwell, *op. cit.,* 477.

17. In "St. Thomas and the Coherence of the Aristotelian Theology," *Mediaeval Studies,* 35 (1973), p. 68, Anton Pegis expresses his surprise with Jean Paulus. In his "La Theorie du premier moteur chez Aristote," *Revue de philosophie,* 33 (1933), p. 263, Paulus claimed that the *Physics* reaches only the soul of a celestial sphere and that he found this interpretation in Aquinas. Two comments. First, Pegis is right to criticize Paulus. Aquinas undoubtedly sees the *Physics* (but I might add — not natural philosophy) as reaching God. Nevertheless, Pegis takes no note of the

metaphysical context of Aquinas' view. Second, Pegis protests too much in saying (pp. 75-6) that there is no doctrine of besouled heavens in the *Physics*. Paulus is correct to attribute besouled heavens both to Aristotle and Aquinas' understanding of Aristotle. Besouled heavens is just the point of *Phys.* VIII, 6: "Now the question whether each of the things that are unmoved but impart motion [e.g., individual souls] is eternal is irrelevant to our present argument; but the following considerations will make it clear that there must necessarily be some such thing,... And let us further suppose it possible that some principles that are unmoved but capable of imparting motion at one time are and at another time are not. Even so this cannot be true of all such principles,..." (258b 12-21) Hence, Aquinas acknowledges: "Secundum est, quod supponitur in praedictis demonstrationibus primum motum, scilicet corpus caeleste, esse motum ex se. Ex quo sequitur ipsum esse animatum." *C.G.* I, 13. Also *In XII Meta.*, lect. 4, no. 2476 and *ibid.*, lect. 8, no. 2536.

18. Weisheipl, *op. cit.*, p. 194. Doig, *op. cit.*, pp. 242-3, also gives this textual argument.

19. Weisheipl, *loc. cit.*, wishes "immobile substance" to include man's rational soul. But in context the reference of the phrase is clearly to immaterial beings other than the soul. These beings are the causes of being as being; in other words, God and the angels. On this point, see John Wippel, "Metaphysics and *Separatio* according to Thomas Aquinas," *Review of Metaphysics*, 31 (1978), p. 452. Nevertheless, Leo Elders, *Faith and Science* (Roma: Herder, 1974), p. 107, finds natural philosophy considering the human soul in the sense of "...yield[ing] the conclusion that there is immaterial being." Elders cites the Thomistic text, *In II Phys.*, lect. 4, no. 175. Yet the text says that natural science only deals with the rational soul insofar as it is a part of a generable and corruptible being, i.e., man. The consideration of the soul as separate from matter belongs to "first philosophy." Also, Aristotelian hesitations exist for making the soul a subject of natural philosophy simply. See Joseph Owens, "The Unity in a Thomistic Philosophy of Man," *Mediaeval Studies*, 25 (1963), pp. 76-8.

20. *In VI Meta.*, lect. 1, no. 1170; trans. by John P. Rowan, *Commentary on the Metaphysics of Aristotle* (Chicago: Henry Regnary Company, 1961), p. 462. See also *In III Meta.*, lect. 4, no. 398, and *In XI Meta.*, lect. 7, n. 2267.

21. That Aquinas' texts on the order of learning the sciences do not by themselves indicate a doctrinal dependency, see Wippel, *op. cit.*, pp. 460-2.

22. *Faith and Science*, p. 108. O'Brien says the same but more cryptically, "Negatively, this is the understanding that to be [*esse*] is not necessarily to be material and changeable. The occasion for such a realization is the discovery that there are beings, existent things, that exist, and are not material." O'Brien, *op. cit.*, p. 160. Likewise V. Smith, *op. cit.*, p. 92: "Mobile being can be known only as an unhyphenated unit until reason, discovering through it[s] ascent to the Prime Mover that the realm of being is not co-terminus with mobile being, can separate the being and the mobile to unveil the subject of metaphysics as a distinct reality. Only at this reach can the philosopher speak of being as mobile or immobile, as material or immaterial—of being precisely as being."

23. V. Smith, *op. cit.*, pp. 90-93.

24. *In de Trin.* V, 1, ad 9m; Maurer, *op. cit.*, pp. 17-18.

25. The above observations are taken from Owens, "Aquinas and the Proof from the *Physics*," pp. 131-2. G. Klubertanz, "St. Thomas on Learning Metaphysics," *Gregorianum*, 35 (1954), p. 11, also fails to see any expression of a doctrinal dependence of metaphysics upon physics.

26. For the texts, see Maurer, *op. cit.*, p. 47, n. 28.

27. One can ask why Aquinas does not allow natural philosophy to demonstrate separate substances. For a possible answer, see the *Divus Thomas* version of this article.

28. For a listing of the texts on the second operation and a discussion of them, see Joseph Owens, "Judgment and Truth in Aquinas," in John R. Catan's edition, *St. Thomas Aquinas on*

the Existence of God (Albany: State University of New York Press, 1980), pp. 42-4. Also my "Thomistic Existentialism and the Silence of the *Quinque Viae,*" *The Modern Schoolman,* 63 (1986), 157-171.

29. See Owens, *Doctrine of Being,* pp. 458-9.

30. For a sketch of a metaphysical interpretation of the *prima via à la* Owens, *see John F. X. Knasas,* "Aquinas: Prayer to an Immutable God," *The New Scholasticism,* 57 (1983), pp. 205-7. Craig, *op. cit.,* p. 172, regards an *esse* for the predicamental accidents as Thomistically "unintelligible." Yet Aquinas does teach it. For the texts, see Joseph Owens, "Actuality in the *Prima Via,"* in Catan, *St. Thomas Aquinas,* pp. 194-6. Finally, for the impact of this article upon the entry into Thomistic metaphysics, again see the *Divus Thomas* version of the article.

Prime Matter in Aquinas

by Mark McGovern

A young Dominican some years ago in Ireland asked his instructor whether he would swear on a Bible that there is such a thing as prime matter. The wise professor responded that he would swear to teach it. It seems that many students through the years have much difficulty coming to grips with the notion of prime matter. In my opinion much of the confusion concerning the concept of prime matter could be avoided by highlighting a basic distinction, which Aquinas himself makes in several places, between prime matter considered as an essence and prime matter considered as it actually is present in things.

A common result of the aforementioned confusion is that prime matter is thought of as having an independent existence,[1] as if God first created prime matter and then gave it form. Another result of the confusion is that authors sometimes assert without further clarification that prime matter is potentially everything. This is, of course, opposed to experience which teaches that any given being is not potentially any other being, at least not immediately.[2] The prime matter of an acorn, e.g., can become an oak but it cannot become a rose; whether it could do so by a succession of forms is a question whose answer will, I hope, be more readily available in the course of this paper.

Other Thomists seek to avoid the confusion by distinguishing between primary and secondary matter. As one author puts it:[3] "Prime matter is the aptitude to receive a form or actualizing principle, secondary matter is the accomplishment of this in the physical order." I will not argue whether this is or is not a valid philosophical concept, but I think it will be clear by the end of this paper that it is not Saint Thomas' concept.

In this paper I wish to show that close attention to the significance of the distinction that Aquinas makes between matter as an essence and as it is in things will go a long way toward clarifying much confusion about prime matter and also will be a great asset in making it an acceptable concept in the philosophical world. My procedure will be to investigate the texts of Aquinas in the order of time in which he wrote them, starting with the *Commentary on the Sentences* which is considered by current scholarship to be his earliest work.[4]

The Distinction in the Commentary on the Sentences

In the section of this work where Aquinas is treating the problem of

221

whether prime matter exists by itself before it receives a form, he remarks:[5]

> ...one can speak of prime matter in two ways: either insofar as *prime* signifies the order of nature or as it signifies the order of time.

Then he explains the difference between the two ways. As to the first way, he says:[6]

> Insofar as it signifies the order of nature, prime matter is that in which stands the ultimate resolution of natural bodies...[In this way prime matter] must be without any form...[A]nd although prime matter so understood does not have any form as part of its essence, still it is never divided from every form...; in fact when it loses one form it acquires another insofar as the corruption of one is the generation of another; and thus prime matter so understood could not precede in time the bodies formed from it.

As to the second way, he says:[7]

> In another way one speaks of prime matter insofar as *prime* signifies the order of time, viz., that which precedes the ordered disposition of the parts of the world as it is now perceived.

In order to understand what Aquinas means here one must realize that, as he himself indicates, he is speaking of the view that holds that the world did not always exist and that in the beginning of time things did not appear with the specific forms they now have. Understood in this way, prime matter has to have some form.[8]

The question of a formless matter arises in light of Genesis 1.2, which states that in the beginning "the earth was void and empty." Aquinas tells us in a later work that Augustine, in his commentary on this verse, interprets "earth" to refer to prime matter. It was because of the simplicity of the people of that time who would not have understood the notion of prime matter, Augustine argues, that the author used the term "earth." Aquinas apparently accepts this explanation and this is the reason why he here explains prime matter in terms of Genesis 1.2.[9] Now, it should be noted that the Latin texts available to Aquinas read *terra erat inanis et vacua*.[10] Does this mean that God first creates a formless matter and then later gives it the distinct forms that are now seen in nature? Someone might argue that this is the position of Augustine since he seems to so state in the *Confessions*.[11] Aquinas argues that Augustine is here referring to prime matter as essence or nature and not as it exists in time; considered as a nature Augustine can say that prime matter is altogether without form (although this is not the position of "the other saints").[12] Then after discussing the views of the Presocratics on prime matter, as well as the views of his contemporaries (*moderni*), Aquinas discusses the views of "the other saints" which seem to him more reasonable, viz., those who posit succession in the work of the six days of creation mentioned in Genesis 1. According to their view, prime matter was created under many substantial forms and all the substantial forms of the essential parts of the world were created in the beginning of creation.[13] Aquinas seems to agree with this view but argues that in the beginning of time, matter as present under the substantial form did not have the "active and passive qualities" that it would later possess.[14] For prime matter, in the beginning, appears under not one form but many; but these are not forms of mixed bodies. The mixed bodies result from the active and passive powers possessed by the forms of "unmixed" bodies. Apparently Aquinas held that, e.g., water, air, and fire have the active and passive qualities that explain how "mixed" bodies are possible.[15]

Suppose that someone argues that prime matter is entirely without form since prime matter is that out of which the elements come to exist and so it itself can have the form of none of them.[16] In answering this argument Aquinas employs the distinction between the two ways of considering prime matter:[17] "...the prime matter which is the same numerically in all elements as part of their essence is altogether unformed considered in its essence." However, considered insofar as prime implies the order of time, prime matter is corporal.

In another place in his *Commentary on the Sentences* Aquinas argues that prime matter is present only in bodies and that its first form is corporeity (*corporeitas*). Nevertheless, prime matter can be considered as free of every form and as such has no diversity since the first substantial form accounts for diversity.[18] Here again we see the distinction between prime matter considered as an essence and as it actually exists in things.

Like the distinction mentioned above, Aquinas employs a similar distinction between absolute matter and matter existing in this thing in discussing the position of some who held that the prime matter in a small body is capable of receiving any quantity in such a way that the whole world could come from a grain of millet. He gives four arguments against this position; in the fourth he says:[19]

> ...when we speak of the matter existing in this thing we have already dismissed the consideration of absolute matter....Wherefore the consideration of the matter of this thing is not a consideration of absolute matter but matter under the dimension of the existent. Whence it is not necessary that what applies to matter insofar as it is absolute and primary applies to the matter existing in this thing as it is understood as

existing in this thing; because by this very fact it is withdrawn from the consideration of prime matter. Thus, the matter which is existing in this thing is not in potency to the entire quantity of the world....

Here he seems to distinguish between prime matter and matter in such a way that "prime matter" is the term used to refer to matter considered absolutely or as an essence and "matter" is the term to be used for matter as it exists in this thing. But in other places, as we have seen above, he does not keep this distinction between "matter" and "prime matter."[20]

The Distinction in the De Veritate

Though there seems to be no place in the *De Veritate* where Aquinas explicitly mentions the distinction we are discussing, nevertheless there are places where what he does say about prime matter assumes the distinction as already made. In q. 8, art. 6, e.g., he says:[21]

...Prime matter is not able to produce any action unless it is perfected by form, and then the action is a kind of emanation of the form itself more than of matter....

Or, to put it in terms of the distinction, prime matter considered as a nature can produce no action, but as it exists in things it does so; but only in conjunction with the form. And in q. 10, art. 8, he says:[22]

For just as prime matter is in potency to all sensible forms, so is our possible intellect to all intelligible forms.

Now, considered as a nature prime matter is in potency to all forms, but here and now as it exists in this being it is limited in that it can receive only certain kinds of forms. The same is true of our possible intellect. Considered as a nature the possible intellect can receive any intelligible form, but the possible intellect as it exists in this person here and now is capable of receiving only certain kinds of intelligible forms; e.g., the possible intellect of a child is more limited than that of an adult.

The Distinction in the Summa Contra Gentiles

In an argument to prove the infinity of God Aquinas argues that "since prime matter is infinite in potentiality God who is pure act is infinite in his actuality."[23] Here again it seems to me to be necessary to keep the distinction in mind. Is prime matter infinite in potentiality as it is in things? If it were then the prime matter of water should be able to become gold. Is this possible even through a succession of forms? If so, no one has discovered the secret. However, prime matter considered as an essence is infinite in potentiality, albeit relatively and not absolutely as we shall see below.

Then when he investigates the question of whether prime matter is directly created by God, he argues that it is and the reason he gives is that it cannot be generated since generation occurs by means of matter and a contrary. Now, since prime matter itself has no contrary it cannot be generated.[24] Aquinas' statement here would be confusing if one did not keep in mind the distinction. It seems to me he has to be speaking here of prime matter considered as a nature. For once prime matter has been created (and it is only created as a composite, not as a nature), then it does have a contrary (i.e., prime matter as it exists in things does have a contrary), and this is what makes future generations and corruptions possible.[25]

I have indicated above that, according to Aquinas, prime matter considered as a nature is in potency to all forms. But prime matter as it exists in time is in potency to forms in a definite order. This is made more explicit in the *Summa Contra Gentiles* where Aquinas says:[26]

> For prime matter is first of all in potency to the form of an element. But as it exists under the form of an element it is in potency to a mixed form....Now, considered under the mixed form it is in potency to the vegetative soul for the soul is the act of such a body. And likewise the vegetative soul is in potency to the sensitive [soul] and the sensitive [soul] to the intellective [soul].

Again the distinction is helpful in understanding Aquinas' meaning here. He says: "...prime matter is first of all in potency to the form of an element." It seems clear that he is speaking of prime matter considered as a nature; for prime matter does not exist before it is present under the form of an element. On the other hand, when he speaks of prime matter "under the form of an element" he is speaking of prime matter as it is in things. And the same is true, obviously, of the rest of the quotation.

In another passage Aquinas remarks that prime matter is indifferently in potency to any form.[27] Now, as we have seen above, prime matter as it is in things is not indifferently in potency to any form since there is a definite order in which forms are received. For example, the prime matter of an acorn is in potency in a different way to the form "oak" than it is to the form "rose" (for the prime matter of an acorn is immediately in potency to "oak"; but even if it were possible that it were somehow in potency to "rose" it would have to be so through a succession of forms). Thus, Aquinas must be speaking in this passage of prime matter considered as a nature.

Elsewhere, Aquinas says that prime matter cannot exist without a form.[28] He is obviously not speaking here of prime matter considered as a nature because he has stated in passages quoted above[29] that prime matter as a nature can be considered without form.

Then when he is discussing whether prime matter is ungenerated and incorruptible, he gives explicit reference to the distinction between prime matter as an essence and as it actually is in things.[30]

> For it remains that prime matter is ungenerated and incorruptible as Aristotle proves....Wherefore, when its form recedes it remains in its essence...but prime matter does not remain actually after the form [recedes] unless by reason of the act of another form.

In other words, as we have seen above, prime matter as an essence can be considered without form; but notice, not in such a way that there are two beings; rather, prime matter and its form exist as one being.[31]

The Distinction in the De Potentia

Aquinas also discusses the question of formless matter in the *De Potentia*. And again it is a question of how to interpret the words of Genesis 1.2.: *terra autem erat inanis et vacua*. Aquinas tells us that some take them to refer to formless matter, i.e., matter without any form, which nevertheless is in potency to every form. Aquinas remarks that matter understood in this sense does not actually exist in nature. For matter does not exist unless "it is determined to a special mode of being (*ad aliquem specialem modum essendi determinetur*)." And this does not occur except through form. In conclusion, he says:[32]

> Wherefore, if formless matter is understood thus [i.e., without form], it is impossible that it precede in time the formation [of things]; rather, it precedes only in the order of nature insofar as that from which something comes to be is naturally prior to it, just as night is created prior [to day]. And this was the opinion of Augustine.

The distinction here parallels that made in the *Sentences*. In addition we learn that something can be prior in the order of nature (prime matter free of every form) but not necessarily prior in the order of time. Or to put it another way, one can *consider* prime matter as free from every form but as such it has no existential reality. For prime matter exists only in things, i.e., under one form or another. Still, one can say that prime matter precedes form in the sense that night precedes day. For in the Genesis account even though night as such is nothing, nevertheless it preceded the creation of light (cf. Gen. 1.2 and 1.3).

However, not all interpreted the words "the earth was void and empty" to refer to matter free from every form. Aquinas tells us that Saints Basil, Gregory Nazianzen, and some others held that these words refer to matter that does not yet have the form it will have in its completeness. In that sense it can be called formless matter. In this case one could assert that "formless matter" preceded the formation of things both in nature *and* in time.[33]

In other places in the *De Potentia* Aquinas employs the distinction between matter as an essence and matter as it exists in time. Sometimes these references are explicit, sometimes implicit. He explicitly states this when he says: "....prime matter considered according to its essence is free from every act."[34] In another place he gives an argument of someone who affirms that prime matter precedes in time its reception of form:[35]

> ...that from which something comes to be precedes even in time what comes from it. But God created the world [Wis. 11.18] "from unseen matter" which is formless matter according to Augustine. There-fore, formless matter precedes in time the formed world.

In rejecting this position Aquinas gives another insight into the distinction between the order of nature and time.[36]

> ...the world is said to be made from unseen matter not because formless matter precedes it in time but in the order of nature. And likewise privation was not at anytime in matter before every form; but [it is true that privation precedes form in the order of nature] because matter understood without form is also understood with privation.

In other words, prime matter as well as privation can be *considered* to precede form in the order of nature but not in time.

A further nuance is added to the notion of prime matter when Aquinas discusses the common subject of change (*mutatio*). He begins by remarking that in any change there must be some common subject of each term of the change. There are, however, at least two cases. (1) For sometimes the one common subject for each term of the mutation or change is something actually existing (e.g., a living or nonliving being). This is the case with motion properly so called as we see in the case of alteration, increase and decrease, and motion from one place to another (i.e., accidental changes). (2) But at other times the one common subject of each term does not actually exist but is only potential (the potential subject is prime matter). This is the case with generation and corruption in the absolute sense (i.e., with substantial change).[37] From this it would seem one should conclude that prime matter does not exist, even as a part of a composite. The most one could say is that it is a potential principle in beings of our experience, which principle is needed to explain substantial change.[38] What then is the significance of the distinction between prime matter as an essence and as it is in time (sometimes he says: "as it exists in things")? Certainly the second part of this distinction (prime matter as it is in time) seems to indicate that prime matter actually exists. Perhaps the answer is that when he uses the distinction between prime matter as essence and as it is in time, Aquinas is concerned with resolving a problem about whether prime matter can exist without form. And when he says that prime matter does not exist except potentially, he is concerned with resolving a problem about substantial change. Perhaps, then, the resolution of the problem is that prime matter does not exist without form; but even then its existence is only potential in the sense that as the common subject of substantial changes it explains how they are possible. If not for a common subject one would have to say that there is no continuity in substantial change.

In yet another place Aquinas makes it clear that though prime matter as an essence does not exist, it does not follow that it does not exist at all.[39] This, again, assumes the distinction between prime matter as an essence and as it is in things; for in the latter case prime matter exists under a form. In q. 4, art. 1, Aquinas summarizes his position on formless matter and in doing so he again employs the aforementioned distinction (and once again it is a question of how to understand *terra erat inanis et vacua*). There are two positions that can be held on formless matter. It is either (1) matter without any form or (2) matter with form but not the forms as they now appear in nature. As to the first, Aquinas says that prime matter in this sense could not precede in time but only in nature the creation of things (he says this is the position of Augustine). As to the second, he argues that in this way formless matter could precede even in time the formation of things (he calls this the position of Basil the Great, Gregory of Nazianzen, et al.).[40]

Then there is the passage in the same article which closely parallels the "formless matter" argument in the *Sentences*. Someone might say that since Augustine argues that the *terra erat inanis et vacua* of Genesis 1.2 refers to earth and water not as earth and water already formed but rather that which is able to be earth and water; therefore, prime matter (=s formless matter) does not always have the species of water or earth but rather is able to have them; and so prime matter exists before it has any form.[41] In responding to this argument Aquinas argues that matter as it actually exists is never without form and so Augustine is speaking here of matter as essence. As Aquinas puts it:[42]

The words of Augustine are not to be understood in such a way that matter was at any time in potency to elementary forms and yet not having any of them; but rather that considered in its essence it [prime matter] actually includes no form and is at the same time in potency to all of them.

In other words, considered as it is in things prime matter does not exist without form, but considered as an essence it does.

The Distinction in the Summa Theologiae

As we have seen, Aquinas explicitly mentions the distinction between prime matter as a nature and as it is in things in his earlier works. Now, someone might argue that he abandoned this distinction in his later works.[43] And so if we can find him employing the distinction in what scholars consider to be his latest work, this would vitiate that argument.[44] What we find is that Aquinas mentions the distinction in dealing with the same problem that he dealt with in the earlier writings, viz., the problem of whether there is a formless matter that precedes in time a "formed" matter. After stating, in the *Summa*, that it is impossible to say that prime matter was created altogether without form, since what has being has act or form,[45] he concludes that prime matter was created under distinct forms.[46] And then, in showing the correctness of Augustine's opinion on this problem, he states:[47]

And so if the formlessness of matter is taken for the condition of prime matter which in itself does not have any form, the formlessness of matter does not precede the formation or distinction of it in time, as Augustine says, but in origin or nature only; in the way in which potency is prior to act and part to the whole.

The distinction occurs also, I think, where Aquinas is responding to the question of whether prime matter is infinite in the way God is. He says it is not and gives the reason.[48]

...prime matter does not exist in nature by itself since it is not actual being but only potential being. Thus, it is something concreated rather than created. Nevertheless, prime matter, even as a potency, is not infinite absolutely but only relatively because its potency does not extend except to natural forms.

This, it seems to me, is the distinction once again between prime matter as it is in things (cf. line 1 of the quote: "prime matter does not exist in nature by itself...") and prime matter as a nature or essence (cf. line 3: "prime matter, even as a potency..."). In other words, while it is certainly true that prime matter as it is in things is not immediately in potency to everything (i.e., all forms), not even is prime matter as an essence (as a potency) in potency to all things because it is in potency only to natural forms.

This distinction could be applied as a hermeneutical principle to other texts as well. Space allows only a few examples. One example is where Aquinas mentions that prime matter does not have a natural existence when it is in potency; it has an "unnatural" existence.[49] And this, I would submit, refers to prime matter insofar as it is considered as an essence or nature. Or, to put it more concretely, I can consider the prime matter of the acorn insofar as it is the potential principle in the acorn which explains how the acorn can become an oak. In this way prime matter does not have a natural existence. I am considering prime matter as an essence. When the acorn becomes an oak, the prime matter now has a natural existence (as part of the composite, not in itself). This is the prime matter as it is in things. So far, so good. But is it not possible also to argue that the prime matter of the acorn already has a form, viz., "acorn," and so this is prime matter as it is in things? Yes, I think this is correct. It all depends on the viewpoint. Are you considering the prime matter of the acorn insofar as it is an acorn and how it became an acorn? Or are you considering the prime matter of the acorn insofar as the acorn can become something else? In the first case, it seems to me, you are considering prime matter as it is in things; in the second prime matter as an essence.

Another example is where Aquinas says that "prime matter is said to be one, not because it has one form as man is one by the unity of the one form, but by removal of all distinguishing forms."[50] Obviously, he is referring here to prime matter considered as an essence since prime matter considered as it is in things is considered insofar as it has form.

Finally, in another place Aquinas compares prime matter to the human intellect and says that "[t]he human intellect...is in potency with respect to all intelligible things just as prime matter [is] with respect to all sensible forms...."[51] As I have indicated above, I would argue that here also to speak of prime matter as being in potency to all natural forms is to speak of prime matter considered as an essence, since prime matter as it is in things is not in potency to all forms.[52] Granted it may be in potency *successively* to all forms (and even this can be questioned since the prime matter of water, e.g., can never receive the form "gold"), nevertheless prime matter as present here and now in this acorn is certainly not *immediately* in potency to all forms.

Significance of the Distinction

As I have indicated earlier, it seems to me that by highlighting this distinction, which Aquinas himself makes, much confusion about the concept of prime matter is avoided and it can become once again what might be called, for lack of a better term, a viable concept. For there are those who argue that the concept of prime matter is no longer needed since modern atomic theory more adequately explains the occurrences in nature. Some Thomists might be tempted to answer that science does not judge philosophy. However, it is one thing to say that science does not judge philosophy since science is a subordinant discipline; it is another thing to say that philosophy need not be aware of what advances occur in the subordinate discipline. The question is whether the advances in atomic theory have done away with the need for the philosophical concept of prime matter. Now, one aspect of the problem is the same whether it is being investigated by the philosopher or by the scientist, viz., what is there about "A" that allows it to become "B"? It is probably true that the modern theory of atoms adequately explains how change takes place on certain levels, such as, e.g., on the level of chemical changes. But there are certain levels that it cannot explain. For example, it cannot explain why an acorn becomes an oak rather than a rose, or why the oak can become ashes but not a man. And there is another problem which the scientist probably is not interested in and could not answer if he were, viz., how can one thing become another without thereby ceasing to exist? This, it seems to me, is a strictly philosophical problem. In my view only a philosophical concept such as prime matter can answer such a problem. This is why I believe it so important to make sure that prime matter is presented in such a way that it is seen as a valid concept. To say, e.g., without further distinction that prime matter is that principle in any being which allows it to become any other being is an oversimplification and leads to the concept being discredited. It is one thing for a concept correctly understood to be discredited but it is another for a concept incorrectly understood to be discredited. I am afraid that the latter has too often been the case with prime matter. It is my hope that this paper will contribute to a better understanding of the concept of prime matter and that if it is to be discredited it will be because it has been correctly understood.[53]

Conclusion

I have tried to show in this paper that by paying attention to an important distinction that Aquinas makes between prime matter as an essence and prime matter as it is in things, followers of the doctrine of Thomas Aquinas will be in a better position to make prime matter an understandable and philosophically significant concept for themselves and for others who might be interested in Thomistic doctrine and its importance in the 20th century.[54]

Notre Dame High School
Cresco, Iowa

NOTES

1. Apparently this was the position of Suarez (cf. *Meta.*, disp. 13 sect. 5; cf. L. De Raeymaeker, *Metaphysica Generalis* [Louvain, 1935], p. 377).

2. Prime matter is not indiscriminately in potency to all forms. It is in potency to all forms successively with one exception in Aquinas' system; for the prime matter of inferior bodies is not in potency to the form of the superior (celestial) bodies (cf. *Summa Theol.*, I, 66, 2). Cf. *Sum. cont. Gent.*, III, 22, where in speaking of prime matter he says: "...tota eius potentia reducatur in actum successive, quod simul fieri non poterat."

3. Cf. Father William Bruckmann in the glossary (s.v. "matter") of vol. 3 of *Summa Theologica*, transl. by Fathers of the English Dominican Province (New York, 1948), p. 3560.

4. Cf. J. Weisheipl, O.P., *Friar Thomas D'Aquino: His Life, Thought, and Work* (Garden City, N.Y., 1974), pp. 355-405.

5. *In II Sent.*, d. 12, 1, 4. Unless otherwise noted the translations are my own.

6. *Ibid.*

7. *Ibid.*

8. *Ibid.*

9. Cf. *Summa Theol.*, I, 66, 1 ad 1; cf. also *De Pot.*, IV, 1 ad 1.

10. Or "invisibilis et incomposita" from the *Septuagint*, "uoratos kai akataskeuastos." Cf. *Summa Theol.*, I, 66, 1 obj. 1.

11. Bk. 12, *cap.* 3; cf. *In II Sent.*, d. 12, 1, 4 obj. 2.

12. *In II Sent.*, d. 12, 1, 4 and 2. Later (cf. *Summa Theol.*, I, 66, 1) he expressly rejects Augustine's position. Also in a later work (cf. *De Pot.*, IV, 1 ad 17) Aquinas tells us more specifically what Augustine's position is. Augustine (*II Super Genes. ad litteram, cap.* VII and VIII) holds that prime matter was created first ("the earth" of Genesis 1.2 which is "void and empty"); on the second day the formation of the celestial bodies took place (Gen. 1.6: "Let there be a firmament..."); on the third day the formation of the inferior elements is signified by the words (Gen. 1.9): "Let the waters...be gathered together." That water receives its form on the third day is also signified here. And the words (Gen. 1.9) "Let the dry land appear" indicate that the earth also received its form on the third day. Augustine also makes much of the words used in the formation of these elements. They were not created as the firmament and the earth (of Gen. 1.1) were. The waters are (vs. 9) "gathered together" and the dry land "appears"; this, says Augustine, is to signify their nearness to formless matter. Aquinas (cf. *De Pot.*, IV, 1 ad 17) prefers the position of Basil who held that the waters were over all the earth in the beginning but not with the depth they had when they were gathered together to form the seas.

13. *In II Sent.*, d. 12, 1, 4.

14. *Ibid.*

15. *Ibid.*, ad 3.

16. *Ibid.*, obj. 1.

17. *In II Sent.*, d. 12, 1 and 1.

18. *In I Sent.*, d. 8, 5, 2; cf. also *In II Sent.*, d. 30, 2, 1.

19. *In II Sent.*, d. 30, 2, 1.

20. Cf. also *In IV Sent.*, d. 49, 2, 1 ad 10. Certainly he is speaking here of "prime matter" as it exists in things.

21. *De Ver.* VIII, 6. In light of this it is difficult for one to understand how some Thomists can

speak of matter limiting form (cf., e.g., C. Hart, *Thomistic Metaphysics: An Inquiry into the Act of Existing* [Englewood Cliffs, N.J., 1959], pp. 119-130).

22. *De Ver.*, X, 8.

23. *Sum. cont. Gent.*, I, 43; n. 361.

24. *Ibid.*, II, 42.

25. Problem: Aquinas says elsewhere (Cf. *De Pot.*, IV, 1 ad s.c. 6) that prime matter as a nature can be considered with a contrary. Solution: As a nature prime matter can be *considered* with a contrary. In point of fact it has a contrary only when it exists as a composite (i.e., in things).

26. *Sum. cont. Gent.*, III, 22; cf. also *ibid.*, II, 89.

27. *Ibid.*, III, 23.

28. *Ibid.*, IV, 63; cf. also *ibid.*, II, 43.

29. Cf. nn. 6, 17 & 18.

30. *Sum. cont. Gent.*, II, 81.

31. *Ibid.*

32. *De Pot.*, IV, 1; cf. Gen. 1.2: "And darkness was on the face of the deep." Then in vs. 3: "And God said: Be light made." Apparently these verses are the source for Aquinas' view that night is created prior to day.

33. *De Pot.*, IV, 1.

34. *Ibid.*, I, 1 obj. 7. Though this is an objection, Aquinas concedes the argument in the reply (cf. *ibid.*, ad 7).

35. *Ibid.*, IV, 1, s.c. 6; cf. Augustine, *lib. I super Gen., cap.* XV.

36. *De Pot.*, IV, 1 ad s.c. 6. In the context it seems to me to be necessary to add the words in the brackets to make sense out of the somewhat cryptic sentence.

37. *Ibid.*, III, 2; cf. also *Summa Theol.*, I, 45, 1 ad 2; *Sum. cont. Gent.*, II, 17, 18 & 19; *In II Sent.*, d. 1, 1, 2.

38. Cf. *In XII Meta.*, lect 2. Aquinas calls prime matter "potential being." E. Glowienka ("Aquinas with the Linguists on 'Matter,'" *Proceedings of the American Catholic Philosophical Association* [LVII (1983)], 180-188) argues that matter is a concept in the same way that immateriality is a concept. There may be some merit in his analogy. The problem is that the concept of immateriality is a quality of something that really exists, e.g., an angel or the soul. The concept of matter, in contrast, is not a quality of anything and it is something which exists only potentially and not actually.

39. *De Pot.*, III, 5 ad 3.

40. *Ibid.*, IV, 1; cf. the same discussion in the *Sum cont. Gent.* section above.

41. *De Pot.*, IV, 1, s.c. 8.

42. *Ibid.*, ad s.c. 8. According to Aquinas' interpretation of Augustine's view (cf. *De Pot.*, IV, 1 ad 17), the earth of Genesis 1.1 is unformed matter (prime matter). The firmament of the second day (vs. 8) refers to the reception of the form of the celestial bodies. On the third day (vs. 9) the forms of earth and water come into being.

43. This methodology has been employed on other of Aquinas' doctrinal points. E.g., B. Garceau (*Judicium. Vocabulaire, sources, doctrine de Saint Thomas d'Aquin* [Montreal & Paris, 1968], pp. 45-46) argues that there is a change in Aquinas' view on "judgment" from his earlier to his later works. While Garceau's book is otherwise very enlightening, I disagree with him on this point which does not affect the validity of his work. In my dissertation (cf. *Aquinas and Scotus on Certitude*, p. 101) I try to show that, at least in the case of judgment, I do not think there is any change or development in Aquinas' thought. I think the same is true of prime matter.

44. Besides the reference in n. 47ff see also *Summa Theol.*, I, 7, 2 ad 3; *ibid.*, 16, 7, 2; *ibid.*, 44, 2 ad 3.

45. *Summa Theol.*, I, 66, 1.

46. *Ibid.*

47. *Ibid.* Cf. Augustine, *Confess.*, bk. 12, c. 29; PL 32, 842-843; *De Gen. ad litt.*, Bk 1, c. 15; PL 34, 257; cf. also *Summa Theol.*, I, 69, 1 and *ibid.*, 66, 4.

48. *Summa Theol.*, I, 7, 2, 3.

49. *Ibid.*, 14, 2 ad 3; cf. also *Quodl.*, III, 1.

50. *Summa Theol.*, I, 16, 7, ad 2.

51. *Ibid.*, I-II, 50, 6.

52. This interpretation seems to be confirmed by *In II Sent.*, d. 30, 2, 1: "...materia prima, quantum in se est, caret omni quantitate et forma; ergo aequaliter se habet ad recipiendum omnes..."; i.e., prime matter considered as an essence is in potency to all forms, but as it is in things it is not.

53. I depend on what Charles S. Pierce (cf. "How to Make Our Ideas Real," in C. S. Pierce *Values in a Universe of Chance*, ed. P. Weiner [Stanford, Calif., 1958], p. 134) has called "the community of investigators" to further clarify and explicate the topic I have rather inadequately initiated in this paper.

54. I find an interesting parallel between prime matter and the concept of the atom correctly understood. Cf. Mortimer Adler's excellent article, "Two Philosophical Mistakes," *The New Scholasticism*, LXIX (1985) 18-19, where he argues that the correct concept of atoms is that they are nothing in themselves but potentially many things.

Report of the Secretary

The sixtieth Annual Meeting of the American Catholic Philosophical Association took place on April 4-6, 1986 at the Baltimore Plaza-Hotel, Baltimore, Maryland. The theme of the meeting, proposed by President Francis J. Lescoe, was "Existential Personalism." Papers read at the convention and reports of the official business of the Association have been edited and are currently being printed as Volume LX of the *Proceedings of the American Catholic Philosophical Association.*

The four regular issues of the *The New Scholasticism* have appeared under the editorship of Ralph McInerny, Jean Oesterle, and Alfred J. Freddoso. The 1986/85 distribution of *The New Scholasticism* is as follows:

	1986	**1985**
Members of the Association	1124	1079
Subscribers	658	662
Exchanges	71	133
Individual Copies Sold	74	93
TOTALS	1927	1967

The secretary acknowledges with deep appreciation the free facilities and the generous services of The Catholic University of America for the secretary and the treasurer/business manager of *The New Scholasticism.* With equally deep gratitude he acknowledges the similar free and generous facilities of the University of Notre Dame for the Editor and Associate Editor of *The New Scholasticism.*

Four editions of the Newsletter of the Personnel Placement Service have appeared on schedule, along with improvements in its nature and appearance. 22 individuals and 14 institutions have formally participated in the Newsletter, indicating their availability and openings, respectively. This compares with 36 individuals and 18 institutions in 1985 and 25 individuals and 25 institutions in 1984.

A total of 75 have applied for membership since April 1986. The total membership equals 1124 (previous year: 1079). From April 1985 to 1986, 78 new members were received. In 1984, 59 new members were received.

The 1986/85 distribution of the *Proceedings* is as follows:

	1986	**1985**
Members of the Association	1124	1079
Subscribers	273	220
Exchanges	6	4
Individual Copies Sold	156	90
TOTALS	1559	1393

In accord with motions passed by the Executive Council Meeting, Volume LX of the *Proceedings* (1986) is being printed according to the traditional type-setting procedures followed in previous years. Also in accord with these motions, for the editing of the *Program* for 1987 the experiment was continued of employing an independent word processor. Because of delays and comparative quality, the recommendation of the secretary is that the traditional type-setting procedures also be followed for the printing of the *Program* in the future.

With the help of Dr. Theresa Sandok, OSM of Bellarmine College and Patrick Bourgeois of Loyola University, commitments have been made to hotels in Louisville (1988) and New Orleans (1989) respectively.

Rev. Francis J. Lescoe has appointed Leonard Kennedy and Theresa Sandok to serve with him on the Aquinas Medal subcommittee of the Executive Council. Nominations for next year's Aquinas Medal have been processed by this subcommittee.

The results of this year's election are as follows: Joseph Boyle (St. Michael's College, University of Toronto) has been elected Vice-President-President Elect, and Lawrence Dewan (College Dominicain), Thérèse-Anne Druart (Georgetown), Mary F. Rousseau (Marquette), Thomas D. Sullivan (College of St. Thomas), and M. Katherine Tillman (Notre Dame) have been elected to the Executive Council. These individuals are to be congratulated, and all of those who have permitted themselves to be nominated for offices in the ACPA deserve special thanks. The ACPA is a voluntary association kept alive by the enthusiasm and support of such individuals alone.

The administrative assistant, responsible for billings, mailings, and business correspondence for the ACPA, Mrs. Sandra Regina, has retired. For the last four years, Mrs. Regina has devoted—and quite literally even contributed—countless hours and hard work to the ACPA's often thankless, workaday operations. During this past year alone she has been instrumental in re-activating several memberships in the ACPA. Her efforts to cut costs, to make deadlines, and to revise the ACPA's transactions with various book and journal distributors handling ACPA publications are much, much appreciated. The ACPA is also indebted to Mrs. Regina for introducing and guiding the current administrative assistant, Ms. Bach-Mai Pham, into the intricacies and responsibilities of the position, thus making a smooth transition between them possible. On behalf of the ACPA I would like to thank Mrs. Regina for her generous and painstaking contributions to the ACPA's well-being over the past four years.

Respectfully submitted,
Daniel O. Dahlstrom, secretary

Minutes of the 1987 Executive Council Meeting

The meeting of the Executive Council meeting opened with a prayer by the Reverend Leonard Kennedy at 1:35. President Wippel, Vice President-President-Elect Caputo, Drs. Dahlstrom, Schrenk, Burke, Jones, Brown, Freddoso, Jordan, Kennedy, Sandok, Coffey, Dougherty, Fauser, Gomez-Lobo, and Lescoe were present.

Minutes of the 1986 Executive Council meeting and Reports of the Secretary and Treasurer were read and approved. At the recommendation of Drs. Brown and Kennedy, the Executive Council advised the secretary to have a framed certificate or its equivalent be presented to Mrs. Regina for her fine service to the ACPA over the past four years. At the recommendation of Drs. Kennedy and Lescoe the treasurer was directed to approach foundations with specific proposals for research funding.

The Executive Council then turned to the election of the secretary and treasurer for the next four-year term of office, commencing at the close of next year's meeting in Louisville. Before proceeding to the election, the Executive Council agreed that the votes of absent members of the Executive Council *not* be counted. Dr. Marilynn Fleckenstein and Dr. Lawrence Schrenk presented themselves before the Executive Council separately for questions. Dr. Schrenk was asked to leave the room during the subsequent discussion. After lengthy discussion the Executive Council held a secret ballot in which Dr. Lawrence Schrenk was elected secretary and Sr. Marian Brady treasurer for the next four-year term. The Executive Council then directed the secretary to express formally its extreme gratitude to Drs. Fleckenstein and Sylvester as well as to the University of Niagara and its Department of Philosophy for its generous offer to carry on the work of the ACPA's national office.

Reports were next made by Dr. Sandok and Caputo on the upcoming meeting in Louisville in 1988. The Executive Council next determined that the primary site for the 1990 meeting would be Toronto, with Montreal and St. Paul as secondary and tertiary (back-up) sites.

Dr. McInerny and Jean Oesterle were invited into the Executive Council meeting for the purpose of discussing their report on *The New Scholasticism.* In the course of making suggestions about the advantages of introducing a desk-top publishing system for *The New Scholasticism* (e.g., increasing the size of the journal, bringing more book reviews back into the journal), Dr. McInerny announced that he would not be available for re-election as Editor of *The New Scholasticism* in 1988. As specified by the ACPA's constitution, the Editor and Associate Editor shall be elected by the Executive Council for three year terms. This election is to take place in 1988 in Louisville. The Executive Council expressed its gratitude to Dr. McInerny and Jean Oesterle for their presentation and for their work on *The New Scholasticism* during the past year. The Executive Council then turned to the proposal for a review committee for *The New Scholasticism*. Dr. Caputo requested that the charges of this committee be enlarged to include a search for a new editor as well as a study of the membership's expectations in regard to *The New Scholasticism*. After considerable discussion, the following motion by Drs. Lescoe and Caputo was passed by the Executive Council:

> "that a *New Scholasticism Search and Review Committee* be set up (1) to review the current and past state of *The New Scholasticism*, (2) to investigate the research interests of the membership of the ACPA at large, and (3) to make recommendations to the Executive Council on the editor and associate editor as part of the agenda of the 1988 Executive Council meeting."

Dr. Burke then proposed that the incoming president appoint this committee. Drs. Jordan and Lescoe indicated that it would be appropriate for the Executive Council members themselves to select members of this important committee. Because of the late hour of the meeting and because of the importance for more reflection on the likely members of such a committee, the following compromise motion was accepted:

> "that the incoming president suggest five names of individuals to constitute *The New Scholasticism Search and Review Committee* and that any members of the Executive Council submit any names for this committee by May 1 to the secretary. The complete list of names will be sent to the members of the Executive Council. The members of the Executive Council will vote for the five individuals on the list, whom they consider most qualified to constitute this committee, and return their votes to the secretary by May 15. The five individuals with the most votes will constitute *The New Scholasticism Search and Review Committee*."

The list of 75 new members of the ACPA was then approved.

The Aquinas Medal Nominating Committee next made its report. The secretary then moved that the rule recommended by this committee be accepted. A motion containing the following recommended rules for awarding the Aquinas Medal was passed.

Recommended rules for awarding the Aquinas Medal:

1. Former recipients are ineligible.

2. The award must not be given to a less-than-worthy recipient, but a serious effort will be made each year to find a worthy one.

3. The recipient should be well known through his or her writings to members of the ACPA, and should be recognized as having contributed significantly to the development of philosophy in the Catholic tradition.

4. Those selecting the recipient will apply the above criteria each according to his or her own judgment, since it is not possible to find an automatic way of making a decision. Of course discussion should precede the choice.

5. Long-standing membership in the ACPA shall count as a favorable factor in assessing nominees.

6. The vote of the ACPA Executive Council shall be by secret ballot. An absolute majority of votes will be required, with the person on the preceding ballot obtaining the fewest votes being dropped from the next ballot until such a majority is reached.

7. Recommendations for the Medal should be made to the Chairperson of the Nominating Committee (the past president) by December 1st, along with supporting documentation.

Dr. Caputo's proposal that he, as incoming president, appoint a committee for review of the role of women in the ACPA was passed, on the condition that not only women serve on the committee.

Finally, the Executive Council moved that, after the experiment of the past two years, the annual *Program* and *Proceedings* be published hereafter according to the traditional process.

The meeting adjourned at 5:40 p.m.

> Respectfully,
> Daniel O. Dahlstrom, secretary

HOYE, GRAVES, BAILEY & ASSOCIATES

ANNAPOLIS, MD

PROFESSIONAL ASSOCIATION
CERTIFIED PUBLIC ACCOUNTANTS
7819 NORFOLK AVENUE
BETHESDA, MARYLAND 20814-5074

(800) 352-1470
(301) 652-5465

ANAHEIM, CA

The American Catholic Philosophical
Association
Washington, District of Columbia

We have reviewed the accompanying balance sheet of THE AMERICAN CATHOLIC PHILOSOPHICAL ASSOCIATION, as of December 31, 1986, and the related statement of support, revenue, expenses and changes in fund balance for the year then ended, in accordance with standards established by the American Institute of Certified Public Accountants. All information included in these financial statements is the representation of management of THE AMERICAN CATHOLIC PHILOSOPHICAL ASSOCIATION.

A review consists principally of inquiries of Association personnel and analytical procedures applied to financial data. It is substantially less in scope than an examination in accordance with generally accepted auditing standards, the objective of which is the expression of an opinion regarding the financial statements taken as a whole. Accordingly, we do not express such an opinion.

Based on our review, we are not aware of any material modifications that should be made to the accompanying financial statements in order for them to be in conformity with generally accepted accounting principles.

Hoye, Graves, Bailey & Associates, P.A.

Certified Public Accountants

Bethesda, Maryland
March 15, 1987

241

THE AMERICAN CATHOLIC PHILOSOPHICAL ASSOCIATION
Balance Sheet
December 31, 1986

ASSETS

CURRENT ASSETS:	
Cash in Bank - Checking	$ 17,746.64
Calvert Group - Variable Rate Fund	29,402.31
Royalty Receivable	309.89
Total Current Assets	$ 47,458.84
INVESTMENTS:	
Marketable Securities (Note 2)	31,601.50
TOTAL ASSETS	$ 79,060.34

LIABILITIES AND FUND BALANCE

CURRENT LIABILITIES:	
Accounts Payable	$ 334.39
Prepaid Dues, Subscriptions	
and Other (Note 4)	31,518.00
Payroll Taxes Payable	219.40
Total Current Liabilities	$ 32,071.79
FUND BALANCE	46,988.55
TOTAL LIABILITIES AND FUND BALANCE	$ 79,060.34

See Accountants' Review Report.
The accompanying notes are an integral part of this statement.

THE AMERICAN CATHOLIC PHILOSOPHICAL ASSOCIATION
Statement of Support, Revenue, Expenses and Changes in Fund Balance
For The Year Ended
December 31, 1986

SUPPORT AND REVENUE:

Membership Dues:		
Constituent and Associate		$ 23,807.00
Student		1,697.00
Institutional		1,088.00
The New Scholasticism:		
Subscriptions		14,119.70
Sales		463.82
Proceedings:		
Subscriptions		2,675.45
Sales		2,179.61
Annual Meeting - Schedule B-2		4,579.11
Dividend Income - Telephone Co. Stocks		1,605.48
Interest Income - Calvert Group		1,121.62
Appreciation in Fair Value		
of Investments		3,727.50
Off Prints		565.89
Royalties		749.79
Postage, Mailing and Labelling Income		1,720.87
Other Income		671.73
Total Support and Revenue		$ 60,772.57
Less: Expenses - Schedule B-1		53,218.15
Revenues Over Expenses		$ 7,554.42
Fund Balance - January 1, 1986	$42,473.60	
Prior Period Adjustment - Note 5	(3,039.47)	
Adjusted Fund Balance - January 1, 1986		39,434.13
Fund Balance - December 31, 1986		$ 46,988.55

See Accountants' Review Report.
The accompanying notes are an integral part of this statement.

THE AMERICAN CATHOLIC PHILOSOPHICAL ASSOCIATION
Schedule of Expenses
For The Year Ended
December 31, 1986

EXPENSES:
  Publications:
    The New Scholasticism $21,156.22
    Proceedings   4,299.39
    Editors Honoraria   1,500.00

      Total Publications $26,955.61

  Accounting Services   1,000.00
  Salaries   12,043.81
  Exchange Loss   200.17
  Printing and Duplicating   899.41
  Postage   3,660.86
  Annual Meeting - Schedule B-2   3,346.22
  Telephone   2,033.66
  Office Supplies and Expenses   1,196.90
  Payroll Taxes   1,127.77
  Miscellaneous   753.74

      Total Expenses $53,218.15

See Accountants' Review Report.
The accompanying notes are an integral part of this schedule.

THE AMERICAN CATHOLIC PHILOSOPHICAL ASSOCIATION
Schedule of Revenue and Expenses of Annual Meeting
For The Year Ended
December 31, 1986

ANNUAL MEETING

REVENUE:
Registration and Banquet	$ 3,187.80
Book Exchange	1,041.31
Donation	350.00
	$ 4,579.11

EXPENSES:
Printing, Program and Mailing	$ 443.64
Banquet Expenses	2,652.58
Award	250.00
	$ 3,346.22

EXCESS OF REVENUE OVER
EXPENSES $ 1,232.89

See Accountants' Review Report.
The accompanying notes are an integral part of this schedule.

245

1. Accounting Policy - The Association's financial statements have been prepared on the accrual basis of accounting. Accrual accounting reports income as it is earned rather than when it is received; and reports expenses as incurred, rather than when they are paid.

2. Investments - Investments are carried at fair market value. Investments include the following:

280 Shares of American Telephone and Telegraph, Inc.	$ 7,000.00
426 Shares of Bell South Corporation	24,601.50
	$31,601.50

3. Income Taxes - The Association is exempt from Federal income taxes under Internal Revenue Code Section 501(c)(3) per letter from the Internal Revenue Service dated January 8, 1958.

4. Prepaid Dues, Subscriptions and Other:

Prepaid Dues for 1987	$20,112.70
Prepaid Subscriptions for 1987	10,620.30
1987 Annual Meeting	785.00
	$31,518.00

5. Prior Period Adjustment:

    In 1981, The De Rance Foundation made a grant of $5,583.94 to the World Union of Catholic Philosophical Societies. This money was to be in the possession of the American Catholic Philosophical Association, but expenditures were to be made at the direction of the World Union. This was an ad hoc arrangement that could be changed. In 1986, the balance of the funds, $3,039.47, was transferred to the World Union. These funds should not have been reported as assets of the Association in prior years.

Business Meeting and Resolutions

The Business Meeting took place at 11:45 a.m. on Saturday, March 28, 1987. The President, Father Wippel, asked Father Schmidt to open the meeting with a prayer. Reports of the Secretary and the Treasurer were read and approved as were the Minutes of the Executive Council Meeting. The meeting adjourned with the Secretary reading the following resolutions, all of which were approved.

Be it resolved that the ACPA:

1. express its appreciation to Dr. Marilynn Fleckenstein and her local committee for their handling of local arrangements for the Annual Meeting in Buffalo, March 27-29, 1987;

2. express its gratitude to Dr. Jorge J. Gracia and his program committee for their efforts in organizing the Buffalo meeting;

3. express its thankfulness to retiring Mrs. Sandra Regina for her generous and painstaking considerations to the ACPA's well-being over the past four years.